MARGARET FULLER: AMERICAN ROMANTIC

PERRY MILLER was born in Chicago and graduated from the University of Chicago, where he received his Ph.D. degree in 1931. That year he became an instructor at Harvard University. He has been Professor of American Literature at Harvard since 1946. During 1962–63, he was at the Institute for Advanced Studies, in Princeton, where he was composing an analysis of the American intellect in the early nineteenth century—the era of Margaret Fuller.

Among his many books are: *Orthodoxy in Massachusetts*; *The New England Mind: The Seventeenth Century*; *Jonathan Edwards*; *Roger Williams*; *The New England Mind: From Colony to Province*; *The American Puritans* (A80); *The American Transcendentalists* (A119); and *The Legal Mind in America* (A313).

MARGARET FULLER
AMERICAN ROMANTIC

A SELECTION FROM
HER WRITINGS AND CORRESPONDENCE

EDITED BY
PERRY MILLER

Anchor Books
Doubleday & Company, Inc.
Garden City, New York
1963

The Anchor Books edition
is the first publication of
Margaret Fuller: American Romantic.

Anchor Books edition: 1963

Library of Congress Catalog Card Number 63–13082

Margaret had so many aspects to her soul that she might furnish material for a hundred biographers, not all could be said even then.

James Freeman Clarke
to Thomas Wentworth Higginson, 1883.

FOREWORD

In the general American memory, Margaret Fuller is recollected—if at all—as the woman who told Thomas Carlyle in London in 1846, "I accept the universe." This legendary version of their conversation implies that she thought she was paying the universe a compliment; so she always appears ridiculous, and posterity cackles over Carlyle's supposed retort, "By Gad, she'd better." Only in recent years have voices been raised (to which I now add my own) arguing that Margaret Fuller comes off from the interchange with honor. For the Carlyle who held that she had better accept the universe as it actually is also contended that the truth of that universe was the rule of unmitigated force, as exemplified in the despotism of Frederick of Prussia, and he tried to lash the populace back to their kennels. Margaret's affirmation—if she did make it—was fully in character: she fought hard and valiantly for a liberalism so positive as immediately to excite Carlyle's ire.

A more reliable documentation of what many of her contemporaries sneeringly termed her "mountainous *me*" is Emerson's report of a remark she delivered in casual simplicity while dining (frugally, we may be sure) at his table: "I now know all the people worth knowing in America, and I find no intellect comparable to my own." When Emerson let this boast appear in his portion of *Memoirs* of *Margaret Fuller*, printed in 1852, it was greeted with the kind of derision that most of the male intellectuals of the nation had learned to heap upon her. Today these men would be astounded to be told that in the prospective of American intellectual history her observation may, in fact, be the simple truth.

She was born in Cambridgeport, Massachusetts, on May 23, 1810. In a manner typical of that time in New England, her father, Timothy Fuller, dominated the family with a tyrannical masculinity that he thought was affection, but that actually amounted to what must be called persecution, or even sadism. The fact that he was unaware of the havoc he was wreaking on the nervous constitution of his eldest child hardly excuses his conduct, even when it is considered in the light of the customs of his day. The letters herein reproduced reveal the ghastly effects of Timothy Fuller's regime, and suggest the amount of covert resentment it left with his loving daughter. However, Margaret came out of this training with a wide knowledge of history, of the works of Thomas Jefferson, of several languages, of English literature, of mathematics, and of Biblical scholarship, far beyond that possessed by the young men of her circle who were moving toward Harvard, where they acquired at best but a modicum of the erudition she so painfully mastered. There was no college for women, and to make the situation worse, in 1833 she was forced to move with her family from the peripheral felicities of residence in Cambridge to the comparatively dead atmosphere of rural Groton.

Upon the death of her father in 1835, Margaret was obliged to support the family. She taught for two years (1837–39) at a school in Providence, Rhode Island, which, in relation to the pedagogy of the time, we might salute as "progressive," although its radicalism aroused among the girl students a fervent, not to say feverish, devotion that put an intolerable strain on Margaret's flagging energy.

Despite the pressing responsibilities, Margaret inaugurated, in 1839, her "Conversations" for the intellectual women of Boston (at a few meetings they admitted male guests), exploring such subjects as classical mythology and "What Is Life?" Margaret Fuller presided over these bacchantic rites in homemade dresses that her adorers thought to be of Oriental magnificence, and at the climax of each session, when she had reduced the others to awed silence, she would close her eyes in an inspired trance and utter unfathomable words, which they thought emanated from some occult or Delphic wisdom.

In 1840, she joined to this activity that of editing the Transcendental journal, the *Dial*. Her racking nerves caused her to resign two years later, although for two years more (all that remained for the *Dial*), while Emerson was titular editor, she still did more than her share of the labor. Then, in the autumn of 1844, Margaret committed her great act of treason in the eyes of the New England intellectuals. She willfully departed out of New England to accept employment from Horace Greeley as book reviewer for his New York *Tribune*. In New York—that Babylon, that citadel of iniquity—she became the first woman member of the "working press."

Boston considered New York a vulgar conglomeration, not worthy to be called a city except insofar as a few strayed New Englanders—chiefly William Cullen Bryant —breathed upon it a faint aura of culture. It was unthinkable that a woman of Margaret Fuller's distinction of mind should soil her fingers with the ink of Greeley's newspaper. The work she was doing there, said Emerson in his most tight-lipped manner, might be "honorable," but "still this employment is not satisfactory to me." He was incapable of realizing that her ephemeral journalism of 1845 and 1846 constitutes a performance in literary criticism far beyond the conventional prowess of the then respected but now forgotten professionals, such as Henry Tuckerman and Edwin P. Whipple, or the ponderous judg-

ments of the *North American Review* and the waspish
puerilities of the *Knickerbocker Magazine*. Only a few of
the better pieces of Edgar Allan Poe can stand beside
the body of her *Tribune* articles.

With the financial help of her friends Marcus and Rebecca Spring, Margaret Fuller departed for Europe on
August 1, 1846, and, as she had arranged with Greeley,
the *Tribune* on that morning ran her "Farewell to New
York" (pp. 250–52). New England was insulted (as was
intended) by the piece that praised the superior intellectual stimulations of the great city. But Margaret also
slyly hinted that New York lacked something as well. She
envisioned a community grander than even the teeming
metropolis could provide, and as her intuition had always
told her, what she wanted she could find only in Europe.

I must limit my selection of Margaret's writings to only
a few reports out of a large and absorbing compilation.
Unless these fragments can of themselves prove her case,
both in respect to her period and to the modern reader,
there is no point in pleading for her. Emerson judged that
her writings were "naught," and for a long time after her
death her friends maintained this fiction. Elizabeth Barrett Browning, who became genuinely fond of her in Florence in 1849, warned, "If I wished anyone to do her justice, I should say, as I have indeed said, 'Never read
what she has written.'" Yet I insist that, in the final
analysis, the publications of Margaret Fuller constitute a
gallant, albeit a minor, chapter in the history of America's
persisting quest for self-realization.

Her "feminist" propaganda is actually a slight contribu-
tion to the campaign for "women's rights." She may easily
be dismissed as an eccentric, as no true voice of American
civilization. In fact, she has thus been consigned, time
after time, to oblivion. Yet she refuses to be eclipsed.
The reason for her pertinacity is not hard to discover:
in Margaret Fuller, daughter as she was of Puritan New
England, we have virtually the only candidate—and in her

case an authentic one—for the role of a native champion
of the Romantic heroine in the grandiose (and so, for an
American, dangerously close to the ludicrous) operatic
manner. Only she could prove an equal combatant in
the wide arena of feminine intellectuality that up to that
time had been pre-empted by Madame de Staël and
George Sand. And it seemed further that she possessed
the only mind among her contemporaries that could have
conversed on a plane of equality (though she brashly self-
assumed this) with Rousseau and Goethe. By sheer force
of intellect—certainly not of physical charm—Margaret Fuller reassured those who most denigrated her that she could
provide them some excuse for their own being. Without
her, they might have had no standard of the "great world"
by which to gauge their own sophistication. As they judged
her, sympathetically or nastily, they ranked themselves in
the inexorable scale of cultivation.

Europe did not recognize Margaret's achievements as
a critic. Her essays were unknown there, and would have
been rated, had they been noticed, as overearnest ventures
into the pontifical. Rather, she came to European attention as the notorious author of *Woman in the Nineteenth
Century.* In this book she proclaimed that women could
be even sea captains if they wished. (Horace Greeley,
although an advocate of women's rights, quoted this sentence when he refused to open a door for her. European
sympathizers preferred to test—and they approved—the sincerity of her radicalism.) Happily, the fame of this
polemic enabled her to meet some of the best minds in
Europe—Carlyle, Landor, the Brownings, Lamennais, and
above all George Sand.

Shortly after her arrival in Europe, Margaret directed
a letter about George Sand to Elizabeth Hoar (pp. 260–
65)—with the queer expectation that Elizabeth would
show it to the Emersonian circle, which was to her the
only part of America that mattered. In this letter, Margaret spoke about herself with her customary alias when

she said that Madame Sand needed no defense, but only to be understood; she had done no more than bravely act out her nature. Upon the assurance of George Sand's personal example, Margaret Fuller acted out *her* nature: she went to Italy, and she fell in love with it.

In retrospect, her friends came to recognize that she was predestined to resolve the tumultuous inner strife of her Romantic compulsions only in Italy. In this respect, she was not without precedent—to name only the greatest, Byron, Shelley, Keats; to name those she recognized as fellow fugitives, Landor and the Brownings; to name the image that loomed over her aesthetically starved girlhood in Cambridgeport, Washington Allston. In the large scope of her tragedy, it appears that she had always been out of place in America, had never belonged to the land of enterprise and industry, where the "Romantic movement" could never penetrate more deeply into the life of the Republic than into the fragile brains of a pathetically few intellectuals.

Emerson sensed the issue when, in 1846, he wrote Carlyle requesting hospitality for "one of my luminaries." He explained that Margaret had long been an exotic in New England, "a foreigner from some more sultry and expansive climate." Bronson Alcott, the most incompetent man in the United States in the realm of practical affairs, was also one of its shrewdest judges of character. Upon hearing of the death of Margaret Fuller, he reflected, "She was a citizen and a socialist, by virtue of constitution, or by womanhood; and here in this particular, she was less American than Greek." Henry James later put the essence of the matter in terms that were for him, if not for Margaret's fellow-Americans, more pertinent. "She had bitten deeply into Rome, or, rather, *been*, like so many others, by the wolf of the Capitol, incurably bitten."

Margaret met Mazzini in London in 1846, and, exemplifying her genius for prophetic divination, she joined his cause. Three years later, when she was working as a nurse in a hospital in Rome with a gallantry and devotion equal to that of Garibaldi in the field, Margaret received a letter from Emerson (serene by now in the meadows of Concord, comprehending nothing of what Margaret was enduring) lamenting that revolutionary Italy lacked a great man. Margaret flared back: "Mazzini is a great man. . . . I dearly love Mazzini." Her service in the siege of Rome would have been enough to prove that she was a heroine. Yet she added to this achievement still another feat. To the amazement, to the bewilderment—in most cases to the consternation—of her friends, she somehow found occasion, in the midst of this turmoil, to acquire both a husband and a child, unnoticed by the close-knit and gossipy community. The husband—or at least she said he was—emerged as one Giovanni Angelo Ossoli, who on somewhat vague premises claimed to be a Marquis. The son was born in deepest secrecy amid the mountains of Rieti, on September 4, 1848. Thus Margaret Fuller, the erstwhile oracle of Boston, was to return to the highly censorious Republic in July 1850 as a Marchioness, or at least as a putative Madame Ossoli.

The incomprehensible component in this fabulous drama—this "underplot," as James neatly termed it—is Ossoli. Those closest to Margaret in Italy could never account for the union. At this distance we can gain nothing by amateur psychology. We gain considerably more by reconstructing the passion as a splendid Romantic gesture in the sublime style of the priestesses of that persuasion, Madame de Staël and George Sand. Ossoli was ten or so years younger than Margaret and not intellectual. He was in every respect the antithesis of the young men of Cambridge—yet possibly for this very reason he was more satisfactory for Margaret. Tender, smiling, courteous, he was clearly devoted to his awkward and ailing wife (he could "with knightly zeal" take her parasol to be mended). Little more is known of him, for her friends were never able to study him closely; when they visited the couple in Florence, ostensibly to discuss metaphysics with Margaret, he would quietly retire to the corner café. All they could report with assurance was that he fought bravely at Rome and that he indisputably begot upon Margaret a man-child.

The story spread rapidly throughout Europe, to America, and eventually to Concord. She performed her strenuous duties under fire while her husband stood in daily peril at his post on the walls, and while she was utterly cut off from news of her son in the desolate mountains. The siege was over, and lost, when perhaps Emerson commenced to comprehend the depths of Margaret's distress as she wrote him: "Let me feel, that, amid the fearful agitations of the world, there are pure hands, with healthful, even pulse, stretched out toward me, if I claim their grasp."

Tidings that Margaret was returning to America preceded her embarcation on the ship *Elizabeth*, at Leghorn, Italy. The "timorous," Emerson recorded, were nervously asking, "What shall we do? How shall she be received, now that she brings a husband and child home?" A large number, not at all timorous, had firm notions as to how they would receive her. Their animosity is reflected in James Russell Lowell's letter to William Wetmore Story:

> The American Eagle is anxiously awaiting the return of Miss F., whom he persists in regarding as the genius of Columbia. A public dinner is to be given her in Boston at which the Bird of our Country will preside.

Emerson's sweet optimism—in this case we must add his loyalty—persuaded him that Margaret "had only to open her mouth and a triumph awaited her." My selections from the letters of her last year show that she had somewhat more realistic expectations. These may well have determined her suicidal action as the ship was foundering on the rocks off Fire Island, near New York City.

Mr. Emerson's healthful, even pulse had permitted him for a brief time, around 1840, a series of epistolary flirtations with Margaret Fuller (examples are here recorded), who at once enchanted and discomforted him. In one instance in the *Memoirs*, he harshly judged that "she looked upon herself as a living statue, which should always stand on a polished pedestal, with rich accessories, and under the most fitting lights." Yet he also acknowledged—perhaps to assuage his conscience for not having aided her more—that while her writings did not justify research, they did express "an interesting hour and group in American cultivation"—thus giving Henry James his clue but also confusing the modern researcher. And in this same vein, he admitted in the so-called *Memoirs*—in a strangely secretive and tardy tribute—that Margaret had been consistently brave and noble, even that she had been (as seldom she was) courteous. All who had come within Margaret's spell remained thereafter both as intrigued and as uncomfortable as was Emerson. Professedly or reluctantly, they betrayed how deeply they were relieved that she was prevented from marching ashore with her husband and child, thus to have trespassed on their pretensions to liberality.

One factor in our settling a public image of Margaret Fuller is that she cannot be dissociated from the hyperbolically female intellectualism of the period, the slightest invocation of which invites our laughter. Descriptions of her presiding over "Conversations" in Boston inevitably classify her with such vanished Sapphos as Delia Bacon and Lydia Sigourney—in the phrase of Henry James, the "glossily ringletted and monumentally breastpinned." Yet the fact remains—despite several efforts at, not quite glorification, but mitigation—that she was monumentally homely. Her hair was stringy and her neck abnormally long. Dr. Oliver Wendell Holmes, who was condemned to sit beside her in Grammar School, remembered her neck as "ophidian." (He also remembered that from her

lips he first heard the withering adjective "trite," the meaning of which he had not then learned!) William Henry
Channing, one of the several boys she guided into the
study of German, tried to palliate the reputation of her
countenance; he succeeded, as did most such defenders,
in making her appear even more terrifying than in the
cartoons of her enemies. Characteristic of her, said Channing, was her habit of contracting her eyelids to a point,
but still more arresting was "the singular pliancy of the
vertebrae and muscles of the neck, enabling her by a mere
movement to denote each varying emotion." Well-inten-
tioned Channing hardly improved his portrait by adding
about this famous neck: "In moments of tenderness, or
pensive feeling, its curves were swan-like, but when she
was scornful or indignant, it contracted, and made swift
turns like a bird of prey." Add to this terrifying accomplishment some of her other mannerisms—"a trick of in-
cessantly opening and shutting her eyelids," said the
candid Emerson, "the nasal tone of her voice"—and we
quite understand why the many who disliked her saw in
her person only the grotesque Miranda of Lowell's *A
Fable for Critics.*

In the homespun Boston of 1840, where ideas were
generously entertained but where Margaret Fuller's cos-
tumes were deemed bizarre, she put on grand performances both of scorn and of indignation. Her friend
Emerson and her foe Lowell imagined that they appreciated her stature as a public figure, and after her death
as a tragic one. Yet neither comprehended how much
she had also wrought for the cause of solid criticism in
the United States. Gradually, in spite of either of them,
her claims to serious consideration as an intellect have
advanced beyond those of the heroine. Now both claims
may be presented as interlinked in the context of the Romantic movement.

Her society had a full-scale model by which to measure
her, by which they could define the role she nearly suc-

ceeded in playing on this provincial stage. It was Madame de Staël's *Corinne*. If Europe ever produced a true spiritual daughter of Rousseau, she was Anne Louise Germaine Necker. And if ever there was a literary creation in the spirit of Rousseau, it was Madame de Staël's *Corinne*, a testament that pointed the way for many young girls to sentimental ecstasy. Emerson had been warned before he met Margaret that she was a "sneering and critical dame." "What," he exclaimed in retrospect, she was nothing of the sort: she "was this new Corinne." And he sketched out what a Corinne-figure comprised: tenderness, counsel, one before whom every mean thing is ashamed—"more variously gifted, wise, sportive, eloquent, who seems to have learned all languages, Heaven knows when or how,—I should think she was born to them, —magnificent, prophetic, reading my life at her will, and puzzling me with riddles like this, 'Yours is an example of a destiny springing from character;' and, again, 'I see your destiny hovering before you, but it always escapes from you.'"

The most poised of sages, whether residing beside the Concord River or the Ganges, might well have been jolted by having riddles of such Orphic profundity proposed to him, and Emerson was not then the perfectly poised Brahma that he would become by the time he surveyed this first encounter. Out of the security into which she along with several others, but chiefly she, had frightened him, he was able to view her abstractly, to cast her as a type. Yet possibly this made it easier for him to deal with one who had lived her life at a rate so much faster than his own that she caused a voice to cry out to him, "*Stand from under!*" Still, William Henry Channing sought the same refuge; Margaret's friendships, he recorded (thus minimizing the danger in which *he* once had stood) had such an air of "romantic exaggeration" that he confessed, "I then suspected her of affecting the part of a Yankee Corinna."

Passages linking New England's Margaret Fuller with the heroine of Madame de Staël's romance of 1807 abound in the literature concerning her. Their frequency indicates that there was something more powerful here than a simple comparison—as Bryant was called "the American Wordsworth" or James Fenimore Cooper labeled "the American Scott": here was not analogy, but identification. The universality of this identification shows, first, that the female avatar was as firmly established in the authors' imaginations as was the corresponding male incarnation, the Byronic hero; and, second, that in the thin atmosphere of America, Margaret Fuller was the best we could offer as an exhibition of feminine variety. The fact that Margaret herself accepted the appellation is conclusive evidence for its appropriateness. It is hardly possible, Margaret wrote, for anyone who has felt the influence of Madame de Staël to criticize the effect with calmness. The beams of her intellect "make the obscurest schoolhouse in New England warmer and lighter to the little rugged girls who are gathered together on its wooden bench." As a little rugged girl who had been warmed by these beams, she revealed their power over her and her friends when she proudly announced, following her first "conversation," that she did not feel what she had dreaded in advance, the sense of being "a paid Corinne."

For Margaret Fuller, the innermost appeal of the *improvvisatrice* of the romance *Corinne* was not alone that she embodied an ideal of womanly genius but that she was patently a dream-image of a plain, monstrously learned, tempestuous, and tormented Germaine. In the American arena—minute as compared with Rome—the public figure that Sarah Margaret Fuller made of herself was as much a dream-fulfillment as was Madame de Staël's Corinne. Indeed, the intermittently astute Emerson wrote Margaret in January, 1841, that one of her self-glorifications (not reproduced here, but in the style of "Mariana") was "a new Corinna with a fervid Southern eloquence that makes me wonder as often before how you fell into Massachusetts." Emerson should not have been so blind: just as Germaine Necker fell into a rationalist France shaken apart by the Revolution, Margaret emerged into Massachusetts when the Puritan mentality was lit—even though from afar—by the flames of European Romanticism. In fact, Isabel Hill's translation of *Corinne,* published in 1807, promptly became a troubling intrusion into all Anglo-Saxon communities. It was perpetually denounced from middle-class pulpits and assiduously read by middle-class daughters in their chambers at night.

In *Corinne,* the raven-haired, the sensuous *improvvisatrice* (this term, albeit not the physical attribute, was repeatedly applied to Margaret Fuller) seeks to explain herself to her stolid English nobleman: "You see, I cannot touch on any of the themes that affect me, without the kind of thrill which is the source of ideal beauty in the arts, or religion in the recluse, generosity in heroes, and disinterestedness among men." It sufficed for Corinne to beseech the pardon of the English: there obviously could be no such woman as she in Britain. But America was faced with Margaret, and the problem occasioned increasing panic: could there be a native Corinne, even one such woman, in an economy infinitely more devoted to utilitarianism than industrial Britain? Having escaped to Rome, Margaret Fuller wailed in 1848, "A little money would have enabled me to come here long ago, and find those that belong to me, or at least to try my experiments; then my health would never have been wasted in useless friction." She discovered there that no more than Ossoli and his son could fully belong to her. Again we marvel at the sagacity of Bronson Alcott: "Imperial creature that she was, and, alike in ideal excellencies and bearing, mythological!"

To many of the band who worshiped Margaret as a martyred saint, her bond with Madame de Staël was an article of faith. We may surmise that several motives,

not all of them compatible, were combined in this gesture.
On the more facile level, a linking of Margaret and Germaine excused them for not having done all that they
might have in Margaret's service. It also assuaged their
consciences for not investing emotional or financial capital in her cause. This harsh remark applies even to Marcus
and Rebecca Spring, who financed her trip to Europe
in 1846, but who left her perilously on her own there
in 1847. Yet her friends must not be assailed. How were
they to know that in the eighteen-forties in America a
native Madame de Staël could actually arise? It was downright idiotic to support what seemed to be Miss Fuller's
mad pretensions. Madame de Staël's Corinne had already
explained the situation: "There are only two distinct
classes of people on this earth, those who espouse enthusiasm and those who despise it." Those who were against
Margaret, including those who supported her only half-
heartedly, were not enthusiasts. She stood for the heart,
even though so terribly endowed with brains.

Margaret complicated the problem for her apologists
by further seeking an alliance of her spirit with that of
Rousseau, and—most scandalously—with that of the then
vibrantly living and utterly subversive George Sand. Indeed, the fictional character Corinne, the historical record
of Madame de Staël, and the figure of George Sand had
become one sublime image in Margaret Fuller's mind
well before her fatal pilgrimage to Europe. The sensibility they shared is described in what Emerson reports as
a transcript from a letter of Margaret's to a friend
(clearly female). Margaret comments on a new work by
George Sand: "I am astonished at her insight into the
life of thought," whereupon adds the disciple of Corinne,
"She must know it through some man." A more than
superficial reader of Madame de Staël would know, as
Margaret preternaturally knew, that to acknowledge this
was not to say that men were superior intellectually.
Women, as Margaret triumphantly continues, do not

understand the life of thought; what matters to them is not the pulsations of the brain but the beatings of the heart, of which Madame de Staël has been the supreme diagnostician. Margaret concluded by paraphrasing Germaine:

> It is easy for women to be heroic in action, but when it comes to interrogating God, the universe, the soul, and above all, trying to live above their own hearts, they dart down to their nests like so many larks, and, if they cannot find them, fret like the French Corinne.

In this passage, written before she went to Italy, Margaret was once more, as she was so frequently and so mysteriously, prophetic about herself.

The parallel of Margaret Fuller's life with that of Madame de Staël proved amazing to Margaret's contemporaries—and so it may be to us. Just as Germaine suffered through a more than Spartan discipline in her scholastic training under the supervision of her dogmatic, rationalist father, the financier Necker, so Margaret was schooled with inhuman severity by *her* rationalist father, the doctrinaire Jeffersonian Timothy Fuller. Madame de Staël discovered the agonies and perversities of passion in flagrant affairs with such capricious characters as Benjamin Constant. Miss Fuller was less prodigal of her body; but she learned almost as much about the intricacies of affection in her more attenuated affairs with the women and men of New England, from her bruising encounter with James Nathan in New York (pp. 202–4), and ultimately in her union with Ossoli. In fact, a treatise on the fluctuations of love that would enchant a Marcel Proust could be composed from the few surviving accounts of her discourses with intimates (I have included some of these).

Furthermore, just as Madame de Staël's *De l'Allemagne* was primarily responsible for introducing Western Europe to German Romantic literature, so Margaret Fuller's essays in the *Dial* and the *Tribune* helped to introduce to America Goethe, Herder, Novalis, Jean-Paul, and other highly suspect Germans. As Madame de Staël defied Napoleon, so Margaret in Rome pitted herself against the forces of reaction from Austria and France. Finally, just as Germaine, all passion spent, married in middle age a Lieutenant Rocca, several years her junior and a man of no intellectual pretensions, so did the American Corinne marry Ossoli. All of this, as Henry James remarked, invests Margaret with "a sharp identity."

The identity, however, presented as many forms of sharpness as there were numbers of beholders. In no mechanical sense was Margaret Fuller the "original" of Zenobia in Nathaniel Hawthorne's *The Blithedale Romance*. Even so, Hawthorne's creature of darkness and sex—clearly another Corinne—owed all her being to his imagining a Corinne in New England. In this sense, Margaret Fuller was at least a provocation.

Hawthorne disliked Margaret intensely, and we may surmise that it was a resentment he had cherished since 1842. When he and his Sophia at last managed to secure their haven at the Old Manse, Margaret actually proposed that her sister Ellen and Ellen's newly acquired husband, Ellery Channing, should move in with them! "Had it been proposed to Adam and Eve," Hawthorne expostulated, "to receive two angels into their Paradise, as *boarders*, I doubt whether they would have been altogether pleased to consent." Nine years after Margaret died, Hawthorne says that he met a sculptor in Rome who recollected Ossoli as a veritable idiot. Recalling his impressions of Margaret, Hawthorne exploded to his journal what must have been long-suppressed rancor: Margaret Fuller was a "great humbug," "a strong and coarse nature," who tried in every way to refine herself, to make something dazzling out of "her strong, heavy, unpliable, and, in many respects, defective and evil nature." He took a salacious delight (as did many of her male associates) in supposing that for the basest of sensual motives she fell "as the weakest of her sisters did." Hawthorne enjoyed a sardonic satisfaction in reflecting that her tragedy was all the sadder "because so much of the ridiculous was mixed up with it." Hawthorne's wife omitted this passage when preparing the *Italian Notebooks* for publication, but their son, Julian, printed it in the second edition in 1884.

Survivors of the Transcendental congregation were outraged, with Bronson Alcott declaiming "we have no woman approaching so near our conception of the ideal woman herself," although this helped little since the evidence he offered for her supremacy was that she, more than anybody in the New England group, had sympathized with his own "drift and purposes." Young Hawthorne, declared Christopher Cranch, a faithful friend from her Cambridge days, "has his quietus, for he sees that public opinion is against him." But the truth is that by 1884 there was little or no public opinion to be aroused over Margaret Fuller.

Yet, just as Margaret's specter haunted all who knew her to the ends of their lives, so she haunts the corridors of the American intellect and frequently disturbs many who looked upon her in life. Henry James is perhaps the most instructive case. He was seven years old when he stood beside his father on a Hudson River excursion boat and heard Washington Irving tell that Margaret Fuller had drowned the day before. Already this boy had become, unlike Emerson, one on whom nothing would be lost. He sensed then that a heroine had gone to a heroic death. James insisted that he did not belong to the "Boston connection"; yet he admitted half a century later that the "Margaret-ghost" was more present to him than images of any other habitués of the conclave. And the way in which she haunted him tells volumes about what Margaret

Fuller represented to the America of her time, and in fact what she should signify for us today.

In *The Portrait of a Lady* (appearing in the *Atlantic* for 1880 and 1881), James has the Countess Gemini explain that her mother, the parent also of the sterile aesthete Osmund, had been a personage of distinction: "She was called the American Corinne." James came back to America, for the last time seeking in his native land a suitable subject, and in 1885 he published *The Bostonians*. In this romance, an indubitably masculine Southerner rescues a beautiful Titian heroine from the stifling clutches of an ultra-feministic, a decadently Transcendental, Boston. The parallels to what did in historical fact happen to Margaret, though skillfully disguised, are obvious. The hero is somewhat more intelligent than Hawthorne said Ossoli was, but he too has been a soldier and is not, in the New England sense, an intellectual. Just a year after Julian Hawthorne disclosed his father's brutal paragraphs about Margaret, James had the hero of *The Bostonians* remark that he too has read about "the *improvvisatrice* of Italy" and that he beholds in Verbena Tarrant "a chastened, modern, American version of the type, a New England Corinna, with a mission instead of a lyre." Hawthorne had written that Margaret surfeited herself with borrowed qualities "which had no root in her" and that she "took credit to herself for having been her own Redeemer if not her own Creator"; hence he exulted that she was rightly betrayed to sensuality, a surrender all the more degrading because Ossoli was a beast. In James' conception of the legend about Margaret, she does not yield to a beast but to a gentleman; still, he is a *man*. James assured the failure of his romance in America by concluding that the marriage could not possibly be a happy one—how could a feminist mystic permanently accept the mundane role of wife? Yet perhaps the major reason for the popular failure of the novel was that the American public of 1885 could no longer appreciate the poignance of the Corinne-figure.

However, the vicarious subjugation of the Corinne-figure in *The Bostonians* no more laid to rest the "Margaret-ghost" for Henry James than it can for us. In 1903, James accepted the job of editing two volumes of *William Wetmore Story and His Friends.* The Storys were stalwart friends to Margaret in the last two strenuous years of her life, and James could not speak of them without confessing how much for him Margaret "still unmistakably walks the passages." He agreed—rather too readily—with Emerson and Mrs. Browning that her writings were "naught." But the woman herself? "Would she," James asked, posing the central question, "with her appetite for ideas and her genius for conversation, have struck us but as a somewhat formidable bore, one of the worst kind, a culture-seeker without a sense of proportion, or, on the contrary, have affected us as a really attaching, a possibly picturesque New England Corinne?" Not that the exquisite Verbena *is* a photograph of ophidian Margaret, any more than is sumptuous Zenobia. Still, what both Verbena and Zenobia—and the still more lovely Milly Theale in *The Wings of the Dove*—owe to the nearsighted, ungainly, doomed Margaret-ghost is worth speculating about.

To Margaret's contemporaries—joyfully to those who loved her, repulsively to those who abhorred her—this is what she was: a Madame de Staël in these stumbling provinces who, not comprehending their predicament, did not know whether they wanted to remain crude and virtuous or to reach toward some dizzy sophistication that surely would carry with it the contagion of corruption. Margaret summoned America to a maturity for which neither it nor she was ready. She was as divided among her own sensibilities as was the culture itself. Yet she tried to come to terms with them, as she defended the majestic gospel of nineteenth-century liberalism and never shrank from its severest imperatives. Identifying herself

xxviii   Margaret Fuller: American Romantic

with the sibylline responsibilities of a Corinne, she acted, to the bitter end, the alternative title Madame de Staël had given to the biography of the original Corinne: "Or, Italy." As Henry James said in summation of her adventures: "These things, let alone the final catastrophe, in short, were not talk but life, and life dealing with the somewhat angular Boston sibyl on its own free lines."

Margaret Fuller proved herself one of the rigorous liberals of her age by criticizing most angrily the cowardice of liberals. The record of her publications and of her letters does not show that her ultimate discovery of marriage and motherhood was a "capitulation." In fact, for a woman in this period, she had been unusually brazen in declaring that she wanted love, that she needed love, that she suffocated without it. As Madame de Staël's heroine had already said, "In seeking glory, I always hoped to find love." The young men of Cambridge, as well as James Nathan in New York, ran away from her; Ossoli did not.

The open secret of the legend behind the Romantic Corinne was that she was named after the classical Corinna, who competed with the local Pindars, won the prize, and advised them "to sow with the hand, not with the sack." Ossoli—according to Hawthorne a boor, a man without any intellectual spark—did his sowing. Margaret was bringing him and the child home to confront Henry James' question. There is evidence that while the *Elizabeth* was breaking upon the rocks of Fire Island on July 19, 1850, she herself might have been rescued, had she wanted to make the effort. If this is so, then in full view of America, she elected to perish with her husband and her baby.

Perry Miller

CONTENTS

Foreword   ix

Chapter I. Cambridge, 1810–1833   1

1. Father   1
2. Childhood   4
3. Mariana   5
4. Reading   24
5. Self-Searching   26
6. Genius   27
7. Self-Consciousness   29

Chapter II. Groton, Providence, Jamaica Plain,
1833–1840   33

1. The Anguish of Groton   33
2. Classical and Romantic   36
3. Genius and Morality   46
4. Passion   49
5. To Ralph Waldo Emerson, September 29, 1840   52
6. To Ralph Waldo Emerson, November, 1840   55

Chapter III. The *Dial*, 1840–1844   57

1. The Editors to the Reader   57
2. Motives for the *Dial*   62
3. A Short Essay on Critics   66
4. A House Guest in Concord   74

5. A Caveat to Pastoralism   75
6. Goethe   77
7. To Ralph Waldo Emerson, October, 1841   108
8. To Ralph Waldo Emerson, from Chicago,
   August 17, 1843   111
9. To Ralph Waldo Emerson, November 12,
   1843   114
10. Summer on the Lakes   116
11. To Ralph Waldo Emerson, July, 1844   132

Chapter IV. New York, 1844–1846   135

1. Woman in the Nineteenth Century   135
2. Emerson's Essays   191
3. Americans and Their Love of Nature   200
4. To James Nathan, March 23, 1845   202
5. A Transcendental Defense of Classical Metres   205
6. American Facts   207
7. Fourth of July, 1845   210
8. Poe's Tales   214
9. The Philosophy of Criticism   215
10. To James Nathan, August 31, 1845   218
11. A Further Caveat to Pastoralism   219
12. Typee   221
13. Charles Brockden Brown   223
14. American Literature. Its Position in the
    Present Time, and Prospects for the Future   227
15. Farewell to New York   250

Chapter V. Europe, 1846–1850   253

1. Poverty in England   253
2. Carlyle   257
3. George Sand   260
4. Nature and Art   265
5. Rousseau   268
6. Americans in Europe   269
7. To Ralph Waldo Emerson, December 20,
   1847   277

Contents

8. The Revolution, March and April, 1848   278
9. To Richard F. Fuller, February 23, 1849   280
10. To Caroline Sturgis Tappan, March 16, 1849   282
11. The Agony of the Revolution   286
12. To Ralph Waldo Emerson, June 10, 1849   295
13. To Ellen Channing, June 19, 1849   298
14. To William Henry Channing, August 28, 1849   299
15. To Emelyn Story, November 30, 1849   300
16. To William Wetmore Story, December 2, 1849   302
17. To Ellen Channing, December 11, 1849   303
18. To Caroline Sturgis Tappan, December 30, 1849   307
19. To Richard F. Fuller, January 8, 1850   310
20. To Marcus and Rebecca Spring, February 5, 1850   312
21. To Emelyn Story, April 11, 1850   314
22. Prophecy   315

Bibliographical Sources and Acknowledgments   317

MARGARET FULLER: AMERICAN ROMANTIC

CHAPTER I

CAMBRIDGE, 1810–1833

1. FATHER

(Date unknown, but clearly in retrospect; text from
Memoirs, I, 14–16.)

*[The brothers of Margaret Fuller would stoutly insist
after her death that Timothy Fuller had subjected his
daughter to no more rigorous training than that given
to a boy preparing for college. Thus they strove to correct his reputation as a monster in the legends of Margaret Fuller. Yet judging him by the most lenient standards of modern "child psychology," we have to conclude
that, although his motives were of the highest order, he
did torture the child. Her descriptions of her nightmares
make horribly clear the ravaging character of her neuroses.
These recitations often verge on the brink of the ridiculous, for Margaret had learned the arts of self-pity; they
are rescued from absurdity by attesting the reality of
her afflictions and demonstrating the courage with which,
although amid whimpers, she endured her pains.]*

My father,—all whose feelings were now concentrated
on me,—instructed me himself. The effect of this was so
far good that, not passing through the hands of many
ignorant and weak persons as so many do at preparatory
schools, I was put at once under discipline of considerable
severity, and, at the same time, had a more than ordinar-

ily high standard presented to me. My father was a man of business, even in literature; he had been a high scholar at college, and was warmly attached to all he had learned there, both from the pleasure he had derived in the exercise of his faculties and the associated memories of success and good repute. He was, beside, well read in French literature, and in English, a Queen Anne's man. He hoped to make me the heir of all he knew, and of as much more as the income of his profession enabled him to give me means of acquiring. At the very beginning, he made one great mistake, more common, it is to be hoped, in the last generation, than the warnings of physiologists will permit it to be with the next. He thought to gain time, by bringing forward the intellect as early as possible. Thus I had tasks given me, as many and various as the hours would allow, and on subjects beyond my age; with the additional disadvantage of reciting to him in the evening, after he returned from his office. As he was subject to many interruptions, I was often kept up till very late; and as he was a severe teacher, both from his habits of mind and his ambition for me, my feelings were kept on the stretch till recitations were over. Thus frequently, I was sent to bed several hours too late, with nerves unnaturally stimulated. The consequence was a premature development of the brain, that made me a "youthful prodigy" by day, and by night a victim of spectral illusions, nightmare, and somnambulism, which at the time prevented the harmonious development of my bodily powers and checked my growth, while, later, they induced continual headache, weakness and nervous affections, of all kinds. As these again re-acted on the brain, giving undue force to every thought and every feeling, there was finally produced a state of being both too active and too intense, which wasted my constitution, and will bring me,—even although I have learned to understand and regulate my now morbid temperament,—to a premature grave.

No one understood this subject of health then. No one

knew why this child, already kept up so late, was still un-
willing to retire. My aunts cried out upon the "spoiled
child, the most unreasonable child that ever was,—if
brother could but open his eyes to see it,—who was never
willing to go to bed." They did not know that, so soon as
the light was taken away, she seemed to see colossal faces
advancing slowly towards her, the eyes dilating, and each
feature swelling loathsomely as they came, till at last,
when they were about to close upon her, she started up
with a shriek which drove them away, but only to return
when she lay down again. They did not know that, when
at last she went to sleep, it was to dream of horses trampling over her, and to awake once more in fright; or, as
she had just read in her Virgil, of being among trees that
dripped with blood, where she walked and walked and
could not get out, while the blood became a pool and
splashed over her feet, and rose higher and higher, till
soon she dreamed it would reach her lips. No wonder the
child arose and walked in her sleep, moaning all over the
house, till once, when they heard her, and came and waked
her, and she told what she had dreamed, her father sharply
bid her "leave off thinking such nonsense, or she would
be crazy,"—never knowing that he was himself the cause
of all these horrors of the night. Often she dreamed of
following to the grave the body of her mother, as she had
done that of her sister, and woke to find the pillow
drenched in tears. These dreams softened her heart too
much, and cast a deep shadow over her young days; for
then, and later, the life of dreams,—probably because
there was in it less to distract the mind from its own
earnestness,—has often seemed to her more real, and been
remembered with more interest, than that of waking
hours.

Poor child! Far remote in time, in thought, from that
period, I look back on these glooms and terrors, wherein I
was enveloped, and perceive that I had no natural childhood.

2. CHILDHOOD

(From a letter to Richard F. Fuller, August 5, 1842; text from *Woman in the Nineteenth Century*, 1874, pp. 365–66.)

[Though a daughter of Puritanism, Margaret Fuller was imbued with a "Romantic" lust for the Sublime. So were many of her contemporaries, who were also striving to cast off the inherited constrictions; yet she seems to have been even more preternaturally endowed than any of them. In a letter to her brother following a trip to the White Mountains in 1842, she underscored the torments that her romantic temperament had to endure in the dull and flat setting of Cambridgeport.]

. . . I want to hear how you enjoyed your journey, and what you think of the world, as surveyed from mountain tops, but suppose you are waiting to hear from me. The heat during my journey was extreme. I suffered from fatigue, and the times I enjoyed were those when we were staying amid the mountains. I feel satisfied, as I thought I should, with reading these bolder lines in the manuscript of nature. Merely gentle and winning scenes are not enough for me. I wish my lot had been cast amid the sources of the streams, where the voice of the hidden torrent is heard by night, where the eagle soars, and the thunder resounds in long peals from side to side, where the grasp of a more powerful emotion has rent asunder the rocks, and the long purple shadows fall like a broad wing upon the valley. All places like all persons I know have beauty which may be discovered by a thoughtful and observing mind, but only in some scenes and with some people can I expand, and feel myself at home. I feel this all the more for having passed my childhood in such a place as Cambridgeport. There I had nothing except the little flower garden behind the house, and the elms before the door. I used to long and pine for beautiful places such as I read of. There was not one walk for me, except over the bridge. I liked that very much, the river, and the city glittering in sunset, and the lovely undulating line all round, and the light smokes seen in some weather. . . .

3. MARIANA

(Presumably written after the visit to Chicago, in the summer of 1843; text from *Life Without and Life Within*, 1874, pp. 258–76.)

[In 1823, Timothy Fuller sent Margaret to a school in Groton, Massachusetts, kept by the Misses Prescott. Evidently Margaret's difficulties with both the teachers and the students there brought on a violent convulsion. This account was obviously written after the event. It is a projection into fantasy and is more revealing as a psychological disclosure than as a piece of autobiography. It is one among several efforts of plain Margaret to act out the role of a beautiful and foredoomed heroine. As an exercise in self-glorification such fantasy has many counterparts in the literature of Romantic Europe, but in America it is a rarity.

It also reveals the fetid intimacy that she cultivated among her female friends. Mariana as the "improvvisatrice" is one of many examples of Margaret's lifelong obsession with Madame de Staël's Corinne.

Since I have deliberately ignored Margaret's unfortunate ventures into verse, I let the concluding stanza in this sketch, attributed to her alter ego, remain as a sample of her ability. This threnody has the added interest of telling us, by its address to "Father," just how lasting was the

*impression upon her of the dominating Timothy Fuller.
The conclusion charmingly, although abruptly, declares
the connection between Margaret's "mountainous me"
and her passionate advocacy of women's rights.]*

MARIANA

Among those whom I met in a recent visit at Chicago
was Mrs. Z., the aunt of an old schoolmate, to whom I
impatiently hasted, to demand news of Mariana. The answer startled me. Mariana, so full of life, was dead. That
form, the most rich in energy and coloring of any I had
ever seen, had faded from the hearth. The circle of youthful associations had given way in the part that seemed the
strongest. What I now learned of the story of this life,
and what was by myself remembered, may be bound together in this slight sketch.

At the boarding school to which I was too early sent,
a fond, a proud, and timid child, I saw among the ranks
of the gay and graceful, bright or earnest girls, only one
who interested my fancy or touched my young heart; and
this was Mariana. She was, on the father's side, of Spanish
Creole blood, but had been sent to the Atlantic coast, to
receive a school education under the care of her aunt,
Mrs. Z.

This lady had kept her mostly at home with herself,
and Mariana had gone from her house to a day school;
but the aunt being absent for a time in Europe, she had
now been unfortunately committed for some time to the
mercies of a boarding school.

A strange bird she proved there—a lonely one, that
could not make for itself a summer. At first, her school-
mates were captivated with her ways, her love of wild
dances and sudden song, her freaks of passion and of wit.
She was always new, always surprising, and, for a time,
charming.

But after a while, they tired of her. She could never

be depended on to join in their plans, yet she expected them to follow out hers with their whole strength. She was very loving, even infatuated in her own affections, and exacted from those who had professed any love for her, the devotion she was willing to bestow.

Yet there was a vein of haughty caprice in her character; and a love of solitude, which made her at times wish to retire entirely; and at these times she would expect to be thoroughly understood, and let alone, yet to be welcomed back when she returned. She did not thwart others in their humors, but she never doubted of great indulgence from them.

Some singular ways she had, which, when new, charmed, but, after acquaintance, displeased her companions. She had by nature the same habit and power of excitement that is described in the spinning dervishes of the East. Like them she would spin until all around her were giddy, while her own brain, instead of being disturbed, was excited to great action. Pausing, she would declaim verses of others, or her own; perform many parts, with strange catch-words and burdens that seemed to act with mystical power on her own fancy, sometimes stimulating her to convulse the hearer with laughter, sometimes to melt him to tears. When her power began to languish, she would spin again till fired to recommence her singular drama, into which she wove figures from the scenes of her earlier childhood, her companions, and the dignitaries she sometimes saw, with fantasies unknown to life, unknown to heaven or earth.

This excitement, as may be supposed, was not good for her. It usually came on in the evening, and often spoiled her sleep. She would wake in the night, and cheat her restlessness by inventions that teased, while they sometimes diverted her companions.

She was also a sleep-walker; and this one trait of her case did somewhat alarm her guardians, who, otherwise, showed the same profound stupidity, as to this peculiar being, usual in the overseers of the young. They consulted a physician, who said she would outgrow it, and prescribed a milk diet.

Meantime, the fever of this ardent and too early stimulated nature was constantly increased by the restraints and narrow routine of the boarding school. She was always devising means to break in upon it. She had a taste, which would have seemed ludicrous to her mates, if they had not felt some awe of her, from a touch of genius and power, that never left her, for costume and fancy dresses; always some sash twisted about her, some drapery, something odd in the arrangement of her hair and dress; so that the methodical preceptress dared not let her go out without a careful scrutiny and remodelling, whose soberizing effects generally disappeared the moment she was in the free air.

At last, a vent for her was found in private theatricals. Play followed play, and in these and the rehearsals she found entertainment congenial with her. The principal parts, as a matter of course, fell to her lot; most of the good suggestions and arrangements came from her, and for a time she ruled masterly and shone triumphant.

During these performances the girls had heightened their bloom with artificial red; this was delightful to them —it was something so out of the way. But Mariana, after the plays were over, kept her carmine saucer on the dressing table, and put on her blushes regularly as the morning.

When stared and jeered at, she at first said she did it because she thought it made her look prettier; but, after a while, she became petulant about it—would make no reply to any joke, but merely kept on doing it.

This irritated the girls, as all eccentricity does the world in general, more than vice or malignity. They talked it over among themselves, till they were wrought up to a desire of punishing, once for all, this sometimes amusing, but so often provoking nonconformist.

Having obtained leave of the mistress, they laid, with

great glee, a plan, one evening, which was to be carried into execution the next day at dinner.

Among Mariana's irregularities was a great aversion to the meal-time ceremonial. So long, so tiresome she found it, to be seated at a certain moment, to wait while each one was served at so large a table, and one where there was scarcely any conversation; from day to day it became more heavy to sit there, or go there at all. Often as possible she excused herself on the ever-convenient plea of headache, and was hardly ever ready when the dinner-bell rang.

To-day the summons found her on the balcony, lost in gazing on the beautiful prospect. I have heard her say afterwards, that she had scarcely in her life been so happy —and she was one with whom happiness was a still rapture. It was one of the most blessed summer days; the shadows of great white clouds empurpled the distant hills for a few moments only to leave them more golden; the tall grass of the wide fields waved in the softest breeze. Pure blue were the heavens, and the same hue of pure contentment was in the heart of Mariana.

Suddenly on her bright mood jarred the dinner bell. At first rose her usual thought, I will not, cannot go; and then the *must*, which daily life can always enforce, even upon the butterflies and birds, came, and she walked reluctantly from her room. She merely changed her dress, and never thought of adding the artificial rose to her cheek.

When she took her seat in the dining-hall, and was asked if she would be helped, raising her eyes, she saw the person who asked her was deeply rouged, with a bright glaring spot, perfectly round, in either cheek. She looked at the next—the same apparition! She then slowly passed her eyes down the whole line, and saw the same, with a suppressed smile distorting every countenance. Catching the design at once, she deliberately looked along her own side of the table, at every schoolmate in turn; every one had joined in the trick. The teachers strove to be grave, but she saw they enjoyed the joke. The servants could not suppress a titter.

When Warren Hastings stood at the bar of Westminster Hall; when the Methodist preacher walked through a line of men, each of whom greeted him with a brickbat or rotten egg,—they had some preparation for the crisis, and it might not be very difficult to meet it with an impassive brow. Our little girl was quite unprepared to find herself in the midst of a world which despised her, and triumphed in her disgrace.

She had ruled like a queen in the midst of her companions; she had shed her animation through their lives, and loaded them with prodigal favors, nor once suspected that a popular favorite might not be loved. Now, she felt that she had been but a dangerous plaything in the hands of those whose hearts she never had doubted.

Yet the occasion found her equal to it; for Mariana had the kind of spirit, which, in a better cause, had made the Roman matron truly say of her death wound, "It is not painful, Poetus." She did not blench—she did not change countenance. She swallowed her dinner with apparent composure. She made remarks to those near her as if she had no eyes.

The wrath of the foe of course rose higher, and the moment they were freed from the restraints of the dining room, they all ran off, gayly calling, and sarcastically laughing, with backward glances, at Mariana, left alone.

Alone she went to her room, locked the door, and threw herself on the floor in strong convulsions. These had sometimes threatened her life, as a child, but of later years she had outgrown them. School hours came, and she was not there. A little girl, sent to her door, could get no answer. The teachers became alarmed, and broke it open. Bitter was their penitence and that of her companions at the state in which they found her. For some hours terrible anxiety was felt; but at last Nature, exhausted, relieved herself by a deep slumber.

From this Mariana arose an altered being. She made no reply to the expressions of sorrow from her companions, none to the grave and kind, but undiscerning comments of her teacher. She did not name the source of her anguish, and its poisoned dart sank deeply in. It was this thought which stung her so.— "What, not one, not a single one, in the hour of trial, to take my part! not one who refused to take part against me!" Past words of love, and caresses little heeded at the time, rose to her memory, and gave fuel to her distempered heart. Beyond the sense of universal perfidy, of burning resentment, she could not get. And Mariana, born for love, now hated all the world.

The change, however, which these feelings made in her conduct and appearance bore no such construction to the careless observer. Her gay freaks were quite gone, her wildness, her invention. Her dress was uniform, her manner much subdued. Her chief interest seemed now to lie in her studies and in music. Her companions she never sought; but they, partly from uneasy, remorseful feelings, partly that they really liked her much better now that she did not oppress and puzzle them, sought her continually. And here the black shadow comes upon her life—the only stain upon the history of Mariana.

They talked to her as girls, having few topics, naturally do of one another. Then the demon rose within her, and spontaneously, without design, generally without words of positive falsehood, she became a genius of discord among them. She fanned those flames of envy and jealousy which a wise, true word from a third person will often quench forever; by a glance, or a seemingly light reply, she planted the seeds of dissension, till there was scarce a peaceful affection or sincere intimacy in the circle where she lived, and could not but rule, for she was one whose nature was to that of the others as fire to clay.

It was at this time that I came to the school, and first saw Mariana. Me she charmed at once, for I was a sentimental child, who, in my early ill health, had been in-

dulged in reading novels till I had no eyes for the common
greens and browns of life. The heroine of one of these,
"the Bandit's Bride," I immediately saw in Mariana. Surely
the Bandit's Bride had just such hair, and such strange,
lively ways, and such a sudden flash of the eye. The
Bandit's Bride, too, was born to be "misunderstood" by all
but her lover. But Mariana, I was determined, should be
more fortunate; for, until her lover appeared, I myself
would be the wise and delicate being who could understand her.

It was not, however, easy to approach her for this purpose. Did I offer to run and fetch her handkerchief, she
was obliged to go to her room, and would rather do it herself. She did not like to have people turn over for her the
leaves of the music book as she played. Did I approach
my stool to her feet, she moved away, as if to give me
room. The bunch of wild flowers which I timidly laid beside her plate was left there.

After some weeks my desire to attract her notice really
preyed upon me, and one day, meeting her alone in the
entry, I fell upon my knees, and kissing her hand, cried,
"O Mariana, do let me love you, and try to love me a little." But my idol snatched away her hand, and laughing
more wildly than the Bandit's Bride was ever described
to have done, ran into her room. After that day her manner to me was not only cold, but repulsive; I felt myself
scorned, and became very unhappy.

Perhaps four months had passed thus, when, one afternoon, it became obvious that something more than common was brewing. Dismay and mystery were written in
many faces of the older girls; much whispering was going
on in corners.

In the evening, after prayers, the principal bade us stay;
and, in a grave, sad voice summoned Mariana to answer
charges to be made against her.

Mariana came forward, and leaned against the chimney-
piece. Eight of the older girls came forward, and pre-

ferred against her charges—alas! too well founded—of calumny and falsehood.

My heart sank within me, as one after the other brought up their proofs, and I saw they were too strong to be resisted. I could not bear the thought of this second disgrace of my shining favorite. The first had been whispered to me, though the girls did not like to talk about it. I must confess, such is the charm of strength to softer natures, that neither of these crises could deprive Mariana of hers in my eyes.

At first, she defended herself with self-possession and eloquence. But when she found she could no more resist the truth, she suddenly threw herself down, dashing her head, with all her force, against the iron hearth, on which a fire was burning, and was taken up senseless.

The affright of those present was great. Now that they had perhaps killed her, they reflected it would have been as well if they had taken warning from the former occasion, and approached very carefully a nature so capable of any extreme. After a while she revived, with a faint groan, amid the sobs of her companions. I was on my knees by the bed, and held her cold hand. One of those most aggrieved took it from me to beg her pardon, and say it was impossible not to love her. She made no reply.

Neither that night, nor for several days, could a word be obtained from her, nor would she touch food; but, when it was presented to her, or any one drew near from any cause she merely turned away her head, and gave no sign. The teacher saw that some terrible nervous affection had fallen upon her—that she grew more and more feverish. She knew not what to do.

Meanwhile, a new revolution had taken place in the mind of the passionate but nobly-tempered child. All these months nothing but the sense of injury had rankled in her heart. She had gone on in one mood, doing what the demon prompted, without scruple and without fear.

But at the moment of detection, the tide ebbed, and

the bottom of her soul lay revealed to her eye. How black, how stained and sad! Strange, strange, that she had not seen before the baseness and cruelty of falsehood, the loveliness of truth! Now, amid the wreck, uprose the moral nature, which never before had attained the ascendant. "But," she thought, "too late sin is revealed to me in all its deformity, and sin-defiled, I will not, cannot live. The main-spring of life is broken."

And thus passed slowly by her hours in that black despair of which only youth is capable. In older years men suffer more dull pain, as each sorrow that comes drops its leaden weight into the past, and, similar features of character bringing similar results, draws up the heavy burden buried in those depths. But only youth has energy, with fixed, unwinking gaze, to contemplate grief, to hold it in the arms and to the heart, like a child which makes it wretched, yet is indubitably its own.

The lady who took charge of this sad child had never well understood her before, but had always looked on her with great tenderness. And now love seemed—when all around were in greatest distress, fearing to call in medical aid, fearing to do without it—to teach her where the only blame was to be found that could have healed this wounded spirit.

One night she came in, bringing a calming draught. Mariana was sitting, as usual, her hair loose, her dress the same robe they put on her at first, her eyes fixed vacantly upon the whited wall. To the proffers and entreaties of her nurse, she made no reply.

The lady burst into tears, but Mariana did not seem even to observe it.

The lady then said, "O, my child, do not despair; do not think that one great fault can mar a whole life! Let me trust you; let me tell you the griefs of my sad life. I will tell you, Mariana, what I never expected to impart to any one."

And so she told her tale: it was one of pain, of shame,

borne, not for herself, but for one near and dear as herself. Mariana knew the lady—knew the pride and reserve of her nature. She had often admired to see how the cheek, lovely, but no longer young, mantled with the deepest blush of youth, and the blue eyes were cast down at any little emotion: she had understood the proud sensibility of the character. She fixed her eyes on those now raised to hers, bright with fast-falling tears. She heard the story to the end, and then, without saying a word, stretched out her hand for the cup.

She returned to life, but it was as one who had passed through the valley of death. The heart of stone was quite broken in her, the fiery life fallen from flame to coal. When her strength was a little restored, she had all her companions summoned, and said to them,—"I deserved to die, but a generous trust has called me back to life. I will be worthy of it, nor ever betray the truth, or resent injury more. Can you forgive the past?"

And they not only forgave, but, with love and earnest tears, clasped in their arms the returning sister. They vied with one another in offices of humble love to the humbled one; and let it be recorded, as an instance of the pure honor of which young hearts are capable, that these facts, known to forty persons, never, so far as I know, transpired beyond those walls.

It was not long after this that Mariana was summoned home. She went thither a wonderfully instructed being, though in ways those who had sent her forth to learn little dreamed of.

Never was forgotten the vow of the returning prodigal. Mariana could not resent, could not play false. The terrible crisis which she so early passed through probably prevented the world from hearing much of her. A wild fire was tamed in that hour of penitence at the boarding school such as has oftentimes wrapped court and camp in a destructive glow.

But great were the perils she had yet to undergo, for

she was one of those barks which easily get beyond sound-
ings, and ride not lightly on the plunging billow.

Her return to her native climate seconded the effects
of inward revolutions. The cool airs of the north had exasperated nerves too susceptible for their tension. Those
of the south restored her to a more soft and indolent
state. Energy gave place to feeling—turbulence to intensity
of character.

At this time, love was the natural guest; and he came
to her under a form that might have deluded one less
ready for delusion.

Sylvain was a person well proportioned to her lot in
years, family, and fortune. His personal beauty was not
great, but of a noble description. Repose marked his slow
gesture, and the steady gaze of his large brown eye; but
it was a repose that would give way to a blaze of energy,
when the occasion called. In his stature, expression, and
heavy coloring, he might not unfitly be represented by the
great magnolias that inhabit the forests of that climate.
His voice, like every thing about him, was rich and soft,
rather than sweet and delicate.

Mariana no sooner knew him than she loved; and her
love, lovely as he was, soon excited his. But O, it is curse
to woman to love first, or most! In so doing she reverses
the natural relations; and her heart can never, never be
satisfied with what ensues.

Mariana loved first, and loved most, for she had most
force and variety to love with. Sylvain seemed, at first, to
take her to himself, as the deep southern night might some
fair star; but it proved not so.

Mariana was a very intellectual being, and she needed
companionship. This she could only have with Sylvain, in
the paths of passion and action. Thoughts he had none,
and little delicacy of sentiment. The gifts she loved to
prepare of such for him he took with a sweet but indolent
smile; he held them lightly, and soon they fell from his
grasp. He loved to have her near him, to feel the glow

and fragrance of her nature, but cared not to explore the little secret paths whence that fragrance was collected.

Mariana knew not this for a long time. Loving so much, she imagined all the rest; and, where she felt a blank, always hoped that further communication would fill it up. When she found this could never be,—that there was absolutely a whole province of her being to which nothing in his answered,—she was too deeply in love to leave him. Often, after passing hours together beneath the southern moon, when, amid the sweet intoxication of mutual love, she still felt the desolation of solitude, and a repression of her finer powers, she had asked herself, Can I give him up? But the heart always passionately answered, No! I may be wretched with him, but I cannot live without him.

And the last miserable feeling of these conflicts was, that if the lover—soon to be the bosom friend—could have dreamed of these conflicts, he would have laughed, or else been angry, even enough to give her up.

Ah, weakness of the strong! of those strong only where strength is weakness! Like others, she had the decisions of life to make before she had light by which to make them. Let none condemn her. Those who have not erred as fatally should thank the guardian angel who gave them more time to prepare for judgment, but blame no children who thought at arm's length to find the moon. Mariana, with a heart capable of the highest Eros, gave it to one who knew love only as a flower or plaything, and bound her heartstrings to one who parted his as lightly as the ripe fruit leaves the bough. The sequel could not fail. Many console themselves for the one great mistake with their children, with the world. This was not possible for Mariana. A few months of domestic life she still was almost happy. But Sylvain then grew tired. He wanted business and the world; of these she had no knowledge, for them no faculties. He wanted in her head of his house; she to make her heart his home. No compromise was pos-

sible between natures of such unequal poise, and which
had met only on one or two points. Through all its stages
she

> felt
>
> The agonizing sense
> Of seeing love from passion melt
> Into indifference;
> The fearfull shame, that, day by day,
> Burns onward, still to burn,
> To have thrown her precious heart away,
> And met this black return,

till death at last closed the scene. Not that she died of
one downright blow on the heart. That is not the way such
cases proceed. I cannot detail all the symptoms, for I was
not there to watch them, and Aunt Z., who described
them, was neither so faithful an observer or narrator as I
have shown myself in the school-day passages; but generally, they were as follows.

Sylvain wanted to go into the world, or let it into his
house. Mariana consented; but, with an unsatisfied heart,
and no lightness of character, she played her part ill there.
The sort of talent and facility she had displayed in early
days were not the least like what is called out in the social
world by the desire to please and to shine. Her excitement
had been muse-like—that of the *improvvisatrice*, whose
kindling fancy seeks to create an atmosphere round it, and
makes the chain through which to set free its electric
sparks. That had been a time of wild and exuberant life.
After her character became more tender and concentrated,
strong affection or a pure enthusiasm might still have
called out beautiful talents in her. But in the first she
was utterly disappointed. The second was not roused
within her mind. She did not expand into various life,
and remained unequal; sometimes too passive, sometimes
too ardent, and not sufficiently occupied with what oc-

cupied those around her to come on the same level with them and embellish their hours.

Thus she lost ground daily with her husband, who, comparing her with the careless shining dames of society, wondered why he had found her so charming in solitude.

At intervals, when they were left alone, Mariana wanted to open her heart, to tell the thoughts of her mind. She was so conscious of secret riches within herself, that sometimes it seemed, could she but reveal a glimpse of them to the eye of Sylvain, he would be attracted near her again, and take a path where they could walk hand in hand. Sylvain, in these intervals, wanted an indolent repose. His home was his castle. He wanted no scenes too exciting there. Light jousts and plays were well enough, but no grave encounters. He liked to lounge, to sing, to read, to sleep. In fine, Sylvain became the kind but preoccupied husband, Mariana the solitary and wretched wife. He was off, continually, with his male companions, on excursions or affairs of pleasure. At home Mariana found that neither her books nor music would console her.

She was of too strong a nature to yield without a struggle to so dull a fiend as despair. She looked into other hearts, seeking whether she could there find such home as an orphan asylum may afford. This she did rather because the chance came to her, and it seemed unfit not to seize the proffered plank, than in hope; for she was not one to double her stakes, but rather with Cassandra power to discern early the sure course of the game. And Cassandra whispered that she was one of those

"Whom men love not, but yet regret;"

and so it proved. Just as in her childish days, though in a different form, it happened betwixt her and these companions. She could not be content to receive them quietly, but was stimulated to throw herself too much into the tie, into the hour, till she filled it too full for them. Like Fortunio, who sought to do homage to his friends by building a fire of cinnamon, not knowing that its perfume would be too strong for their endurance, so did Mariana. What she wanted to tell they did not wish to hear; a little had pleased, so much over-powered, and they preferred the free air of the street, even, to the cinnamon perfume of her palace.

However, this did not signify; had they staid, it would not have availed her. It was a nobler road, a higher aim, she needed now; this did not become clear to her.

She lost her appetite, she fell sick, had fever. Sylvain was alarmed, nursed her tenderly; she grew better. Then his care ceased; he saw not the mind's disease, but left her to rise into health, and recover the tone of her spirits, as she might. More solitary than ever, she tried to raise herself; but she knew not yet enough. The weight laid upon her young life was a little too heavy for it. One long day she passed alone, and the thoughts and presages came too thick for her strength. She knew not what to do with them, relapsed into fever, and died.

Notwithstanding this weakness, I must ever think of her as a fine sample of womanhood, born to shed light and life on some palace home. Had she known more of God and the universe, she would not have given way where so many have conquered. But peace be with her; she now, perhaps, has entered into a larger freedom, which is knowledge. With her died a great interest in life to me. Since her I have never seen a Bandit's Bride. She, indeed, turned out to be only a merchant's. Sylvain is married again to a fair and laughing girl, who will not die, probably, till their marriage grows a "golden marriage."

Aunt Z. had with her some papers of Mariana's, which faintly shadow forth the thoughts that engaged her in the last days. One of these seems to have been written when some faint gleam had been thrown across the path only to make its darkness more visible. It seems to have been suggested by remembrance of the beautiful ballad, *Helen of Kirconnel Lee*, which once she loved to recite, and in

tones that would not have sent a chill to the heart from
which it came.

                                 Death
Opens her sweet white arms, and whispers, Peace;
Come, say thy sorrows in this bosom! This
Will never close against thee, and my heart,
Though cold, cannot be colder much than man's.

DISAPPOINTMENT

"I wish I were where Helen lies."
    A lover in the times of old,
Thus vents his grief in lonely sighs,
    And hot tears from a bosom cold.

But, mourner for thy martyred love,
    Couldst thou but know what hearts must feel,
Where no sweet recollections move,
    Whose tears a desert fount reveal!

When "in thy arms bird Helen fell,"
    She died, sad man, she died for thee;
Nor could the films of death dispel
    Her loving eye's sweet radiancy.

Thou wert beloved, and she had loved,
    Till death alone the whole could tell;
Death every shade of doubt removed,
    And steeped the star in its cold well.

On some fond breast the parting soul
    Relies—earth has no more to give!
Who wholly loves has known the whole;
    The wholly loved doth truly live.

But some, sad outcasts from this prize,
    Do wither to a lonely grave;
All hearts their hidden love despise,
    And leave them to the whelming wave.

They heart to heart have never pressed,
    Nor hand in holy pledge have given,
By father's love were ne'er caressed,
    Nor in a mother's eye saw heaven.

A flowerless and fruitless tree,
    A dried-up stream, a mateless bird,
They live, yet never living be,
    They die, their music all unheard.

I wish I were where Helen lies,
    For there I could not be alone;
But now, when this dull body dies,
    The spirit still will make its moan.

Love passed me by, nor touched my brow;
    Life would not yield one perfect boon;
And all too late it calls me now—
    O, all too late, and all too soon.

If thou couldst the dark riddle read
    Which leaves this dart within my breast,
Then might I think thou lov'st indeed,
    Then were the whole to thee confest.

Father, they will not take me home;
    To the poor child no heart is free;
In sleet and snow all night I roam;
    Father, was this decreed by thee?

I will not try another door,
    To seek what I have never found;
Now, till the very last is o'er,
    Upon the earth I'll wander round.

I will not hear the treacherous call
    That bids me stay and rest a while,
For I have found that, one and all,
    They seek me for a prey and spoil.

They are not bad; I know it well;
>   I know they know not what they do;
They are the tools of the dread spell
>   Which the lost lover must pursue.

In temples sometimes she may rest,
>   In lonely groves, away from men,
There bend the head, by heats distressed,
>   Nor be by blows awoke again.

Nature is kind, and God is kind;
>   And, if she had not had a heart,
Only that great discerning mind,
>   She might have acted well her part.

But O this thirst, that nought can fill,
>   Save those unfounden waters free!
The angel of my life must still
>   And soothe me in eternity!

It marks the defect in the position of woman that one
like Mariana should have found reason to write thus. To a
man of equal power, equal sincerity, no more!—many resources would have presented themselves. He would not
have needed to seek, he would have been called by life,
and not permitted to be quite wrecked through the affections only. But such women as Mariana are often lost,
unless they meet some man of sufficiently great soul to
prize them.

Van Artevelde's Elena, though in her individual nature
unlike my Mariana, is like her in a mind whose large impulses are disproportioned to the persons and occasions
she meets, and which carry her beyond those reserves
which mark the appointed lot of woman. But, when she
met Van Artevelde, he was too great not to revere her
rare nature, without regard to the stains and errors of its
past history; great enough to receive her entirely, and
make a new life for her; man enough to be a lover! But

as such men come not so often as once an age, their presence should not be absolutely needed to sustain life.

4. READING

(Text from *Memoirs*, I, 30–32; evidently from pages that were intended to become an autobiography.)

[Emerson said that Margaret read as extensively as Gibbon. She was probably even better read. Her father, in a childhood scene she recollects all too minutely, forbade her to read Shakespeare on Sunday—peremptorily sending her to bed when she disobeyed him—but precociously she indulged herself with Shakespeare, Cervantes, and Molière. On first thought, these seem a rather strange trinity for so romantic a soul, but actually they each had a special appeal to the romantic sensibility, which customarily strove to check the vehemence of its emotional drive by a devout worship of the exquisitely concrete. Margaret, like Thoreau and Francis Parkman, was constantly struggling to reconcile these polarities, and hence adopted the three men as her intellectual ideals. Yet, characteristic of the Romantic, Margaret impugns her masters, as her father, for having aroused her to larger expectations of life than life could fulfill—although not a moment of the anguish would she willingly forgo!]

. . . These men were all alike in this,—they loved the *natural history* of man. Not what he should be, but what he is, was the favorite subject of their thought. Whenever a noble leading opened to the eye new paths of light, they rejoiced; but it was never fancy, but always fact, that inspired them. They loved a thorough penetration of the murkiest dens, and most tangled paths of nature; they did not spin from the desires of their own special natures, but reconstructed the world from materials which they collected on every side. Thus their influence upon me was not to prompt me to follow out thought in myself so much as to detect it everywhere, for each of these men is not only a nature, but a happy interpreter of many natures. They taught me to distrust all invention which is not based on a wide experience. Perhaps, too, they taught me to overvalue an outward experience at the expense of inward growth; but all this I did not appreciate till later.

It will be seen that my youth was not unfriended, since those great minds came to me in kindness. A moment of action in one's self, however, is worth an age of apprehension through others; not that our deeds are better, but that they produce a renewal of our being. I have had more productive moments and of deeper joy, but never hours of more tranquil pleasure than those in which these demi-gods visited me,—and with a smile so familiar, that I imagined the world to be full of such. They did me good, for by them a standard was early given of sight and thought, from which I could never go back, and beneath which I cannot suffer patiently my own life or that of any friend to fall. They did me harm, too, for the child fed with meat instead of milk becomes too soon mature. Expectations and desires were thus early raised, after which I must long toil before they can be realized. How poor the scene around, how tame one's own existence, how meagre and faint every power, with these beings in my mind! Often I must cast them quite aside in order to grow in my small way, and not sink into despair. Certainly I do not wish that instead of these masters I had read baby books, written down to children, and with such ignorant dulness that they blunt the senses and corrupt the tastes of the still plastic human being. But I do wish that I had read no books at all till later,—that I had lived with toys, and played in the open air. Children should not cull the fruits of reflection and observation, but expand in the sun, and let thoughts come to them. They should not through books antedate their actual experiences, but should take them gradually, as sympathy and interpretation are needed. With me, much of life was devoured in the bud.

5. SELF-SEARCHING

(Probably written around 1829; text from *Memoirs*, I, 135–36.)

[Margaret Fuller's papers abound with an extravagance of self-analysis that can become, even to the sympathetic reader, a bore. Yet when these passages are viewed as a manifestation not alone of her preoccupation with herself but of that frenzy of self-absorption to which, as she would have happily acknowledged, the spiritual progeny of Rousseau were condemned, they become eloquent footnotes to the fantasy of "Mariana." Again, they show this crude, native genius groping toward the grandeur of romantic selfhood, toward the Byronic. This desire would obsess Margaret Fuller, but it also would plague her, as she would never be able to ignore completely her New England Puritan heritage. Here she announces the utter failure of any Christian solution to her problem—or rather, she rejects any such formulation.]

My pride is superior to any feelings I have yet experienced: my affection is strong admiration, not the necessity of giving or receiving assistance or sympathy. When disappointed, I do not ask or wish consolation,—I wish to know and feel my pain, to investigate its nature and its source; I will not have my thoughts diverted, or my feelings soothed; 'tis therefore that my young life is so singularly barren of illusions. I know I feel the time must come when this proud and impatient heart shall be stilled, and turn from the ardors of Search and Action, to lean on something above. But—shall I say it?—the thought of the calmer era is to me a thought of deepest sadness; so remote from my present being is that future existence, which still the mind may conceive. I believe in Eternal Progression. I believe in a God, a Beauty and Perfection to which I am to strive all my life for assimilation. From these two articles of belief, I draw the rules by which I strive to regulate my life. But, though I reverence all religions as necessary to the happiness of man, I am yet ignorant of the religion of Revelation. Tangible promises! well defined hopes! are things of which I do not *now* feel the need. At present, my soul is intent on this life, and I think of religion as its rule; and, in my opinion, this is the natural and proper course from youth to age. What I have written is not hastily concocted, it has a meaning. I have given you, in this little space, the substance of many thoughts, the clues to many cherished opinions. 'Tis a subject on which I rarely speak. I have here given you all I know, or think, on the most important of subjects— could you but read understandingly!

6. GENIUS

(Passage is dated May 4, 1830; text from *Memoirs*, I, 69–70.)

[Every epoch in Western culture has held up to the admiration of the multitude an image of superiority, called genius. But no age so exalted the word itself, let alone the wonder-working prowess of this natural, yet supernaturally endowed, creature as did that of the French Revolution and of Napoleon, Goethe, and Byron.

Of all American youths, Margaret Fuller, by temperament and literary stimulation, probably responded most

to the lure of this ideal—although others named Poe, Mel-
ville, Thoreau, Hawthorne, and even Emerson felt its at-
traction. Margaret here casts her glorified self—as she
frequently did—into a masculine image, but she is obvi-
ously celebrating her own apotheosis. She was not to be
permitted to live it out in the terms she here envisions.
Possibly the most poignant comment upon her vision is
that this passage is virtually a prefiguration of the hero of
Herman Melville's Pierre, *whom Americans firmly rejected*
in 1852.]

. . . I have greatly wished to see among us such a person
of genius as the nineteenth century can afford—i.e., one
who has tasted in the morning of existence the extremes
of good and ill, both imaginative and real. I had imagined
a person endowed by nature with that acute sense of
Beauty, (i.e., Harmony or Truth,) and that vast capacity
of desire, which give soul to love and ambition. I had
wished this person might grow up to manhood alone (but
not alone in crowds); I would have placed him in a situation so retired, so obscure, that he would quietly, but
without bitter sense of isolation, stand apart from all sur-
rounding him. I would have had him go on steadily, feeding his mind with congenial love, hopefully confident that
if he only nourished his existence into perfect life, Fate
would, at fitting season, furnish an atmosphere and orbit
meet for his breathing and exercise. I wished he might
adore, not fever for, the bright phantoms of his mind's
creation, and believe them but the shadows of external
things to be met with hereafter. After this steady intellectual growth had brought his powers to manhood, so
far as the ideal can do it, I wished this being might be
launched into the world of realities, his heart glowing
with the ardor of an immortal perfection, his eyes searching everywhere to behold it; I wished he might collect
into one burning point those withering, palsying convictions, which, in the ordinary routine of things, so gradu-

ally pervade the soul; that he might suffer, in brief space, agonies of disappointment commensurate with his unpreparedness and confidence. And I thought, thus thrown back on the representing pictorial resources I supposed him originally to possess, with such material, and the need he must feel of using it, such a man would suddenly dilate into a form of Pride, Power, and Glory,—a centre, round which asking, aimless hearts might rally,—a man fitted to act as interpreter to the one tale of many-languaged eyes!

What words are these! Perhaps you will feel as if I sought but for the longest and strongest. Yet to my ear they do but faintly describe the imagined powers of such a being.

7. SELF-CONSCIOUSNESS

(From a letter printed in *Memoirs*, I, 98–101, apparently before the removal to Groton.)

[James Freeman Clarke quotes this letter in the section on "Cambridge Friendship" in the Memoirs. *He did not know to whom it was addressed. Whether to a man or to a woman we cannot tell, but whichever the case, it is a typical disclosure of Margaret's temperament.]*

. . . From a very early age I have felt that I was not born to the common womanly lot. I knew I should never find a being who could keep the key of my character; that there would be none on whom I could always lean, from whom I could always learn; that I should be a pilgrim and sojourner on earth, and that the birds and foxes would be surer of a place to lay the head than I. You understand me, of course; such being can only find their homes in hearts. All material luxuries, all arrangements of society, are mere conveniences to them.

This thought, all whose bearing I did not, indeed, understand, affected me sometimes with sadness, sometimes with pride. I mourned that I never should have a thorough experience of life, never know the full riches of my being; I was proud that I was to test myself in the sternest way, that I was always to return to myself, to be my own priest, pupil, parent, child, husband, and wife. All this I did not understand as I do now; but this destiny of the thinker, and (shall I dare to say it?) of the poetic priestess, sibylline, dwelling in the cave or amid the Lybian sands, lay yet enfolded in my mind. Accordingly, I did not look on any of the persons, brought into relation with me, with common womanly eyes.

Yet, as my character is, after all, still more feminine than masculine, it would sometimes happen that I put more emotion into a state than I myself knew. I really was capable of attachment, though it never seemed so till the hour of separation. And if a connexion was torn up by the roots, the soil of my existence showed an unsightly wound, which long refused to clothe itself in verdure.

With regard to yourself, I was to you all that I wished to be. I knew that I reigned in your thoughts in my own way. And I also lived with you more truly and freely than with any other person. We were truly friends, but it was not friends as men are friends to one another, or as brother and sister. There was, also, that pleasure, which may, perhaps, be termed conjugal, of finding oneself in an alien nature. Is there a tinge of love in this? Possibly! At least, in comparing it with my relation to——, I find *that* was strictly fraternal. I valued him for himself. I did not care for an influence over him, and was perfectly willing to have one or fifty rivals in his heart. . . .

. . . I think I may say, I never loved. I but see my possible life reflected on the clouds. As in a glass darkly, I have seen what I might feel as child, wife, mother, but I have never really approached the close relations of life.

A sister I have truly been to many,—a brother to more,—
a fostering nurse to, oh how many! The bridal hour of
many a spirit, when first it was wed, I have shared, but
said adieu before the wine was poured out at the banquet.
And there is one I always love in my poetic hour, as the
lily looks up to the star amid the waters; and another
whom I visit as the bee visits the flower, when I crave
sympathy. Yet those who live would scarcely consider that
I am among the living,—and I am isolated, as you say.

My dear——, all is well; all has helped me to decipher
the great poem of the universe. I can hardly describe to
you the happiness which floods my solitary hours. My
actual life is yet much clogged and impeded, but I have
at last got me an oratory, where I can retire and pray.
With your letter, vanished a last regret. You did not act
or think unworthily. It is enough. As to the cessation of
our confidential intercourse, circumstances must have accomplished that long ago; my only grief was that you
should do it with your own free will, and for reasons that
I thought unworthy. I long to honor you, to be honored
by you. Now we will have free and noble thoughts of one
another, and all that is best of our friendship shall remain.

CHAPTER II

GROTON, PROVIDENCE, JAMAICA PLAIN
1833–1840

1. THE ANGUISH OF GROTON

(From a letter to her brother Richard, August 11, 1842; Fuller MSS, Harvard College Library.)

[In 1833, Timothy Fuller conceived what proved to be the disastrous notion of retiring from practice and retreating to a farm at Groton, Massachusetts. From her unhappy term at the Prescott school in 1823, Margaret already had miserable associations with the town. Now she was brutally abducted from the circle of the young intellectuals of Harvard with whom she was forming stimulating scholarly ties, and sentenced to a dismal isolation, an exile which at that time the thirty miles between Groton and Cambridge made virtually absolute. She was condemned to serve as tutor to the four youngest children, and only on rare occasions permitted an escape to the metropolis.

Shortly after the family arrived, her brother Arthur almost died, and in 1835 Margaret herself fell dangerously ill of a "brain fever" and for several days hovered near death. She was just beginning to recover when her father suddenly died on October 2, 1835. He left a sadly diminished estate, and Margaret had to give up her plans to go to Europe, and take up the burden of supporting her

*family. In this letter she looks back upon those years,
which she could by now view objectively, although she
indicates how much of an ordeal they were, coming on
the heels of the agonies of her childhood. Yet in April
of 1842 she wrote to an intimate friend that while destiny,
in the phrase of George Herbert, still "cross biases me,"
refusing her solitude and quiet, it had rewarded her "with
many new and sweet thoughts, an extending hope, and
a clear faith."]*

. . . You do not speak of Groton. That place is very
beautiful in its way, but I never admired it much, both
because the scenery is too tamely smiling and sleepy, and
because it jarred my mood. My associations with the place
are painful. The first passage of our lives there was Arthur's misfortune, my first weeks were passed in Arthur's
chamber. There darkened round us the consequences of
our father's ill-judged exchange.

Father's removal there was ill-judged, at least as regarded himself, your mother, and myself. The younger
ones were not violently rent from all their former life and
cast on toils for which they were unprepared. There your
mother's health was injured and mine destroyed; there
your father died, but not till the cares of a narrowed income, and collisions with his elder sons which would not
have ended there had so embittered his life and made
him so over anxious that I have never regretted that he
did not stay longer to watch the turning of the tide, for
his life up to 1830 had been one of well-earned prosperity,
which, after that time, was rapidly ebbing from him, and
I do not think adversity would have done him good. He
could not reconcile himself to it, his feeling was that after
thirty years' labor and self-denial he was entitled to peace
and he would not have had it.

You are too young to feel how trying are the disorders
of a house which has lost its head, the miserable perplexities which arose in our affairs, the wounds your

mother underwent in that time of deep dejection from the
unfeeling and insolent conduct of many who had been
kept in check by respect for your father, her loneliness
and sense of unfitness for the new and heavy burden of
care. It will be many years before you can appreciate the
conflicts of my mind, as I doubted whether to give up all
which my heart desired for a path for which I had no
skill, and no call, except that *some one* must tread it,
none else was ready.

The Peterborough hills and the Waschusetts are associated in my mind with many hours of anguish, as great
I think as I am capable of feeling. I used to look at them,
towering to the sky, and feel that I, too, from my birth
had longed to rise, but I felt crushed to earth; yet again
a nobler spirit said *that* could never be. The good knight
may come forth scarred and maimed from the unequal
contest, shorn of his strength and unsightly to the careless eye, but the same fire burns within and deeper than
ever, and he may be conquered but *never subdued.*

But if these beautiful hills, and wide, rich fields saw
this sad lore well learned they also saw some precious
lessons given too, of faith, of fortitude, of self-command,
and a less selfish love. There too in solitude the mind
acquired more power of concentration, and discerned the
beauty of a stricter method. There the heart was awakened to sympathize with the ignorant, to pity the vulgar,
and hope for the seemingly worthless; for a need was felt
of realizing the only reality, the divine soul of this visible
creation, which cannot err and will not sleep, which cannot permit evil to be permanent or its aim of beauty to
be eventually frustrated in the smallest particular.

2. CLASSICAL AND ROMANTIC

(From the _Western Messenger_, I, December 1835, pp. 398–432.)

[_Sir Henry Taylor's_ Philip Van Artevelde, _published in 1834, is a "closet" drama which, for reasons unfathomed by us, was enthusiastically received by the most advanced intelligences of the period as an equal to Goethe's_ Faust. _In America it aroused violent hostility—at least in the public notices. It, like_ Faust, _was accused of corrupting our youth. In the play, Artevelde turns from a life of meditation to one of action for the sake of his people, but he becomes intoxicated with political power and goes down to defeat in a blaze of Napoleonic egotism. We need to remember that Andrew Jackson was then President of the United States, and that Margaret Fuller was a Democrat._

Margaret was still in Groton when she wrote a review of this controversial drama for the Messenger, _a periodical that her friend from Cambridge, William Henry Channing, was striving to publish in the frontier outpost of Cincinnati. Although Margaret had successfully written two articles for the periodical prior to this, and although Channing was courageous in giving space to any discussion of_ Artevelde _in Cincinnati, it was utterly foolhardy of him to entrust a New England maiden with the task._

The differentiation between Classical and Romantic, which had been a commonplace in German critical theory for a generation, was still barely known in the United States when this piece appeared. What little Americans apprehended of it, they instinctively rejected as a threat to native institutions. Along with everything else emanating from Germany, it seemed to them somehow slyly immoral.

Oddly enough, Margaret Fuller, Emerson, and others in the Transcendental band, who were beginning to grasp the distinction and who were quickly accused by the general public of being contaminated by the "German disease," liked to consider themselves Classical rather than Romantic. They were all children of Rousseau, but most of them strove to suppress the delirious elements of their genius. In this piece, Margaret contends against the Romantic ego and appeals to the "Classical" virtues of Goethe's Iphigenia, although she is exceptional among the Transcendentalists in her ultimate willingness to recognize her true spiritual paternity.]

The natural process of the mind in forming a judgment is comparison. The office of sound criticism is to teach that this comparison should be made, not between the productions of differently-constituted minds, but between any one of these and a fixed standard of perfection. Nevertheless it is not contrary to the canon to take a survey of the labors of many artists with reference to one, if we value them, not according to the degree of pleasure we have experienced from them, which must always depend upon our then age, the state of the passions and relations with life, but according to the success of the artist in attaining the object he himself had in view. To illustrate: In the same room hang two pictures, Raphael's Madonna and Martin's Destruction of Nineveh. A person enters, capable of admiring both, but young, excitable; he is delighted with the Madonna, but probably far more so with the other, because his imagination is at that time more developed than the pure love for beauty which is the characteristic of a taste in a higher state of cultivation. He prefers the Martin, because it excites in his mind a thousand images of sublimity and terror, recalls the brilliancy of Oriental history, and the stern pomp of the old prophetic day, and rouses his mind to a high state of action, *then* as congenial with its wants as at a later day would be the feeling of contented absorption, of perfect satisfaction with a production of the human soul, which one of Raphael's calmly beautiful creations is fitted to cause. Now, it would be very unfair for this person to pronounce the Martin superior to the Raphael, because it then gave him more pleasure. But if he said, the one is intended to excite the imagination, the other to gratify the taste, that which fulfils its object most completely must be the best, whether it give me most pleasure or no; he would be on the right ground, and might consider the two pictures relatively to one another, without danger of straying very far from the truth.

This is the ground we would assume in a hasty sketch, which will not, we hope, be deemed irrelevant, of the most prominent essays to which the last sixty years have given rise in the department of the work now before us, previous to stating our opinion of its merits. Many, we are aware, ridicule the idea of filling reviews with long dissertations, and say they only want brief accounts of such books as are coming out, by way of saving time. With such we cannot agree. We think the office of the reviewer is, indeed, in part, to point out to the public attention deserving works, which might otherwise slumber too long unknown on the bookseller's shelves, but still more to present to the reader as large a cluster of objects round one point as possible, thus, by suggestion, stimulating him to take a broader or more careful view of the subject than his indolence or his business would have permitted.

The terms Classical and Romantic, which have so long divided European critics, and exercised so powerful an influence upon their decisions, are not much known or heeded among us,—as, indeed, *belles-lettres* cannot, generally, in our busy state of things, be important or influential, as among a less free and more luxurious people, to whom the more important truths are proffered through those indirect but alluring mediums. Here, where everything may be spoken or written, and the powers that be, abused without ceremony on the very highway, the Muse has nothing to do with dagger or bowl; hardly is the censor's wand permitted to her hand. Yet is her lyre by no means unheeded, and if it is rather by refining our tastes than by modelling our opinions that she influences us, yet is that influence far from unimportant. And the time is coming, perhaps in our day, we may (if war do not untimely check the national progress) even see and temper its beginning, when the broad West shall swarm with an active, happy, and cultivated population; when the South, freed from the incubus which now oppresses her best energies, shall be able to do justice to the resources of her soil and of her mind; when the East, gathering from every breeze the riches of the old world, shall be the unwearied and loving agent to those regions which lie far away from the great deep, our bulwark and our minister. Then will the division of labor be more complete; then will a surplus of talent be spared from the mart, the forum, and the pulpit; then will the fine arts assume their proper dignity, as the expression of what is highest and most ethereal in the mind of a people. Then will our quarries be thoroughly explored, and furnish materials for stately fabrics to adorn the face of all the land, while our ports shall be crowded with foreign artists flocking to take lessons in the school of American architecture. Then will our floral treasures be arranged into harmonious gardens, which, environing tasteful homes, shall dimple all the landscape. Then will our Allstons and our Greenoughs preside over great academies, and be raised far above any need, except of giving outward form to the beautiful ideas which animate them; and ornament from the exhaustless stores of genius the marble halls where the people meet to rejoice, or to mourn, or where dwell those wise and good whom the people delight to honor. Then shall music answer to and exalt the national spirit, and the poet's brows shall be graced with the civic as well as the myrtle crown. Then shall we have an American mind, as well as an American system, and, no longer under the sad necessity of exchanging money for thoughts, traffic on perfectly equal terms with the other hemisphere. Then—ah, not yet!—shall our literature make its own laws, and give its own watchwords; till then we must learn and borrow from that of nations who possess a higher degree of cultivation though a much lower one of happiness.

The term Classical, used in its narrow sense, implies a servile adherence to the Unities, but in its wide and best sense, it means such a simplicity of plan, selection of actors and events, such judicious limitations on time and range of subject, as may concentrate the interest, perfect the illusion, and make the impression most distinct and forcible. Although no advocates for the old French school, with its slavish obedience to rule, which introduces follies greater than those it would guard against, we lay the blame, not on their view of the drama, but on the then bigoted nationality of the French mind, which converted the Mussulman prophet into a De Retz, the Roman princess into a French grisette, and infected the clear and buoyant atmosphere of Greece with the vapors of the Seine. We speak of the old French Drama: with the modern we do not profess to be acquainted, having met with scarcely any specimens in our own bookstores or libraries; but if it has been revolutionized with the rest of their literature, it is probably as unlike as possible to the former models.

We shall speak of productions in the classical spirit first; because Mr. Taylor is a disciple of the other school, though otherwise we should have adopted a contrary course.

The most perfect specimens of this style with which we are acquainted are the Filippo, the Saul, and the Myrrha of Alfieri; the Wallenstein of Schiller; the Tasso and the Iphigenia of Gœthe. England furnishes nothing of the sort. She is thoroughly Shakespearian.

There is no higher pleasure than to see a genius of a

wild, impassioned, many-sided eagerness, restraining its exuberance by its sense of fitness, taming its extravagance beneath the rule its taste approves, exhibiting the soul within soul, and the force of the will over all that we inherit. The *abandon* of genius has its beauty—far more beautiful its voluntary submission to wise law. A picture, a description, has beauty, the beauty of life; these pictures, these descriptions, arranged upon a plan, made subservient to a purpose, have a higher beauty—that of the mind of man acting upon life. Art is nature, but nature new-modelled, condensed, and harmonized. We are not merely like mirrors, to reflect our own times to those more distant. The mind has a light of its own, and by it illumines what it re-creates.

This is the ground of our preference for the classical school, and for Alfieri beyond all pupils of that school. We hold that if a vagrant bud of poesy here and there be blighted by conforming to its rules, our loss is more than made up to us by our enjoyment of plan, of symmetry, of the triumph of genius over multiplied obstacles.

It has been often said that the dramas of Alfieri contrast directly with his character. This is, perhaps, not true; we do but see the depths of that volcano which in early days boiled over so fiercely. The wild, infatuated youth often becomes the stern, pitiless old man. Alfieri did but bend his surplus strength upon literature, and became a despot to his own haughty spirit, instead of domineering over those of others.

We have selected his three masterpieces, though he, to himself an inexorable critic, has shown no indulgence to his own works, and the least successful of those which remain to us, Maria Stuarda, is marked by great excellence.

Filippo has been so ably depicted in a work now well known, Carlyle's "Life of Schiller," that we need not dwell upon it. All the light of the picture, the softer feelings of the hapless Carlos and Elizabeth, is so cast, as to make more visible the awing darkness of the tyrant's perverted mind, deadened to all virtue by a false religion, cold and hopeless as the dungeons of his own Inquisition, and relentless as death. Forced by the magic wand of genius into the stifling precincts of this mind, horror-struck that we must sympathize with such a state as possible to humanity, we rush from the contemplation of the picture, and would gladly curtain it over in our hall of imagery forever. Yet stigmatize not our poet as a dark master, courting the shade, and hating the glad lights which love and hope cast upon human nature. The drama has a holy meaning, a patriot moral, and we, above all, should reverence him, the aristocrat by birth, by education, and by tastes, whose love of liberty could lead him to such conclusions.

In "Saul," a bright rainbow rises, by the aid of the Sun of Righteousness, above the commotion of the tempest. David, the faithful, the hopeful, combining the æsthetic culture, the winged inspiration of the poet with the noble pride of Israel's chosen warrior, contrasts finely with the unfortunate Saul, his mind darkened and convulsed by jealousy, vain regrets, and fear of the God he has forgotten how to love. The other three actors shade in the picture without attracting our attention from the two principal personages. The Hebrew spirit breathes through the whole. The beauty of the lyric effusions is so generally felt, that encomium is needless; we shall only observe that in them Alfieri's style, usually so severe, becomes flexible, melodious, and glowing; thus we may easily perceive what he might have done, had not the simplicity of his genius disdained the foreign aid of ornament upon its Doric proportions.

Myrrha is, however, the highest exertion of his genius. The remoteness of time and manners, the subject, at once so hackneyed and so revolting, these great obstacles he seizes with giant grasp, and moulds them to his purpose. Our souls are shaken to the foundation; all every-day barriers fall with the great convulsion of passion. We sorrow, we sicken, we die with the miserable girl, so pure under her involuntary crime of feeling, pursued by a malignant deity in her soul's most sacred recesses, torn from all communion with humanity, and the virtue she was framed to adore. The perfection of plan, the matchless skill with which every circumstance is brought out! The agonizing rapidity with which her misery "va camminando al fine"! No! never was higher tragic power exhibited; never were love, terror, pity, fused into a more penetrating draught! Myrrha is a favorite acting-play in Italy—a fact inconceivable to an English or American mind; for (to say nothing of other objections) we should think such excess of emotion unbearable. But in those meridian climes they drink deep draughts of passion too frequently to taste them as we do.

We pass to works of far inferior power, but of greater beauty. We have selected Iphigenia and Tasso as the most finished results of their author's mature views of art. On his plays in the Romantic style, we shall touch in another place. If any one ask why we do not class Faust with either, we reply, *that* is a work without a parallel; one of those few originals which have their laws within themselves, and should always be discussed singly.

The unity of plan in Iphigenia is perfect. There is one pervading idea. The purity of Iphigenia's mind must be kept unsullied, that she may be a fit intercessor to the gods in behalf of her polluted family. Gœthe, in his travels through Italy, saw a picture of a youthful Christian saint—Agatha, we think; struck by the radiant purity of her expression, he resolved his heathen priestess should not have one thought which could revolt the saint of the true religion. This idea is wonderfully preserved throughout a drama so classic in its coloring and manners. The happiest development of character, an interest in the denouement which is only so far tempered by our trust in the lovely heroine, as to permit us to enjoy all the minuter beauties on our way, (this the breathless interest of Alfieri's dramas hardly allows, on a fourth or fifth reading,) exquisite descriptive touches, and expressions of sentiment, unequalled softness and harmony of style, distinguish a drama not to be surpassed in its own department. Torquato Tasso is of inferior general, but greater particular beauty. The two worldly, the two higher characters, with that of Alphonso halting between, are shaded with equal delicacy and distinctness. The inward-turning imagination of the ill-fated bard, and the fantastic tricks it plays with life, are painted as only a poet's soul of equal depth, of greater versatility, could have painted them. In analysis of the passions, and eloquent descriptions of their more hidden workings, some parts may vie with Rousseau; while several effusions of feeling are worthy of Tasso's own lyre, with its "breaking heartstring's tone." The conduct of the piece being in perfect accordance with the plan, gives the satisfaction we have mentioned in speaking of Raphael's Madonna.

Schiller's Wallenstein does not strictly belong to this class, yet we are disposed to claim it as observing the unities of time and interest; the latter especially is entire, notwithstanding the many actors and side-scenes which are introduced. Numberless touches of nature arrest our attention, bright lights are flashed across many characters, but our interest, momently increasing, is for Wallenstein —for the perversion, the danger, the ruin of that monarch soul, that falling son of the morning. Even that we feel in Max, with his celestial bloom of heart, in Thekla's sweet trustfulness, is subsidiary. This work, generally known to the reader through Mr. Coleridge's translation, affords an imperfect illustration of our meaning. Miss Baillie's plays on the passions hold a middle place. Unity of purpose there is—no unity of plan or conduct. Bold, fine outline —very bad coloring. Profound, beautifully-expressed reflections on the passions—utter want of skill in showing them out; a thorough feeling, indeed, of the elements of trag-

edy,—had but the vitalizing energy been added. Her plays
are failures; but since she has given us nothing else, we
cannot but rejoice in having these. 'Tis great pity that the
authoress of De Montfort and Basil should not have attempted a narrative poem.

Coleridge and Byron are signal instances how peculiar
is the kind of talent required for the drama; one a philosopher, both men of great genius and uncommon mastery
over language, both conversant with each side of human
nature, both considering the drama in its true light as one
of the highest departments of literature, both utterly
wanting in simplicity, pathos, truth of passion and liveli-
ness of action—in that thrilling utterance of heart to heart,
whose absence *here*, no other excellence can atone for. Of
Maturin and Knowles we do not speak, because theirs,
though very good acting plays, are not, like Mr. Taylor's,
written for the closet; of Milman, because not sufficiently
acquainted with his plays. We would here pay a tribute to
our countryman Hillhouse, whose Hadad, read at a very
early age, we remember with much delight. Probably our
judgment now might be different; but a work which could
make so deep an impression on any age, must have genius.
We are sorry we have never since met it in any library or
parlor, and are not competent to speak of it more particularly.

It will be seen that Mr. Taylor has not attempted the
sort of dramatic poetry which we consider the highest,
but has labored in that which the great wizard of Avon
adopted, because it lay nearest at hand to clothe his spells
withal, and consecrated it, with his world-embracing genius, to the (in our judgment) no small detriment of his
country's taste. Having thus declared that we cannot grant
him our very highest meed of admiration, (though we
will not say that he might not win it if he made the essay,)
we hasten to meet him on his own ground. "Dramatica
Poesis est veluti Historia spectabilis," is his motto, taken
from Bacon, who formed his taste on Shakespeare. We

would here mention that Gœthe's earlier works, Gœtz
von Berlichingen and Egmont are of this school—brilliant
fragments of past days, ballads acted out, historical scenes
and personages clustered round a hero; and we have seen
that his ripened taste preferred the form of Iphigenia and
Tasso.

We cannot too strongly express our approbation of the
opinions maintained in his short preface to this work. We
rejoice to see a leader coming forward who is likely to
un-Hemansize and un-Cornwallize literature. We too have
been sick, we too have been intoxicated with *words* till we
could hardly appreciate thoughts; perhaps our present
writing shows traces of this Lower-Empire taste; but we
have sense enough left to welcome the English Phocion,
who would regenerate public feeling. The candor and modest dignity with which these opinions are offered charm
us. The remarks upon Shelley, whom we have loved, and
do still love passing well, brought truth home to us in a
definite shape. With regard to the lowness of Lord Byron's
standard of character, every thing indeed has been said
which could be, but not as Mr. Taylor has said it; and
we opine that his refined and gentle remarks will find their
way to ears which have always been deaf to the harsh
sarcasms unseasoned by wit, which have been current on
this topic.

3. GENIUS AND MORALITY

(Two passages from letters to James Freeman Clarke;
the first is dated January 8, 1839; the second is probably
of about the same time; text from *Memoirs*, I, 73, 129.)

*[James Freeman Clarke was one of the young men with
whom Margaret maintained such perfervid discourse before her exile to Groton and with renewed intensity upon*

her return to civilization. The young New Englanders were as fascinated with genius as were all youths touched by the spirit of Romanticism, and all of them aspired to possess it. In 1839, after having assisted Bronson Alcott with his Temple School, read German with the venerable William Ellery Channing, and labored for two harrowing years (1837–39) at the Greene Street School in Providence, Margaret set up a home for herself and her mother in Jamaica Plain, Massachusetts, and she commenced her famous and widely ridiculed "Conversations" in Boston. In these she cast herself in the role of genius, and cultivated the arts of the "improvvisatrice" (under the spell of Corinne), by which she dazzled the intellectual ladies of that intellectual capital.

For her the supreme genius was Goethe, a man who had lived as flagrant a life as Byron in the eyes of staid New England. It required audacity for a New England virgin to propose writing a "life" of him. She had constantly to beseech her male companions to overcome their shyness and tell her about Goethe's mistresses. Considering the uninhibited range of her reading and her later experiences of love, we can judge in retrospect that although she was incarcerated in the code of her time, Margaret had an intuitive knowledge of sexual passion which none of these boys would ever attain.]

. . . Genius seems to me excusable in taking the public for a confidant. Genius is universal, and can appeal to the common heart of man. But even here I would not have it too direct. I prefer to see the thought or feeling made universal. How different the confidence of Goethe, for instance, from that of Byron!

But us lesser people, who write verses merely as vents for the overflowings of a personal experience, which in every life of any value craves occasionally the accompaniment of the lyre, it seems to me that all the value of this utterance is destroyed by a hasty or indiscriminate publicity. The moment I lay open my heart, and tell the fresh feeling to any one who chooses to hear, I feel profaned.

When it has passed into experience, when the flower has gone to seed, I don't care who knows it, or whither they wander. I am no longer it,—I stand on it. I do not know whether this is peculiar to me, or not, but I am sure the moment I cease to have any reserve or delicacy about a feeling, it is on the wane. . . .

. . . How am I to get the information I want, unless I go to Europe? To whom shall I write to choose my materials? I have thought of Mr. Carlyle, but still more of Goethe's friend, Von Muller. I dare say he would be pleased at the idea of a life of G. written in this hemisphere, and be very willing to help me. If you have anything to tell me, you will, and not mince matters. Of course, my impressions of Goethe's works cannot be influenced by information I get about his *life*; but, as to this latter, I suspect I must have been hasty in my inferences. I apply to you without scruple. There are subjects on which men and women usually talk a great deal, but apart from one another. You, however, are well aware that I am very destitute of what is commonly *called* modesty. With regard to this, how fine the remark of our present subject: "Courage and modesty are virtues which every sort of society reveres, because they are virtues which cannot be counterfeited; also, they are known by the *same hue*." When that blush does not come naturally to my face, I do not drop a veil to make people think it is there. All this may be very unlovely, but it is *I*. . . .

4. PASSION

(From Fuller MSS, Harvard College Library; a hand other than Margaret's has written at the top, "I believe in the first days of Sept. 1839.")

[The Memoirs have a fascination beyond that of their content: they tantalize us with the question of whether the three noble gentlemen who compiled them—Emerson, Clarke, and William Henry Channing—had any real notion of the range or vehemence of Margaret's emotions.

In his portion of the volumes, Emerson does offer several startling observations. Maybe he was not as innocent as the public image of him supposes; on the other hand, his innocence may have been the sort that takes everything in its stride. She wore her friends, he memorably said, "as a necklace of diamonds about her neck." "Persons were her game," he continued, and in every house where she came as a guest she "seemed like the queen of some parliament of love." Since Margaret Fuller had often been a guest in the Emerson household, he spoke from experience.

Possibly, then, Emerson wrote deliberately when he commented that "The loveliest and the highest endowed women were eager to lay their beauty, their grace, the hospitalities of sumptuous homes, and their costly gifts, at her feet," and that according to one of these infatuated creatures, had Margaret been a man, any one of them would have married her—they were all in love with her. Indeed, Emerson's summation of Margaret's reputation in this respect is just short of clinical: "Her friendships, as a girl with girls, as a woman with women, were not unmingled with passion, and had passages of romantic sacrifice and of ecstatic fusion, which I have heard with

*the ear, but could not trust my profane pen to report."
He had penetrated deeply enough into the Romantic cult
of friendship to note that in these affairs there were "ebbs
and recoils from the other party," that the "mortal" often
proved unequal to converse with an "immortal," and that
what Margaret denounced as ingratitude was more truly
an incapacity for love at her tempo.*

*Both Emerson (Memoirs, I, 283) and her brother Ar-
thur (Woman in the Nineteenth Century, p. 342) had access to an entry in Margaret's journal, now lost, which
commences, "It is so true that a woman may be in love
with a woman, and a man with a man. I like to be sure
of it, for it is the same which angels feel." She describes
one of her own absorptions with a girl friend, and notes
that these reflections were started by an engraving of
Madame Récamier in her boudoir. "I have so often
thought over the intimacy between her and Madame de
Staël."*

*We cannot doubt that the hothouse atmosphere of Mar-
garet's "Conversations"—the temperature can be felt even
in the crude transcriptions that survive—was a concentration of femininity. This letter, remaining among the
manuscripts and never before published, is the best example I have found of this blast of female passion. It
fully documents Emerson's perceptiveness.]*

. . . You love me no more.— How did you pray me to
draw near to you! What words were spoken in impatience
of separation! How did you promise to me, ay, and doubt-
less to yourself, too, of all we might be to one another!
We were near and with spring's fairest flowers I poured
out my heart to you.—At an earlier period I would fain
have broke the tie that bound us, for I knew myself incapable of feeling or being content to inspire an ordinary
attachment. As soon as I saw a flaw I would have broke
the tie. You would not—you resented, yet with what pa-
thetic grace, any distrust on my part. Forever, ever are

words of which you have never been, are not now afraid.

You call me your best of friends, your dearest friend, you say that you always find yourself with me. I doubt not the depth of your attachment, doubt not that you feel my worth. But the confiding sweetness, the natural and prompt expression are gone—are they gone forever?

You do not wish to be with me; why try to hide it from me, from yourself? You are not interested in any of my interests; my friends, my pursuits are not yours. If you tell me of yours, it is like a matter of duty, not because you cannot help it, and must write or speak to relieve the full heart and mind.

The sympathizing contemplation of the beautiful in Nature, in Art is over for us, that for which I loved you first, and which made that love a shrine at which I could rest upon my weary pilgrimage. Now—moons wax and wane, suns rise and set, the summer segment of the beautiful circle is filled, and since the first flush on the cheek of June we have not once seen, felt, admired together. You come here—to go away again, and make a call upon me in the parlor while you stay! You write to me—to say you could not write before and ask me why I do not write. You write me to go and see Michel's work by myself! You send me your books and pictures to ask me what I think of them! Thus far at least we have walked no step together and my heart deceives me widely if this be love, or if we live as friends should live!

Yet spite of all this, sometimes I believe when I am with you, and, come what may, I will be faithful myself, I will not again draw back, it shall be all your fault if we break off again. I will wait—I will not complain. I will exact nothing. I will make every allowance for the restlessness of a heart checked in its love, a mind dissatisfied with its pursuits. I will bear in mind that my presence is like to recall all you have need to forget and will try to believe that you would not be with me, that I "spoil you for your part on life's dull scene," or as you have said, "call up the woman in you."

You say you love me as ever, forever. I will, if I can, rely upon your word, believing you must deem me entitled to unshrinking frankness.

You have given me the sacred name of Mother, and I will be as indulgent, as tender, as delicate (if possible) in my vigilance, as if I had borne you beneath my heart instead of in it. But oh, it is waiting like the Mother beside the sepulchre for the resurrection, for all I loved in you is at present dead and buried, only a light from the tomb shines now and then in your eyes. . . .

5. TO RALPH WALDO EMERSON,
September 29, 1840

(Text from Ralph L. Rusk, *The Letters of Ralph Waldo Emerson*, 1939, II, pp. 340–41.)

[Emerson probably first met Margaret Fuller at the house of Mrs. John Farrar in 1835. Mrs. Farrar, wife of a distinguished and wealthy professor at Harvard, a dedicated patroness of "genius," and a hostess in as grand a manner as Cambridge could then afford, had offered Margaret the trip to Europe that was prevented by the disastrous events at Groton.

Clearly, Margaret adored him. In 1834 she had written Frederic Hedge that she expected to find in Emerson—he had not yet published anything—a mind that could be "useful" for her researches on Goethe. In July 1836, Margaret came to Concord. For the next six years she made repeated assaults upon Emerson's attention that can be described only as a sexual duel. She was foredoomed to defeat—especially since the resolutely uxorious Emerson had

*very little to give her, and since she herself hardly knew
what she wanted.*

In the summer of 1840, Emerson carried on an animated—a perilously animated—correspondence with Margaret, but also with Margaret's dearest friend, Caroline
Sturgis. By October 19th, he could tell his businesslike
brother, William, that he had recovered from his summer's indulgence "in writing romances of letters," and
was settling down to proofreading his Essays, a task that
he found "hard and mechanical" by comparison.

The memorials of this strange romance between Emerson and Margaret Fuller are copious. The relationship
has not yet been fully or perceptively expounded, and the
dangers of misstatement are multitudinous. There is no
need in this volume to explore the psychology of the participants; it is enough to give a few of Margaret's letters
that display her personality and her aggressive genius—
although in reading these we must, of course, bear in mind
the peculiar provocations offered by Mr. Emerson.]

29 Sept. 1840

. . . I have felt the impossibility of meeting far more
than you; so much, that, if you ever know me well, you
will feel that the fact of my abiding by you thus far, affords a strong proof that we are to be much to one another. How often have I left you despairing and forlorn.
How often have I said, This light will never understand
my fire; this clear eye will never discern the law by which
I am filling my circle; this simple force will never interpret my need of manifold being. . . .

Dear friend on one point misunderstand me less. I do
not love power other than every vigorous nature delights
to feel itself living. To violate the sanctity of relations—
I am as far from it as you can be. I make no claim. I have
no wish which is not dictated by a feeling of truth. Could
I lead the highest angel captive by a look, that look I
would not give, unless prompted by true love: I am no

usurper. I ask only mine own inheritance. If it be found that I have mistaken its boundaries, I will give up the choicest vineyard, the fairest flowergarden, to its lawful owner. . . .

In me I did not think you saw the purity, the single-ness, into which, I have faith that all this darting motion, and restless flame shall yet be attempered and subdued. I felt that you did not for me the highest office of friend-ship, by offering me the clue of the labyrinth of my own being. Yet I thought you appreciated the fearlessness which shrinks from no truth in myself and others, and trusted me, believing that I knew the path for myself. O it must be that you have felt the worth of that truth which has never hesitated to infringe our relation, or aught else, rather than not vindicate itself. If you have not seen this stair on which God has been so untiringly leading me to himself, you have indeed been wholly ignorant of me. Then indeed, when my soul, in its childish agony of prayer, stretched out its arms to you as a father,—did you not see what was meant by this crying for the moon; this sullen rejection of playthings which had become unmean-ing? Did you then say, "I know not what this means; per-haps this will trouble me; the time will come when I shall hide my eyes from this mood;"—then you are not the friend I seek.

But did you not ask for a "foe" in your friend? Did you not ask for a "large formidable nature"? But a beauti-ful foe, I am not yet, to you. Shall I ever be? I know not. My life is now prayer. Through me sweetest harmonies are momently breathing. Shall they not make me beauti-ful,—Nay, beauty? Shall not all vehemence, all eccentric-ity, be purged by these streams of divine light? I have, in these hours, but one pain; the sense of the infinite ex-hausts and exalts: it cannot therefore possess me wholly; else, were I also one wave of gentlest force. Again I shall cease to melt and flow; again I shall seek and pierce and rend asunder.

But oh, I am now full of such sweet certainty. Never never more can it be utterly shaken. All things have I given up to the Central Power, myself, you also; yet, I cannot forbear adding, dear friend. I am now so at home, I know not how again to wander and grope, seeking my place in another soul. I need to be recognized. After this, I shall be claimed, rather than claim, yet if I speak of facts, it must be as I see them.

To L[idian] my love. In her, I have always recognized the saintly element. *That,* better than a bible in my hand, shows that it cannot be wholly alien. Yet I am no saint, no anything, but a great soul born to know all, before it can return to the creative fount. . . .

6. TO RALPH WALDO EMERSON,
November, 1840

(Text from Rusk, *The Letters of Ralph Waldo Emerson,* II, pp. 366–67.)

[Emerson might have decided to call a halt to his "romances," but he still had to deal with the intellectual challenges of Margaret Fuller. As his colleague in editing the Dial, *she had more than one weapon in her arsenal. Margaret made some severely critical comments on his draft of "Thoughts on Art," which was later printed in the issue of January 1841; and affecting dismay at her own temerity, she followed them with this note, half apologetic and half defiant, to which he amiably but circumspectly replied on December 8th. As is strangely true of Margaret's more impetuous utterances, this seems to us ironically prophetic. In her last years, the distance between her and Emerson in the realm of intellectual affairs would become infinitely more vast than the merely geographical span between Rome and Concord.]*

Tuesday eveg.

. . . I wrote you last night, and today the lines about your Essay seem so dull, so cold, and so impertinent withal that I have a mind to burn the paper—yet let them go—I should have *said* the same, and the office of our best sentiments is to make us altogether better and not induce us to suppress the worst or select the best of ourselves.

Yet there is something obviously wrong in this attempt to measure one another, or one another's act. It seems as if we could not help it in this our present stage, as if we should jostle and bruise one another, if we had not some idea of our respective paths and places. . . . But surely there will come a purer mode of being even in the world of Form. We shall move with an unerring gentleness, we shall read in an eye beam whether other beings have any thing for us; on those who have not our only criticism will be to turn our eyes another way. Then there will be no more negations, we shall learn to be ourselves by the achievements of other natures and not by their failures. Then our actions will not be hieroglyphics any more but perfect symbols. Then parting and meeting will be equally beautiful, for both will be in faith. Then there will be no more explanations but with every instant revelations. Then will be no more intercourse, but perfect communion with full-eyed love,— But then—we shall write no essays on Art, more than cavils at them.

Adieu—*en* Dieu

CHAPTER III

THE DIAL, 1840–1844

1. THE EDITORS TO THE READER

(Text from the *Dial*, I, July 1840, pp. 1–4.)

[After long, intricate, and often muddleheaded negotiations among the "Transcendentalists," a magazine was organized in 1840 as a vehicle for their point of view. Emerson was chiefly responsible for the enterprise, but he initially remained behind the scenes. George Ripley agreed to serve as managing editor, and Margaret Fuller accepted the task of official editor until 1842, when her health forced her to resign. The magazine lasted just four years and achieved a circulation of only two or three hundred; but because it was the voice of many of the most prominent intellectuals of that era, its volumes have become collectors' items.

Emerson did not like Margaret's introductory address for the Dial, *and their argument over this piece continued throughout the spring of 1840. The published version of it probably includes more of Emerson's prose than it does of Margaret's (although he never acknowledged this); yet the basic position taken in the essay so closely reflects Margaret's views that it belongs with her writings even more than with Emerson's.]*

We invite the attention of our countrymen to a new design. Probably not quite unexpected or unannounced will our Journal appear, though small pains have been taken to secure its welcome. Those, who have immediately acted in editing the present Number, cannot accuse themselves of any unbecoming forwardness in their undertaking, but rather of a backwardness, when they remember how often in many private circles the work was projected, how eagerly desired, and only postponed because no individual volunteered to combine and concentrate the freewill offerings of many coöperators. With some reluctance the present conductors of this work have yielded themselves to the wishes of their friends, finding something sacred and not to be withstood in the importunity which urged the production of a Journal in a new spirit.

As they have not proposed themselves to the work, neither can they lay any the least claim to an option or determination of the spirit in which it is conceived, or to what is peculiar in the design. In that respect, they have obeyed, though with great joy, the strong current of thought and feeling, which, for a few years past, has led many sincere persons in New England to make new demands on literature, and to reprobate that rigor of our conventions of religion and education which is turning us to stone, which renounces hope, which looks only backward, which asks only such a future as the past, which suspects improvement, and holds nothing so much in horror as new views and the dreams of youth.

With these terrors the conductors of the present Journal have nothing to do,—not even so much as a word of reproach to waste. They know that there is a portion of the youth and of the adult population of this country, who have not shared them; who have in secret or in public paid their vows to truth and freedom; who love reality too well to care for names, and who live by a Faith too earnest and profound to suffer them to doubt the eternity of its object, or to shake themselves free from its authority. Under the fictions and customs which occupied others, these have explored the Necessary, the Plain, the True, the Human,—and so gained a vantage ground, which commands the history of the past and the present.

No one can converse much with different classes of society in New England, without remarking the progress of a revolution. Those who share in it have no external organization, no badge, no creed, no name. They do not vote, or print, or even meet together. They do not know each other's faces or names. They are united only in a common love of truth, and love of its work. They are of all conditions and constitutions. Of these acolytes, if some are happily born and well bred, many are no doubt ill dressed, ill placed, ill made—with as many scars of hereditary vice as other men. Without pomp, without trumpet, in lonely and obscure places, in solitude, in servitude, in compunctions and privations, trudging beside the team in the dusty road, or drudging a hireling in other men's cornfields, schoolmasters, who teach a few children rudiments for a pittance, ministers of small parishes of the obscurer sects, lone women in dependent condition, matrons and young maidens, rich and poor, beautiful and hard-favored, without concert or proclamation of any kind, they have silently given in their several adherence to a new hope, and in all companies do signify a greater trust in the nature and resources of man, than the laws or the popular opinions will well allow.

This spirit of the time is felt by every individual with some difference,—to each one casting its light upon the objects nearest to his temper and habits of thought;—to one, coming in the shape of special reforms in the state; to another, in modifications of the various callings of men, and the customs of business; to a third, opening a new scope for literature and art; to a fourth, in philosophical insight; to a fifth, in the vast solitudes of prayer. It is in every form a protest against usage, and a search for principles. In all its movements, it is peaceable, and in the very lowest marked with a triumphant success. Of course, it rouses the opposition of all which it judges and con-

demns, but it is too confident in its tone to comprehend
an objection, and so builds no outworks for possible defence against contingent enemies. It has the step of Fate,
and goes on existing like an oak or a river, because it must.

In literature, this influence appears not yet in new books
so much as in the higher tone of criticism. The antidote
to all narrowness is the comparison of the record with
nature, which at once shames the record and stimulates
to new attempts. Whilst we look at this, we wonder how
any book has been thought worthy to be preserved. There
is somewhat in all life untranslatable into language. He
who keeps his eye on that will write better than others,
and think less of his writing, and of all writing. Every
thought has a certain imprisoning as well as uplifting quality, and, in proportion to its energy on the will, refuses
to become an object of intellectual contemplation. Thus
what is great usually slips through our fingers, and it seems
wonderful how a lifelike word ever comes to be written. If
our Journal share the impulses of the time, it cannot now
prescribe its own course. It cannot foretell in orderly propositions what it shall attempt. All criticism should be
poetic; unpredictable; superseding, as every new thought
does, all foregone thoughts, and making a new light on
the whole world. Its brow is not wrinkled with circum-
spection, but serene, cheerful, adoring. It has all things
to say, and no less than all the world for its final audience.

Our plan embraces much more than criticism; were it
not so, our criticism would be naught. Everything noble
is directed on life, and this is. We do not wish to say
pretty or curious things, or to reiterate a few propositions
in varied forms, but, if we can, to give expression to that
spirit which lifts men to a higher platform, restores to
them the religious sentiment, brings them worthy aims
and pure pleasures, purges the inward eye, makes life less
desultory, and, through raising man to the level of nature,
takes away its melancholy from the landscape, and recon-
ciles the practical with the speculative powers.

But perhaps we are telling our little story too gravely. There are always great arguments at hand for a true action, even for the writing of a few pages. There is nothing but seems near it and prompts it,—the sphere in the ecliptic the sap in the apple tree,—every fact, every appearance seem to persuade to it.

Our means correspond with the ends we have indicated. As we wish not to multiply books, but to report life, our resources are therefore not so much the pens of practised writers, as the discourse of the living, and the portfolios which friendship has opened to us. From the beautiful recesses of private thought; from the experience and hope of spirits which are withdrawing from all old forms, and seeking in all that is new somewhat to meet their inappeasable longings; from the secret confession of genius afraid to trust itself to aught but sympathy; from the conversation of fervid and mystical pietists; from tear-stained diaries of sorrow and passion; from the manuscripts of young poets; and from the records of youthful taste commenting on old works of art; we hope to draw thoughts and feelings, which being alive can impart life.

And so with diligent hands and good intent we set down our Dial on the earth. We wish it may resemble that instrument in its celebrated happiness, that of measuring no hours but those of sunshine. Let it be one cheerful rational voice amidst the din of mourners and polemics. Or to abide by our chosen image, let it be such a Dial, not as the dead face of a clock, hardly even such as the Gnomon in a garden, but rather such a Dial as is the Garden itself, in whose leaves and flowers and fruits the suddenly awakened sleeper is instantly apprised not what part of dead time, but what state of life and growth is now arrived and arriving.

2. MOTIVES FOR THE *DIAL*

(Text from *Memoirs*, II, 26–31, where it is dated simply 1840 and the recipient of the letter is not named.)

[Although the formal "Address to the Reader" contained nothing contrary to what Margaret believed, chances are that Emerson tamed down her version. What she had in mind, and how grandly she conceived the Dial's mission to be in elevating American culture, she made clear in a somewhat disorderly manner in this letter of 1840, probably addressed to one of her female admirers. I suspect that William Henry Channing tampered with the original of this letter when editing his section of Margaret's Memoirs. Even so, it is a sharp reminder that Margaret's conception of culture differed from that of the Transcendentalists. Her readiness to accept Goethe's libertinism and her admiration for both Madame de Staël and George Sand indicate an ethical boldness not possessed by the other members of her group. She could view the problems of the intellect in this country on a national rather than a merely regional scale. She commenced, it is true, from the good Transcendental proposition that the inward is superior to the outward, but she distrusted the lack of "practical sagacity" among the apostles; and she insisted that the "natural part" of man—and of woman!—should not be denigrated. On this point, she would become convinced that Emerson's nature and views, in particular, differed radically from her own.]

. . . Since the Revolution; there has been little, in the circumstances of this country, to call out the higher sentiments. The effect of continued prosperity is the same on nations as on individuals—it leaves the nobler faculties undeveloped. The need of bringing out the physical resources of a vast extent of country, the commercial and political fever incident to our institutions, tend to fix the eyes of men on what is local and temporary, on the external advantages of their condition. The superficial diffusion of knowledge, unless attended by a correspondent deepening of its sources, is likely to vulgarize rather than to raise the thought of a nation, depriving them of another sort of education through sentiments of reverence, and leading the multitude to believe themselves capable of judging what they but dimly discern. They see a wide surface, and forget the difference between seeing and knowing. In this hasty way of thinking and living they traverse so much ground that they forget that not the sleeping railroad passenger, but the botanist, the geologist, the poet, really see the country, and that to the former, "a miss is as good as a mile." In a word, the tendency of circumstances has been to make our people superficial, irreverent, and more anxious to get a living than to live mentally and morally. This tendency is no way balanced by the slight literary culture common here, which is mostly English, and consists in a careless reading of publications of the day, having the same utilitarian tendency with our own proceedings. The infrequency of acquaintance with any of the great fathers of English lore marks this state of things.

New England is now old enough,—some there have leisure enough,—to look at all this; and the consequence is a violent reaction, in a small minority, against a mode of culture that rears such fruits. They see that political freedom does not necessarily produce liberality of mind, nor freedom in church institutions—vital religion; and, seeing that these changes cannot be wrought from without inwards, they are trying to quicken the soul, that they may work from within outwards. Disgusted with the vulgarity of a commercial aristocracy, they become radicals; disgusted with the materialistic working of "rational" religion, they become mystics. They quarrel with all that is, because it is not spiritual enough. They would, perhaps, be patient if they thought this the mere sensuality of childhood in our nation, which it might outgrow; but they think that they see the evil widening, deepening,—not only debasing the life, but corrupting the thought of our people, and they feel that if they know not well what should be done, yet that the duty of every good man is to utter a protest against what is done amiss.

Is this protest undiscriminating? are these opinions crude? do these proceedings threaten to sap the bulwarks on which men at present depend? I confess it all, yet I see in these men promise of a better wisdom than in their opponents. Their hope for man is grounded on his destiny as an immortal soul, and not as a mere comfort-loving inhabitant of earth, or as a subscriber to the social contract. It was not meant that the soul should cultivate the earth, but that the earth should educate and maintain the soul. Man is not made for society, but society is made for man. No institution can be good which does not tend to improve the individual. In these principles I have confidence so profound, that I am not afraid to trust those who hold them, despite their partial views, imperfectly developed characters, and frequent want of practical sagacity. I believe, if they have opportunity to state and discuss their opinions, they will gradually sift them, ascertain their grounds and aims with clearness, and do the work this country needs. I hope for them as for "the leaven that is hidden in the bushel of meal, till all be leavened." The leaven is not good by itself, neither is the meal; let them combine, and we shall yet have bread.

Utopia it is impossible to build up. At least, my hopes for our race on this one planet are more limited than those of most of my friends. I accept the limitations of human nature, and believe a wise acknowledgment of them one of the best conditions of progress. Yet every noble scheme, every poetic manifestation, prophesies to man his eventual destiny. And were not man ever more sanguine than facts at the moment justify, he would remain torpid, or be sunk in sensuality. It is on this ground that I sympathize with what is called the "Transcendental party," and that I feel their aim to be the true one. They acknowledge in the nature of man an arbiter for his deeds,— a standard transcending sense and time,—and are, in my view, the true utilitarians. They are but at the beginning of their course, and will, I hope, learn how to make use of the past, as well as to aspire for the future, and to be true in the present moment.

My position as a woman, and many private duties which have filled my life, have prevented my thinking deeply on several of the great subjects which these friends have at heart. I suppose, if ever I become capable of judging, I shall differ from most of them on important points. But I am not afraid to trust any who are true, and in intent noble, with their own course, nor to aid in enabling them to express their thoughts, whether I coincide with them or not.

On the subject of Christianity, my mind is clear. If Divine, it will stand the test of any comparison. I believe the reason it has so imperfectly answered to the aspirations of its Founder is, that men have received it on external grounds. I believe that a religion, thus received, may give the life an external decorum, but will never open the fountains of holiness in the soul.

One often thinks of Hamlet as the true representative of idealism in its excess. Yet if, in his short life, man be liable to some excess, should we not rather prefer to have the will palsied like Hamlet, by a deep-searching tendency and desire for poetic perfection, than to have it enlightened by worldly sagacity, as in the case of Julius Caesar, or made intense by pride alone, as in that of Coriolanus?

After all, I believe it is absurd to attempt to speak on these subjects within the limits of a letter. I will try to say what I mean in print some day. Yet one word as to "the material," in man. Is it not the object of all philosophy, as well as of religion and poetry, to prevent its prevalence? Must not those who see most truly be ever making statements of the truth to combat this sluggishness, or worldliness? What else are sages, poets, preachers, born to do? Men go an undulating course,—sometimes on the hill, sometimes in the valley. But he only is in the right who in the valley forgets not the hill-prospect, and knows in darkness that the sun will rise again. This is the real life which is subordinated to, not merged in, the ideal; he is only wise who can bring the lowest act of his life into sympathy with its highest thought. And this I take to be the one only aim of our pilgrimage here. I agree with those who think that no true philosophy will try to ignore or annihilate the material part of man, but will rather seek to put it in its place, as servant and minister to the soul.

3. A SHORT ESSAY ON CRITICS

(Text, the first piece in the *Dial*, I, July 1840, pp. 5–11, after the salutation to the "Reader.")

[As Margaret Fuller and Emerson said in 1840 in their "Address to the Reader" in the Dial, *there did not seem to be much hope at that time for summoning from America a body of creative writing. But from their vantage point, they would at least promote healthy criticism. Indeed, criticism—in the sense of tutoring and refining an inchoate American taste—was precisely what the nation most needed.*

Margaret Fuller, out of her passions, her frustrations, and out of her eagerness (as always) to get on with the business of the magazine, endeavored in the first num-

ber of the Dial *to inform the public about the sort of
criticism it could expect from the* Dial.]

An essay on Criticism were a serious matter; for, though
this age be emphatically critical, the writer would still
find it necessary to investigate the laws of criticism as a
science, to settle its conditions as an art. Essays entitled
critical are epistles addressed to the public through which
the mind of the recluse relieves itself of its impressions.
Of these the only law is, "Speak the best word that is in
thee." Or they are regular articles, got up to order by
the literary hack writer, for the literary mart, and the only
law is to make them plausible. There is not yet deliberate
recognition of a standard of criticism, though we hope
the always strengthening league of the republic of letters
must ere long settle laws on which its Amphictyonic coun-
cil may act. Meanwhile let us not venture to write on
criticism, but by classifying the critics imply our hopes,
and thereby our thoughts.

First, there are the subjective class, (to make use of a
convenient term, introduced by our German benefactors.)
These are persons to whom writing is no sacred, no rever-
end employment. They are not driven to consider, not
forced upon investigation by the fact, that they are deliberately giving their thoughts an independent existence,
and that it may live to others when dead to them. They
know no agonies of conscientious research, no timidities
of self-respect. They see no Ideal beyond the present hour,
which makes its mood an uncertain tenure. How things
affect them now they know; let the future, let the whole
take care of itself. They state their impressions as they
rise, of other men's spoken, written, or acted thoughts.
They never dream of going out of themselves to seek the
motive, to trace the law of another nature. They never
dream that there are statures which cannot be measured
from their point of view. They love, they like, or they hate;
the book is detestable, immoral, absurd, or admirable,

noble, of a most approved scope;—these statements they
make with authority, as those who bear the evangel of
pure taste and accurate judgment, and need be tried before no human synod. To them it seems that their present
position commands the universe.

Thus the essays on the works of others, which are called
criticisms, are often, in fact, mere records of impressions.
To judge of their value you must know where the man
was brought up, under what influences,—his nation, his
church, his family even. He himself has never attempted
to estimate the value of these circumstances, and find a
law or raise a standard above all circumstances, permanent
against all influence. He is content to be the creature of
his place, and to represent it by his spoken and written
word. He takes the same ground with the savage, who
does not hesitate to say of the product of a civilization on
which he could not stand, "It is bad," or "It is good."

The value of such comments is merely reflex. They
characterize the critic. They give an idea of certain influences on a certain act of men in a certain time or place.
Their absolute, essential value is nothing. The long review, the eloquent article by the man of the nineteenth
century are of no value by themselves considered, but
only as samples of their kind. The writers were content to
tell what they felt, to praise or to denounce without needing to convince us or themselves. They sought not the
divine truths of philosophy, and she proffers them not,
if unsought.

Then there are the apprehensive. These can go out of
themselves and enter fully into a foreign existence. They
breathe its life; they live in its law; they tell what it
meant, and why it so expressed its meaning. They reproduce the work of which they speak, and make it better
known to us in so far as two statements are better than
one. There are beautiful specimens in this kind. They
are pleasing to us as bearing witness of the genial sympathies of nature. They have the ready grace of love with

somewhat of the dignity of disinterested friendship. They sometimes give more pleasure than the original production of which they treat, as melodies will sometimes ring sweetlier in the echo. Besides there is a peculiar pleasure in a true response; it is the assurance of equipoise in the universe. These, if not true critics, come nearer the standard than the subjective class, and the value of their work is ideal as well as historical.

Then there are the comprehensive, who must also be apprehensive. They enter into the nature of another being and judge his work by its own law. But having done so, having ascertained his design and the degree of his success in fulfilling it, thus measuring his judgment, his energy, and skill, they do also know how to put that aim in its place, and how to estimate its relations. And this the critic can only do who perceives the analogies of the universe, and how they are regulated by an absolute, invariable principle. He can see how far that work expresses this principle as well as how far it is excellent in its details. Sustained by a principle, such as can be girt within no rule, no formula, he can walk around the work, he can stand above it, he can uplift it, and try its weight. Finally he is worthy to judge it.

Critics are poets cut down, says some one by way of jeer; but, in truth, they are men with the poetical temperament to apprehend, with the philosophical tendency to investigate. The maker is divine; the critic sees this divine, but brings it down to humanity by the analytic process. The critic is the historian who records the order of creation. In vain for the maker, who knows without learning it, but not in vain for the mind of his race.

The critic is beneath the maker, but is his needed friend. What tongue could speak but to an intelligent ear, and every noble work demands its critic. The richer the work, the more severe would be its critic; the larger its scope, the more comprehensive must be his power of scrutiny. The critic is not a base caviller, but the younger brother of genius. Next to invention is the power of interpreting invention; next to beauty the power of appreciating beauty.

And of making others appreciate it; for the universe is a scale of infinite gradation, and below the very highest, every step is explanation down to the lowest. Religion, in the two modulations of poetry and music, descends through an infinity of waves to the lowest abysses of human nature. Nature is the literature and art of the divine mind; human literature and art the criticism on that; and they, too, find their criticism within their own sphere.

The critic, then, should be not merely a poet, not merely a philosopher, not merely an observer, but tempered of all three. If he criticize the poem, he must want nothing of what constitutes the poet, except the power of creating forms and speaking in music. He must have as good an eye and as fine a sense; but if he had as fine an organ for expression also, he would make the poem instead of judging it. He must be inspired by the philosopher's spirit of inquiry and need of generalization, but he must not be constrained by the hard cemented masonry of method to which philosophers are prone. And he must have the organic acuteness of the observer, with a love of ideal perfection, which forbids him to be content with mere beauty of details in the work or the comment upon the work.

There are persons who maintain, that there is no legitimate criticism, except the reproductive; that we have only to say what the work is or is to us, never what it is not. But the moment we look for a principle, we feel the need of a criterion, of a standard; and then we say what the work is *not*, as well as what it *is*; and this is as healthy though not as grateful and gracious an operation of the mind as the other. We do not seek to degrade but to classify an object by stating what it is not. We detach the part from the whole, lest it stand between us and the whole. When we have ascertained in what degree it manifests the whole we may safely restore it to its place, and love or admire it there ever after.

The use of criticism in periodical writing is to sift, not to stamp a work. Yet should they not be "sieves and drainers for the use of luxurious readers," but for the use of earnest inquirers, giving voice and being to their objections, as well as stimulus to their sympathies. But the critic must not be an infallible adviser to his reader. He must not tell him what books are not worth reading, or what must be thought of them when read, but what he read in them. Wo to that coterie where some critic sits despotic, intrenched behind the infallible "We." Wo to that oracle who has infused such soft sleepiness, such a gentle dulness into his atmosphere, that when he opes his lips no dog will bark. It is this attempt at dictatorship in the reviewers, and the indolent acquiescence of their readers, that has brought them into disrepute. With such fairness did they make out their statements, with such dignity did they utter their verdicts, that the poor reader grew all too submissive. He learned his lesson with such docility, that the greater part of what will be said at any public or private meeting can be foretold by any one who has read the leading periodical works for twenty years back. Scholars sneer at and would fain dispense with them altogether; and the public, grown lazy and helpless by this constant use of props and stays, can now scarce brace itself even to get through a magazine article, but reads in the daily paper laid beside the breakfast plate a short notice of the last number of the long established and popular review, and thereupon passes its judgment and is content.

Then the partisan spirit of many of these journals has made it unsafe to rely upon them as guide-books and expurgatory indexes. They could not be content merely to stimulate and suggest thought, they have at last become powerless to supersede it.

From these causes and causes like these, the journals

have lost much of their influence. There is a languid feeling about them, an inclination to suspect the justice of their verdicts, the value of their criticisms. But their golden age cannot be quite past. They afford too convenient a vehicle for the transmission of knowledge; they are too natural a feature of our time to have done all their work yet. Surely they may be redeemed from their abuses, they may be turned to their true uses. But how?

It were easy to say what they should *not* do. They should not have an object to carry or a cause to advocate, which obliges them either to reject all writings which wear the distinctive traits of individual life, or to file away what does not suit them, till the essay, made true to their design, is made false to the mind of the writer. An external consistency is thus produced, at the expense of all salient thought, all genuine emotion of life, in short, and living influences. Their purpose may be of value, but by such means was no valuable purpose ever furthered long. There are those, who have with the best intention pursued this system of trimming and adaptation, and thought it well and best to

"Deceive their country for their country's good."

But their country cannot long be so governed. It misses the pure, the full tone of truth; it perceives that the voice is modulated to coax, to persuade, and it turns from the judicious man of the world, calculating the effect to be produced by each of his smooth sentences to some earnest voice which is uttering thoughts, crude, rash, ill-arranged it may be, but true to one human breast, and uttered in full faith, that the God of Truth will guide them aright.

And here, it seems to me, has been the greatest mistake in the conduct of these journals. A smooth monotony has been attained, an uniformity of tone, so that from the title of a journal you can infer the tenor of all its chapters. But nature is ever various, ever new, and so should be her daughters, art and literature. We do not want merely a polite response to what we thought before, but by the freshness of thought in other minds to have new thought awakened in our own. We do not want stores of information only, but to be roused to digest these into knowledge. Able and experienced men write for us, and we would know what they think, as they think it not for us but for themselves. We would live with them, rather than be taught by them how to live; we would catch the contagion of their mental activity, rather than have them direct us how to regulate our own. In books, in reviews, in the senate, in the pulpit, we wish to meet thinking men, not schoolmasters or pleaders. We wish that they should do full justice to their own view, but also that they should be frank with us, and, if now our superiors, treat us as if we might some time rise to be their equals. It is this true manliness, this firmness in his own position, and this power of appreciating the position of others, that alone can make the critic our companion and friend. We would converse with him, secure that he will tell us all his thought, and speak as man to man. But if he adapts his work to us, if he stifles what is distinctively his, if he shows himself either arrogant or mean, or, above all, if he wants faith in the healthy action of free thought, and the safety of pure motive, we will not talk with him, for we cannot confide in him. We will go to the critic who trusts Genius and trusts us, who knows that all good writing must be spontaneous, and who will write out the bill of fare for the public as he read it for himself,—

"Forgetting vulgar rules, with spirit free
    To judge each author by his own intent,
    Nor think one standard for all minds is meant."

Such an one will not disturb us with personalities, with sectarian prejudices, or an undue vehemence in favor of petty plans or temporary objects. Neither will he disgust us by smooth obsequious flatteries and an inexpressive, lifeless gentleness. He will be free and make free from the mechanical and distorting influences we hear complained of on every side. He will teach us to love wisely what we before loved well, for he knows the difference between censoriousness and discernment, infatuation and reverence; and, while delighting in the genial melodies of Pan, can perceive, should Apollo bring his lyre into audience, that there may be strains more divine than those of his native groves.

4. A HOUSE GUEST IN CONCORD

(Text from a letter to Richard F. Fuller, Concord, May 25, 1841, Fuller MSS, Harvard College Library.)

[On May 6, 1841, Emerson invited Margaret to visit him and Mrs. Emerson in a tone faintly reminiscent of his more unguarded letters of the previous summer.

Come, O my friend, with your earliest convenience, I pray you, and let us seize the void betwixt two atoms of air, the vacation between two moments of time to decide how we will steer on this torrent which is called Today. (Rusk, Letters, II, 399–400.)

Margaret spent a fortnight in the Emerson house. In this month Henry Thoreau also came to live with the Emersons, and as the letter indicates, Margaret met him for the first time. Thoreau promptly signified his incompatibility with the voraciously feminine Margaret. Apparently Mrs. Emerson was away part of this time, for on June 1st Emerson wrote his brother that he was planning an excursion to Plymouth "to recruit our too pensive careful and melancholy wife." (Ibid., 402.)]

. . . I am living here the quiet country life you would enjoy. There are hens, cows, pigs; and what I like better,

wildflowers and a host of singing birds. By the way, I
don't think you could gratify Mrs. Ward more than on
the Sunday you go to Jamaica to get her a bouquet of
wildflowers. Borrow a tin pail or box and wet them when
you put them in: they may thus be brought to town perfectly fresh. Mr. Emerson works five or six hours a day
in his garden and his health which was in a very low state
this spring improves day by day. He has a friend with
him of the name of Henry Thoreau who has come to
live with him and be his working man this year. H. T.
is three and twenty, has been through college and kept a
school, is very fond of classic studies and an earnest
thinker, yet intends being a farmer. He has a great deal of
practical sense, and as he has bodily strength to book, he
may look to be a successful and happy man. He has a
boat which he made himself, and rows me out on the
pond. Last night I went out quite late and staid till the
moon was almost gone, heard the whip-poor-will for the
first time this year. There was a sweet breeze full of apple-
blossom fragrance which made the pond swell almost into
waves. I had great pleasure. I think of you in these scenes
because I know you love them too. By and by when the
duties are done, we may expect to pass summer days together . . .

5. A CAVEAT TO PASTORALISM

(Text from a letter to Richard F. Fuller that is headed
only "Thursday morning," but that can be dated, by comparison of the handwriting and paper with other letters,
1841.)

[*Although Margaret Fuller shared the Transcendentalists' adoration of nature and regarded Emerson's little
volume entitled* Nature *as her Bible, she was a restive*

disciple. In this letter to her more "orthodox" brother, she permitted herself to utter a heresy that would have caused Emerson to grieve and Thoreau to sneer. A Romantic strain of rebellion was so deeply embedded in Margaret's being that she could rebel in a grand manner against the Romantic exaltation of nature over the city. Thus she again prefigures her pilgrimage to New York and to Rome.]

. . . I take great pleasure in that feeling of the living presence of beauty which your letters show. But you, who have now lived long enough to see some of my prophecies fulfilled, will not deny though you may not yet believe the truth of my words when I say you go to an extreme in your denunciations of cities and the social institutions. *These* are a growth also, and, as well as the diseases which come upon them, under the control of the one spirit as much as the great tree on which the insects prey, and in whose bark the busy bird has made many a wound.

When we get the proper perspective of these things we shall find man, however artificial, still a part of Nature. Meanwhile, let us trust, and, while it is the soul's duty ever to bear witness to the best it knows, let us not be hasty to conclude that in what suits us not there can be no good. Nay let us be sure there *must* be eventual good, could we but see far enough to discern it. In maintaining perfect truth to ourselves and choosing that mode of being which suits us, we had best leave others alone as much as may be. You, dear R, prefer the country, and I doubt not it is on the whole a better condition of life to live there, but at Mr. Frost's sociable you saw that no circumstances will keep people from being frivolous. One may be gossiping and vulgar, and idle in the country,—earnest, wise and noble in the city. Nature cannot be kept from us while there is a sky above, with so much as one star to remind us of prayer in the silent night.

As I walked home this evening at sunset, over the Mill-
Dam, towards the city, I saw very distinctly that the city
also is a bed in God's garden. More of this some other
time. . . .

6. GOETHE

(Text from the *Dial*, II, July 1841, pp. 23–51.)

*[Margaret Fuller's essay on Goethe was the most pre-
tentious and (in the opinion of the fraternity) the most
erudite piece to appear in the journal. Today it occupies
at best a minor place in the body of Goethe scholarship,
as a pioneering but much too emotional exposition of
Goethe's thought.*

*For the historian of American thought, however, this
fact is irrelevant. What is important is that it was written
in this country and actually published here.* At that
time the general American public, without having read a
line of him, was convinced that Goethe was a monster of*

---

* The only other endeavor in the period that can stand beside
Margaret Fuller's is John Lothrop Motley's in the *New York
Reviews*, III, October 1838, pp. 397–442. Since this fine journal
(much neglected by students of the American mind) was published under the auspices of the Protestant Episcopal Church,
contributors did not have to worry so much about being considered suspect by the religious public. Under the editorship of
Joseph Cogswell (1786–1871)—the best German scholar in the
country, a thorough New Englander who had studied at Göt-
tingen, where he became a friend of Goethe—the *New York Review* did yeoman service in fighting against the popular antipathy
to anything German. Even so, Motley's piece is not so bold as
Margaret's, as it is restricted to a defense of Goethe against the
charge of unconscionable "Egotism." Motley's argument, like
Margaret Fuller's, suggests that efforts in America—as in England
—to excuse Goethe's egotism were secretly inspired, not by a
dislike of it, but by an envy of its magnificence.

egoistic immorality. Anyone who ventured to excuse his profligacy, let alone defend it, automatically became a subverter of the national morality. And when the culprit turned out to be a woman, she could only be branded a shameless hussy.

So Margaret Fuller's essay must not be dismissed as a slightly comical effort to play the cosmopolite. The strain that Margaret was under in exposing her convictions is clear in this as in all the Transcendentalists' genuflections before Goethe, as most pathetically it is in Emerson's endeavor to make the demigod a "Representative Man." Let us say, then, that Margaret accepted the challenge more directly than the rest of them.

After Margaret's death, Emerson admitted that Goethe was "the pivotal mind in modern literature" and therefore would rightly have been for her the most powerful of "mental reagents," but he still hedged, adding, whether for "food or poison." Emerson recognized that whatever the nature of the influence, there clearly was "a strict affinity" between Margaret and Goethe, and he acknowledged that "Nowhere did Goethe find a braver, more intelligent, or more sympathetic reader."

This called for audacity; it called more stringently for courage. At many points she wavered and sought refuge in sentimentality. Still, on the whole she stood her ground amid the ethical rigidities of New England. She confronted Goethe with the same gallant intellect she would bring to the ordeal of social revolution and sexual freedom in Rome a few years later.

Fragments of her journals and letters quoted in the *Memoirs* reveal how deeply she was preoccupied with Goethe. Apparently she thought of him as the father that her own parent failed to be: "How often I have thought, if I could see Goethe, and tell him my state of mind, he would support and guide me!" While teaching in Providence, she translated Eckermann's *Conversations* with Goethe, which George Ripley published in 1839, and in

*her preface she defended Goethe even more militantly
than in this essay (considerations of space prevent me from
giving both). In the third number of the* Dial, *January
1841, she vehemently denounced the strictures on
Goethe's lack of patriotism in Professor Felton's translation of Wolfgang Menzel's* History of German Literature.
Sections of Woman in the Nineteenth Century *summon
Goethe and his heroines to support the cause of female
suffrage. But the noblest voicing of her adoration of the
Master is undoubtedly this impassioned oration.*

Here Margaret brashly defends Werther *against the prevailing American opinion that it was a foul corrupter of
youth; and she praises* The Elective Affinities, *which
American men regarded as the nadir of sensual depravity,
to be kept away from the attention of their wives and
daughters. Viewed in this perspective, Margaret's essay
is a basic document in the history of intellectual freedom
in the United States.]*

"Nemo contra Deum nisi Deus ipse."

"Wer Grosses will muss sich zusammen raffen;
  In der Beschrankung zeigt sich erst der Meister,
  Und der Gesetz nur Kann uns Freiheit geben."*

The first of these mottoes is that prefixed by Gœthe to
the last books of "Dichtung und Wahrheit." These books
record the hour of turning tide in his life, the time when
he was called on for a choice at the "Parting of the Ways."
From these months, which gave the sun of his youth, the
crisis of his manhood, date the birth of Egmont, and of
Faust too, though the latter was not published so early.
They saw the rise and decline of his love for Lili, apparently the truest love he ever knew. That he was not himself dissatisfied with the results to which the decisions of

* "He who would do great things must quickly draw together
his forces. The master can only show himself such through limitation, and the law alone can give us freedom." [M.F.'s note]

this era led him, we may infer from his choice of a motto, and from the calm beauty with which he has invested the record.

The Parting of the Ways! The way he took led to court-favor, wealth, celebrity, and an independence of celebrity. It led to large performance, and a wonderful economical management of intellect. It led Faust, the Seeker, from the heights of his own mind to the trodden ways of the world. There, indeed, he did not lose sight of the mountains, but he never breathed their keen air again.

After this period we find in him rather a wide and deep Wisdom, than the inspiration of Genius. His faith, that all *must* issue well, wants the sweetness of piety, and the God he manifests to us is one of law or necessity, rather than of intelligent love. As this God makes because he must, so Gœthe, his instrument, observes and re-creates because he must, observing with minutest fidelity the outward exposition of Nature; never blinded by a sham, or detained by a fear, he yet makes us feel that he wants insight to her sacred secret. The calmest of writers does not give us repose, because it is too difficult to find his centre. Those flame-like natures, which he undervalues, give us more peace and hope, through their restless aspirations, than he with his hearth-enclosed fires of steady fulfilment. For, true as it is, that God is every where, we must not only see him, but see him acknowledged. Through the consciousness of man, "shall not Nature interpret God?" We wander in diversity, and with each new turning of the path, long anew to be referred to the One.

Of Gœthe, as of other natures, where the intellect is too much developed in proportion to the moral nature, it is difficult to speak without seeming narrow, blind, and impertinent. For such men *see* all that others *live*, and, if you feel a want of a faculty in them, it is hard to say they have it not, lest, next moment, they puzzle you by giving some indication of it. Yet they are not, nay, *know* not; they only discern. The difference is that between sight and life, prescience and being, wisdom and love. Thus with Gœthe. Naturally of a deep mind and shallow heart, he felt the sway of the affections enough to appreciate their workings in other men, but never enough to receive their inmost regenerating influence.

How this might have been had he ever once abandoned himself entirely to a sentiment, it is impossible to say. But the education of his youth seconded, rather than balanced, his natural tendency. His father was a gentlemanly martinet; dull, sour, well-informed, and of great ambition as to externals. His influence on the son was wholly artificial. He was always turning his powerful mind from side to side in search of information, for the attainment of what are called accomplishments. The mother was a delightful person in her way; open, genial, playful, full of lively talent, but without earnestness of soul. She was one of those charming, but not noble persons, who take the day and the man as they find them, seeing the best that is there already, but never making the better grow in its stead. His sister, though of graver kind, was social and intellectual, not religious or tender. The mortifying repulse of his early love checked the few pale buds of faith and tenderness that his heart put forth. His friends were friends of the intellect merely; altogether, he seemed led by destiny to the place he was to fill.

Pardon him, World, that he was too worldly. Do not wonder, Heart, that he was so heartless. Believe, Soul, that one so true, as far as he went, must yet be initiated into the deeper mysteries of Soul. Perhaps even now he sees that we must accept limitations only to transcend them; work in processes only to detect the organizing power which supersedes them; and that Sphinxes of fifty-five volumes might well be cast into the abyss before the single word that solves them all.

Now, when I think of Gœthe, I seem to see his soul, all the variegated plumes of knowledge, artistic form "und so weiter," burnt from it by the fires of divine love, wingless, motionless, unable to hide from itself in any subterfuge of labor, saying again and again, the simple words which he would never distinctly say on earth—God beyond Nature—Faith beyond Sight—the Seeker nobler than the *Meister*.

For this mastery that Gœthe prizes seems to consist rather in the skilful use of means than in the clear manifestation of ends. His Master, indeed, makes acknowledgment of a divine order, but the temporal uses are always uppermost in the mind of the reader. But of this, more at large in reference to his works.

Apart from this want felt in his works, there is a littleness in his aspect as a character. Why waste his time in Weimar court entertainments? His duties as minister were not unworthy of him, though it would have been, perhaps, finer, if he had not spent so large a portion of that prime of intellectual life, from five and twenty to forty, upon them.

But granted that the exercise these gave his faculties, the various lore they brought, and the good they did to the community, made them worth his doing,—why that perpetual dangling after the royal family? Why all that verse-making for the albums of serene highnesses, and those pretty poetical entertainments for the young princesses, and that cold setting himself apart from his true peers, the real sovereigns of Weimar—Herder, Wieland, and the others? The excuse must be found in circumstances of his time and temperament, which made the character of man of the world and man of affairs more attractive to him than the children of nature can conceive it to be in the eyes of one who is capable of being a consecrated bard.

The man of genius feels that literature has become too much a craft by itself. No man should live by or for his pen. Writing is worthless except as the record of life; and no great man ever was satisfied thus to express all his being. His book should be only an indication of himself. The obelisk should point to a scene of conquest. In the

present state of division of labor, the literary man finds
himself condemned to be nothing else. Does he write a
good book? it is not received as evidence of his ability
to live and act, but rather the reverse. Men do not offer
him the care of embassies, as an earlier age did to Petrarca;
they would be surprised if he left his study to go forth
to battle like Cervantes. We have the swordsman, and
statesman, and penman, but it is not considered that the
same mind which can rule the destiny of a poem, may
as well that of an army or an empire.* Yet surely it
should be so. The scientific man may need seclusion from
the common affairs of life, for he has his materials before
him; but the man of letters must seek them in life, and
he who cannot act will but imperfectly appreciate action.

The literary man is impatient at being set apart. He
feels that monks and troubadours, though in a similar
position, were brought into more healthy connection with
man and nature, than he who is supposed to look at them
merely to write them down. So he rebels; and Sir
Walter Scott is prouder of being a good sheriff and farmer,
than of his reputation as the Great Unknown. Byron
piques himself on his skill in shooting and swimming.
Sir H. Davy and Schlegel would be admired as dandies,
and Gœthe, who had received an order from a publisher
"for a dozen more dramas in the same style as Gœtz von
Berlichingen," and though (in sadder sooth) he had already Faust in his head asking to be written out, thought
it no degradation to become premier in the little Duchy
of Weimar.

"Straws show which way the wind blows," and a comment may be drawn from the popular novels, where the
literary man is obliged to wash off the ink in a violet
bath, attest his courage in the duel, and hide his idealism
beneath the vulgar nonchalance and coxcombry of the
man of fashion.

* Except in "La belle France." [M.F.'s note]

If this tendency of his time had some influence in making Gœthe find pleasure in tangible power and decided relations with society, there were other causes which worked deeper. The growth of genius in its relations to men around must always be attended with daily pain. The enchanted eye turns from the far-off star it has detected to the short-sighted bystander, and the seer is mocked for pretending to see what others cannot. The large and generalizing mind infers the whole from a single circumstance, and is reproved by all around for its presumptuous judgment. Its Ithuriel temper pierces shams, creeds, covenants, and chases the phantoms which others embrace, till the lovers of the false Florimels hurl the true knight to the ground. Little men are indignant that Hercules, yet an infant, declares he has strangled the serpent; they demand a proof; they send him out into scenes of labor to bring thence the voucher that his father is a god. What the ancients meant to express by Apollo's continual disappointment in his loves, is felt daily in the youth of genius. The sympathy he seeks flies his touch, the objects of his affection sneer at his sublime credulity, his self-reliance is arrogance, his far sight infatuation, and his ready detection of fallacy fickleness and inconsistency. Such is the youth of genius, before the soul has given that sign of itself which an unbelieving generation cannot controvert. Even then he is little benefited by the transformation of the mockers into worshippers. For the soul seeks not adorers, but peers; not blind worship, but intelligent sympathy. The best consolation even then is that which Gœthe puts into the mouth of Tasso: "To me gave a God to tell what I suffer." In "Tasso" Goethe has described the position of the poetical mind in its prose relations with equal depth and fulness. We see what he felt must be the result of entire abandonment to the highest nature. We see why he valued himself on being able to understand the Alphonsos, and meet as an equal the Antonios of every-day life.

But, you say, there is no likeness between Gœthe and Tasso. Never believe it; such pictures are not painted from observation merely. That deep coloring which fills them with light and life is given by dipping the brush in one's own life-blood. Gœthe had not from nature that character of self-reliance and self-control in which he so long appeared to the world. It was wholly acquired, and so highly valued because he was conscious of the opposite tendency. He was by nature as impetuous, though not as tender, as Tasso, and the disadvantage at which this constantly placed him was keenly felt by a mind made to appreciate the subtlest harmonies in all relations. Therefore was it that when he at last cast anchor, he was so reluctant again to trust himself to wave and breeze.

I have before spoken of the antagonistic influences under which he was educated. He was driven from the severity of study into the world, and then again drawn back, many times in the course of his crowded youth. Both the world and the study he used with unceasing ardor, but not with the sweetness of a peaceful hope. Most of the traits which are considered to mark his character at a later period were wanting to him in youth. He was very social, and continually perturbed by his social sympathies. He was deficient both in outward self-possession and mental self-trust. "I was always," he says, "either *too volatile or too infatuated,* so that those who looked kindly on me did by no means always honor me with their esteem." He wrote much and with great freedom. The pen came naturally to his hand, but he had no confidence in the merit of what he wrote, and much inferior persons to Merck and Herder might have induced him to throw aside as worthless what it had given him sincere pleasure to compose. It was hard for him to isolate himself, to console himself, and, though his mind was always busy with important thoughts, they did not free him from the pressure of other minds. His youth was as sympathetic and impetuous as any on record.

The effect of all this outward pressure on the poet is recorded in Werther—a production that he afterwards undervalued, and to which he even felt positive aversion. It was natural that this should be. In the calm air of the cultivated plain he attained, the remembrance of the miasma of sentimentality was odious to him. Yet sentimentality is but sentiment diseased, which to be cured must be patiently observed by the wise physician; so are the morbid desire and despair of Werther, the sickness of a soul aspiring to a purer, freer state, but mistaking the way.

The best or the worst occasion in man's life is precisely that misused in Werther, when he longs for more love, more freedom, and a larger development of genius than the limitations of this terrene sphere permit. Sad is it indeed if, persisting to grasp too much at once, he lose all, as Werther did. He must accept limitation, must consent to do his work in time, must let his affections be baffled by the barriers of convention. Tantalus-like, he makes this world a Tartarus, or, like Hercules, rises in fires to heaven, according as he knows how to interpret his lot. But he must only use, not adopt it. The boundaries of the man must never be confounded with the destiny of the soul. If he does not decline his destiny, as Werther did, it is his honor to have felt its unfitness for his eternal scope. He was born for wings; he is held to walk in leading-strings; nothing lower than faith must make him resigned, and only in hope should he find content—a hope not of some slight improvement in his own condition or that of other men, but a hope justified by the divine justice, which is bound in due time to satisfy every want of his nature.

Schiller's great command is, "Keep true to the dream of thy youth." The great problem is how to make the dream real, through the exercise of the waking will.

This was not exactly the problem Gœthe tried to solve. To *do* somewhat, became too important, as is indicated both by the second motto to this essay, and by his maxim,

"It is not the knowledge of what *might be,* but what *is,* that forms us."

Werther, like his early essays now republished from the Frankfort Journal, is characterized by a fervid eloquence of Italian glow, which betrays a part of his character almost lost sight of in the quiet transparency of his later productions, and may give us some idea of the mental conflicts through which he passed to manhood.

The acting out the mystery into life, the calmness of survey, and the passionateness of feeling, above all the ironical baffling at the end, and want of point to a tale got up with such an eye to effect as he goes along, mark well the man that was to be. Even so did he demand in Werther; even so resolutely open the door in the first part of Faust; even so seem to play with himself and his contemporaries in the second part of Faust and Wilhelm Meister.

Yet was he deeply earnest in his play, not for men, but for himself. To himself as a part of nature it was important to grow, to lift his head to the light. In nature he had all confidence; for man, as a part of nature, infinite hope; but in him as an individual will, seemingly, not much trust at the earliest age.

The history of his intimacies marks his course; they were entered into with passionate eagerness, but always ended in an observation of the intellect, and he left them on his road, as the snake leaves his skin. The first man he met of sufficient force to command a large share of his attention was Herder, and the benefit of this intercourse was critical, not genial. Of the good Lavater he soon perceived the weakness. Merck, again, commanded his respect; but the force of Merck also was cold.

But in the Grand Duke of Weimar he seems to have met a character strong enough to exercise a decisive influence upon his own. Gœthe was not so politic and worldly that a little man could ever have become his Mæcenas. In the Duchess Amelia and her son he found that practical sagacity, large knowledge of things as they are, active force, and genial feeling, which he had never before seen combined.

The wise mind of the duchess gave the first impulse to the noble course of Weimar. But that her son should have availed himself of the foundation she laid is praise enough, in a world where there is such a rebound from parental influence that it generally seems that the child makes use of the directions given by the parent only to avoid the prescribed path. The duke availed himself of guidance, though with a perfect independence in action. The duchess had the unusual wisdom to know the right time for giving up the reins, and thus maintained her authority as far as the weight of her character was calculated to give it.

Of her Goethe was thinking when he wrote, "The admirable woman is she, who, if the husband dies, can be a father to the children."

The duke seems to have been one of those characters which are best known by the impression their personal presence makes on us, resembling an elemental and pervasive force, rather than wearing the features of an individuality. Goethe describes him as *"Dämonische,"* that is, gifted with an instinctive, spontaneous force, which at once, without calculation or foresight, chooses the right means to an end. As these beings do not calculate, so is their influence incalculable. Their repose has as much influence over other beings as their action, even as the thunder cloud, lying black and distant in the summer sky, is not less imposing than when it bursts and gives forth its quick lightnings. Such men were Mirabeau and Swift. They had also distinct talents, but their influence was from a perception in the minds of men of this spontaneous energy in their natures. Sometimes, though rarely, we see such a man in an obscure position; circumstances have not led him to a large sphere; he may not have expressed in words a single thought worth recording; but by his eye and voice he rules all around him.

He stands upon his feet with a firmness and calm security which make other men seem to halt and totter in their gait. In his deep eye is seen an infinite comprehension, an infinite reserve of power. No accent of his sonorous voice is lost on any ear within hearing; and, when he speaks, men hate or fear perhaps the disturbing power they feel, but never dream of disobeying. But hear Gœthe himself.

"The boy believed in nature, in the animate and inanimate, the intelligent and unconscious, to discover somewhat which manifested itself only through contradiction, and therefore could not be comprehended by any conception, much less defined by a word. It was not divine, for it seemed without reason; not human, because without understanding; not devilish, because it worked to good; not angelic, because it often betrayed a petulant love of mischief. It was like chance, in that it proved no sequence; it suggested the thought of Providence, because it indicated connection. To this all our limitations seem penetrable; it seemed to play at will with all the elements of our being; it compressed time and dilated space. Only in the impossible did it seem to delight, and to cast the possible aside with disdain.

"This existence which seemed to mingle with others, sometimes to separate, sometimes to unite, I called the Dämonische, after the example of the ancients, and others who have observed somewhat similar."—*Dichtung und Wahrheit*.

"The Dämonische is that which cannot be explained by reason or understanding; it lies not in my nature, but I am subject to it.

"Napoleon was a being of this class, and in so high a degree that scarce any one is to be compared with him. Also our late grand duke was such a nature, full of unlimited power of action and unrest, so that his own dominion was too little for him, and the greatest would have been too little. Demoniac beings of this sort the Greeks reckoned among their demigods."—*Conversations with Eckermann.*

This great force of will, this instinctive directness of action, gave the duke an immediate ascendency over Gœthe which no other person had ever possessed. It was by no means mere sycophancy that made him give up the next ten years, the prime of his manhood, to accompanying the grand duke in his revels, or aiding him in his schemes of practical utility, or to contriving elegant amusements for the ladies of the court. It was a real admiration for the character of the genial man of the world and its environment.

Whoever is turned from his natural path may, if he will, gain in largeness and depth what he loses in simple beauty; and so it was with Gœthe. Faust became a wiser if not a nobler being. Werther, who must die because life was not wide enough and rich enough in love for him, ends as the Meister of the Wanderjahre, well content to be one never inadequate to the occasion, "help-full, comfort-full."

A great change was, during these years, perceptible to his friends in the character of Gœthe. From being always "either too volatile or infatuated," he retreated into a self-collected state, which seemed at first even icy to those around him. No longer he darted about him the lightnings of his genius, but sat Jove-like and calm, with the thunderbolts grasped in his hand, and the eagle gathered to his feet. His freakish wit was subdued into a calm and even cold irony; his multiplied relations no longer permitted him to abandon himself to any; the minister and courtier could not expatiate in the free regions of invention, and bring upon paper the signs of his higher life, without subjecting himself to an artificial process of isolation. Obliged to economy of time and means, he made of his intimates not objects of devout tenderness, of disinterested

care, but the crammers and feeders of his intellect. The
world was to him an arena or a studio, but not a temple.

"Ye cannot serve God and Mammon."

Had Gœthe entered upon practical life from the dictate
of his spirit, which bade him not be a mere author, but
a living, loving man, that had all been well. But he must
also be a man of the world, and nothing can be more
unfavorable to true manhood than this ambition. The
citizen, the hero, the general, the poet, all these are in
true relations; but what is called being a man of the
world is to truckle to it, not truly to serve it.

Thus fettered in false relations, detained from retirement upon the centre of his being, yet so relieved from
the early pressure of his great thoughts as to pity more
pious souls for being restless seekers, no wonder that he
wrote,—

"Es ist dafür gesorgt dass die Bäume nicht in den Him-
mel wachsen."

"Care is taken that the trees grow not up into the
heavens." Ay, Gœthe, but in proportion to their force
of aspiration is their height.

Yet never let him be confounded with those who sell all
their birthright. He became blind to the more generous
virtues, the nobler impulses, but ever in self-respect was
busy to develop his nature. He was kind, industrious,
wise, gentlemanly, if not manly. If his genius lost sight
of the highest aim, he is the best instructor in the use
of means; ceasing to be a prophet poet, he was still a
poetic artist. From this time forward he seems a listener
to nature, but not himself the highest product of nature,
—a priest to the soul of nature. His works grow out of
life, but are not instinct with the peculiar life of human
resolve, as are Shakespeare's or Dante's.

Faust contains the great idea of his life, as indeed there
is but one great poetic idea possible to man—the progress
of a soul through the various forms of existence.

All his other works, whatever their miraculous beauty

of execution, are mere chapters to this poem, illustrative
of particular points. Faust, had it been completed in the
spirit in which it was begun, would have been the Divina
Commedia of its age.

But nothing can better show the difference of result
between a stern and earnest life, and one of partial ac-
commodation, than a comparison between the Paridiso
and that of the second part of Faust. In both a soul,
gradually educated and led back to God, is received at
last not through merit, but grace. But O the difference between the grandly humble reliance of old Catholicism,
and the loophole redemption of modern sagacity! Dante
was a *man*, of vehement passions, many prejudices, bitter
as much as sweet. His knowledge was scanty, his sphere
of observation narrow, the objects of his active life petty,
compared with those of Gœthe. But, constantly retiring
to his deepest self, clearsighted to the limitations of man,
but no less so to the illimitable energy of the soul, the
sharpest details in his work convey a largest sense, as
his strongest and steadiest flights only direct the eye to
heavens yet beyond.

Yet perhaps he had not so hard a battle to wage, as this
other great poet. The fiercest passions are not so dangerous foes to the soul as the cold scepticism of the understanding. The Jewish demon assailed the man of Uz with
physical ills, the Lucifer of the middle ages tempted his
passions; but the Mephistopheles of the eighteenth century bade the finite strive to compass the infinite, and
the intellect attempt to solve all the problems of the
soul.

This path Faust had taken: it is that of modern necro-
mancy. Not willing to grow into God by the steady worship
of a life, men would enforce his presence by a spell; not
willing to learn his existence by the slow processes of
their own, they strive to bind it in a word, that they
may wear it about the neck as a talisman.

Faust, bent upon reaching the centre of the universe

through the intellect alone, naturally, after a length of trial, which has prevented the harmonious unfolding of his nature, falls into despair. He has striven for one object, and that object eludes him. Returning upon himself, he finds large tracts of his nature lying waste and cheerless. He is too noble for apathy, too wise for vulgar content with the animal enjoyments of life. Yet the thirst he has been so many years increasing is not to be borne. Give me, he cries, but a drop of water to cool my burning tongue. Yet, in casting himself with a wild recklessness upon the impulses of his nature yet untried, there is a disbelief that any thing short of the All can satisfy the immortal spirit. His first attempt was noble, though mistaken, and under the saving influence of it, he makes the compact, whose condition cheats the fiend at last.

> Kannst du mich schmeichelnd je belügen
> Dass ich mir selbst gefallen mag,
> Kannst du mich mit Genuss betrügen:
> Das sey für mich der letzte Tag.

> Werd ich zum Augenblicke sagen:
> Verweile doch! du bist so schön!
> Dann magst du mich in Fesseln schlagen,
> Dann will ich gern zu Grunde gehen.

> Canst thou by falsehood or by flattery
> Make me one moment with myself at peace,
> Cheat me into tranquillity? Come then
> And welcome, life's last day.
> Make me but to the moment say,
> O fly not yet, thou art so fair,
> Then let me perish, &c.

But this condition is never fulfilled. Faust cannot be content with sensuality, with the charlatanry of ambition, nor with riches. His heart never becomes callous, nor his moral and intellectual perceptions obtuse. He is saved at last.

With the progress of an individual soul is shadowed
forth that of the soul of the age; beginning in intellectual scepticism; sinking into license; cheating itself with
dreams of perfect bliss, to be at once attained by means
no surer than a spurious paper currency; longing itself
back from conflict between the spirit and the flesh, induced by Christianity, to the Greek era with its harmonious development of body and mind; striving to reëmbody
the loved phantom of classical beauty in the heroism of
the middle age; flying from the Byron despair of those
who die because they cannot soar without wings, to
schemes however narrow, of practical utility,—redeemed
at last through mercy alone.

The second part of Faust is full of meaning, resplendent
with beauty; but it is rather an appendix to the first part
than a fulfilment of its promise. The world, remembering the powerful stamp of individual feeling, universal
indeed in its application, but individual in its life, which
had conquered all its scruples in the first part, was vexed
to find, instead of the man Faust, the spirit of the age,—
discontented with the shadowy manifestation of truths
it longed to embrace, and, above all, disappointed that
the author no longer met us face to face, or riveted the
ear by his deep tones of grief and resolve.

When the world shall have got rid of the still overpowering influence of the first part, it will be seen that
the fundamental idea is never lost sight of in the second.
The change is that Gœthe, though the same thinker, is
no longer the same person.

The continuation of Faust in the practical sense of
the education of a man is to be found in Wilhelm Meister.
Here we see the change by strongest contrast. The main-
spring of action is no longer the impassioned and noble
seeker, but a disciple of circumstance, whose most marked
characteristic is a *taste* for virtue and knowledge. Wilhelm
certainly prefers these conditions of existence to their
opposites, but there is nothing so decided in his character

as to prevent his turning a clear eye on every part of that variegated world-scene which the writer wished to place before us.

To see all till he knows all sufficiently to put objects into their relations, then to concentrate his powers and use his knowledge under recognized conditions,—such is the progress of man from Apprentice to Master.

'Tis pity that the volumes of the Wanderjahre have not been translated entire, as well as those of the Lehrjahre, for many, who have read the latter only, fancy that Wilhelm becomes a master in that work. Far from it; he has but just become conscious of the higher powers that have ceaselessly been weaving his fate. Far from being as yet a Master, he but now begins to be a Knower. In the Wanderjahre we find him gradually learning the duties of citizenship, and hardening into manhood, by applying what he has learned for himself to the education of his child. He converses on equal terms with the wise and beneficent; he is no longer duped and played with for his good, but met directly mind to mind.

Wilhelm is a master when he can command his actions, yet keep his mind always open to new means of knowledge; when he has looked at various ways of living, various forms of religion and of character, till he has learned to be tolerant of all, discerning of good in all; when the astronomer imparts to his equal ear his highest thoughts, and the poor cottager seeks his aid as a patron and counsellor.

To be capable of all duties, limited by none, with an open eye, a skilful and ready hand, an assured step, a mind deep, calm, foreseeing without anxiety, hopeful without the aid of illusion,—such is the ripe state of manhood. This attained, the great soul should still seek and labor, but strive and battle never more.

The reason for Gœthe's choosing so negative a character as Wilhelm, and leading him through scenes of vulgarity and low vice, would be obvious enough to a person of any depth of thought, even if he himself had not announced it. He thus obtained room to paint life as it really is, and bring forward those slides in the magic lantern which are always known to exist, though they may not be spoken of to ears polite.

Wilhelm cannot abide in tradition, nor do as his fathers did before him, merely for the sake of money or a standing in society. The stage, here an emblem of the ideal life as it gleams before unpractised eyes, offers, he fancies, opportunity for a life of thought as distinguished from one of routine. Here, no longer the simple citizen, but Man, all Men, he will rightly take upon himself the different aspects of life, till poet-wise, he shall have learned them all.

No doubt the attraction of the stage to young persons of a vulgar character is merely the brilliancy of its trappings; but to Wilhelm, as to Gœthe, it was this poetic freedom and daily suggestion which seemed likely to offer such an agreeable studio in the greenroom.

But the ideal must be rooted in the real, else the poet's life degenerates into buffoonery or vice. Wilhelm finds the characters formed by this would-be ideal existence more despicable than those which grew up on the track, dusty and bustling and dull as it had seemed, of common life. He is prepared by disappointment for a higher ambition.

In the house of the count he finds genuine elegance, genuine sentiment, but not sustained by wisdom, or a devotion to important objects. This love, this life, is also inadequate.

Now, with Teresa he sees the blessings of domestic peace. He sees a mind sufficient for itself, finding employment and education in the perfect economy of a little world. The lesson is pertinent to the state of mind in which his former experiences have left him, as indeed our deepest lore is won from reaction. But a sudden change of scene introduces him to the society of the sage and learned uncle, the sage and beneficent Natalia. Here he finds the same virtues as with Teresa, and enlightened by a larger wisdom.

A friend of mine says that his ideal of a friend is a worthy aunt, one who has the tenderness without the blindness of a mother, and takes the same charge of the child's mind as the mother of its body. I don't know but this may have a foundation in truth, though, if so, auntism, like other grand professions, has sadly degenerated. At any rate, Gœthe seems to be possessed with a similar feeling. The Count de Thorane, a man of powerful character, who made a deep impression on his childhood, was, he says, "reverenced by me as an uncle." And the ideal wise man of this common life epic stands before us as "The Uncle."

After seeing the working of just views in the establishment of the uncle, learning piety from the Confessions of a Beautiful Soul, and religious beneficence from the beautiful life of Natalia, Wilhelm is deemed worthy of admission to the society of the Illuminati, that is, those who have pierced the secret of life, and know what it is to be and to do.

Here he finds the scroll of his life "drawn with large, sharp strokes," that is, these truly wise read his character for him, and "mind and destiny are but two names for one idea."

He now knows enough to enter on the Wanderjahre.

Gœthe always represents the highest principle in the feminine form. Woman is the Minerva, man the Mars. As in the Faust, the purity of Gretchen, resisting the demon always, even after all her faults, is announced to have saved her soul to heaven; and in the second part she appears, not only redeemed herself, but by her innocence and forgiving tenderness hallowed to redeem the being who had injured her.

So in the Meister, these women hover around the narrative, each embodying the spirit of the scene. The frail Philina, graceful though contemptible, represents the deg-

radation incident to an attempt at leading an exclusively
poetic life. Mignon, gift divine as ever the Muse be-
stowed on the passionate heart of man, with her soft,
mysterious inspiration, her pining for perpetual youth,
represents the high desire that leads to this mistake, as
Aurelia, the desire for excitement; Teresa, practical wisdom, gentle tranquillity, which seem most desirable after
the Aurelia glare. Of the beautiful soul and Natalia we
have already spoken. The former embodies what was suggested to Gœthe by the most spiritual person he knew
in youth—Mademoiselle von Klettenberg, over whom, as
he said, in her invalid loneliness the Holy Ghost brooded
like a dove.

Entering on the Wanderjahre, Wilhelm becomes acquainted with another woman, who seems the complement
of all the former, and represents the idea which is to
guide and mould him in the realization of all the past
experience.

This person, long before we see her, is announced in
various ways as a ruling power. She is the last hope in
cases of difficulty, and, though an invalid, and living in
absolute retirement, is consulted by her connections and
acquaintance as an unerring judge in all their affairs.

All things tend towards her as a centre; she knows all,
governs all, but never goes forth from herself.

Wilhelm at last visits her. He finds her infirm in body,
but equal to all she has to do. Charity and counsel to
men who need her are her business, astronomy her
pleasure.

After a while, Wilhelm ascertains from the Astronomer, her companion, what he had before suspected, that
she really belongs to the solar system, and only appears
on earth to give men a feeling of the planetary harmony.
From her youth up, says the Astronomer, till she knew
me, though all recognized in her an unfolding of the
highest moral and intellectual qualities, she was supposed
to be sick at her times of clear vision. When her thoughts

were not in the heavens, she returned and acted in obedience to them on earth; she was then said to be well.

When the Astronomer had observed her long enough, he confirmed her inward consciousness of a separate existence and peculiar union with the heavenly bodies.

Her picture is painted with many delicate traits, and a gradual preparation leads the reader to acknowledge the truth; but, even in the slight indication here given, who does not recognize thee, divine Philosophy, sure as the planetary orbits, and inexhaustible as the fountain of light, crowning the faithful Seeker at last with the privilege to possess his own soul.

In all that is said of Macaria,* we recognize that no thought is too religious for the mind of Goethe. It was indeed so; you can deny him nothing, but only feel that his works are not instinct and glowing with the central fire, and, after catching a glimpse of the highest truth, are forced again to find him too much afraid of losing sight of the limitations of nature to overflow you or himself with the creative spirit.

While the apparition of the celestial Macaria seems to announce the ultimate destiny of the soul of man, the practical application of all Wilhelm has thus painfully acquired is not of pure Delphian strain. Goethe draws, as he passes, a dart from the quiver of Phœbus, but ends as Æsculapius or Mercury. Wilhelm, at the school of the Three Reverences, thinks out what can be done for man in his temporal relations. He learns to practise moderation, and even painful renunciation. The book ends, simply indicating what the course of his life will be, by making him perform an act of kindness, with good judgment and at the right moment.

* The name of Macaria is one of noblest association. It is that of the daughter of Hercules, who devoted herself a voluntary sacrifice for her country. She was adored by the Greeks as the true Felicity. [M.F.'s note]

Surely the simple soberness of Gœthe should please at least those who style themselves, preëminently, people of common sense. . . .

But those who demand from him a life-long continuance of the early ardor of Faust, who wish to see, throughout his works, not only such manifold beauty and subtle wisdom, but the clear assurance of divinity, the pure white light of Macaria, wish that he had not so variously unfolded his nature, and concentred it more. They would see him slaying the serpent with the divine wrath of Apollo, rather than taming it to his service, like Æsculapius. They wish that he had never gone to Weimar, had never become a universal connoisseur and dilettante in science, and courtier as "graceful as a born nobleman," but had endured the burden of life with the suffering crowd, and deepened his nature in loneliness and privation, till Faust had conquered, rather than cheated the devil, and the music of heavenly faith superseded the grave and mild eloquence of human wisdom.

The expansive genius which moved so gracefully in its self-imposed fetters, is constantly surprising us by its content with a choice low, in so far as it was not the highest of which the mind was capable. The secret may be found in the second motto of this slight essay.

"He who would do great things must quickly draw together his forces. The master can only show himself such through limitation, and the law alone can give us freedom."

But there is a higher spiritual law always ready to supersede the temporal laws at the call of the human soul. The soul that is too content with usual limitations will never call forth this unusual manifestation.

If there be a tide in the affairs of men, which must be taken at the right moment to lead on to fortune, it is the same with inward as with outward life. He who, in the crisis hour of youth, has stopped short of himself, is not likely to find again what he has missed in one life, for there are a great number of blanks to a prize in each lottery.

But the pang we feel that "those who are so much are not more," seems to promise new spheres, new ages, new crises to enable these beings to complete their circle.

Perhaps Gœthe is even now sensible that he should not have stopped at Weimar as his home, but made it one station on the way to Paradise; not stopped at humanity, but regarded it as symbolical of the divine, and given to others to feel more distinctly the centre of the universe, as well as the harmony in its parts. It is great to be an Artist, a Master, greater still to be a Seeker till the Man has found all himself.

What Gœthe meant by self-collection was a collection of means for work, rather than to divine the deepest truths of being. Thus are these truths always indicated, never declared; and the religious hope awakened by his subtle discernment of the workings of nature never gratified, except through the intellect.

He whose prayer is only work will not leave his treasure in the secret shrine.

One is ashamed when finding any fault with one like Gœthe, who is so great. It seems the only criticism should be to do all he omitted to do, and that none who cannot is entitled to say a word. Let that one speak who was all Gœthe was not,—noble, true, virtuous, but neither wise nor subtle in his generation, a divine ministrant, a baffled man, ruled and imposed on by the pygmies whom he spurned, an heroic artist, a democrat to the tune of Burns:

"The rank is but the guinea's stamp;
The man's the gowd for a' that."

Hear Beethoven speak of Gœthe on an occasion which brought out the two characters in strong contrast.

Extract from a letter of Beethoven to Bettina Brentano, Töplitz, 1812.

"Kings and princes can indeed make professors and privy councillors, and hang upon them titles; but great men they cannot make; souls that rise above the mud of the world, these they must let be made by other means than theirs, and should therefore show them respect. When two such as I and Gœthe come together, then must great lords observe what is esteemed great by one of us. Coming home yesterday we met the whole imperial family. We saw them coming, and Gœthe left me and insisted on standing one side; let me say what I would, I could not make him come on one step. I pressed my hat upon my head, buttoned my surtout, and passed on through the thickest crowd. Princes and parasites made way; the Archduke Rudolph took off his hat; the empress greeted me first. Their highnesses KNOW ME. I was well amused to see the crowd pass by Gœthe. At the side stood he, hat in hand, low bowed in reverence till all had gone by. Then I scolded him well; I gave no pardon, but reproached him with all his sins, most of all those towards you, dearest Bettina; we had just been talking of you."

If Beethoven appears, in this scene, somewhat arrogant and bearish, yet how noble his extreme compared with the opposite! Gœthe's friendship with the grand duke we respect, for Karl August was a strong man. But we regret to see at the command of any and all members of the ducal family, and their connections, who had nothing but rank to recommend them, his time and thoughts, of which he was so chary to private friends. Beethoven could not endure to teach the Archduke Rudolph, who had the soul duly to revere his genius, because he felt it to be "hofdienst," court service. He received with perfect nonchalance the homage of the sovereigns of Europe. Only the Empress of Russia and the Archduke Karl, whom he esteemed as individuals, had power to gratify him by their attentions. Compare with Gœthe's obsequious pleasure at being able gracefully to compliment such high personages, Beethoven's conduct with regard to the famous Heroic Symphony. This was composed at the suggestion of Bernadotte, while Napoleon was still in his first glory. He was then the hero of Beethoven's imagination, who hoped from him the liberation of Europe. With delight the great artist expressed in his eternal harmonies the progress of the Hero's soul. The symphony was finished, and even dedicated to Bonaparte, when the news came of his declaring himself Emperor of the French. The first act of the indignant artist was to tear off his dedication and trample it under foot; nor could he endure again even the mention of Napoleon until the time of his fall.

Admit that Gœthe had a natural taste for the trappings of rank and wealth, from which the musician was quite free, yet we cannot doubt that both saw through these externals to man as a nature; there can be no doubt on whose side was the simple greatness, the noble truth. We pardon thee, Gœthe,—but thee, Beethoven, we revere, for thou hast maintained the worship of the Manly, the Permanent, the True!

The clear perception which was in Gœthe's better nature of the beauty of that steadfastness, of that singleness and simple melody of soul, which he too much sacrificed to become "the many-sided One," is shown most distinctly in his two surpassingly beautiful works, The Elective Affinities and Iphigenia.

Not Werther, not the Nouvelle Héloise, have been assailed with such a storm of indignation as the first-named of these works, on the score of gross immorality.

The reason probably is the subject; any discussion of the validity of the marriage vow making society tremble to its foundation; and, secondly, the cold manner in which it is done. All that is in the book would be bearable to most minds if the writer had had less the air of a spectator, and had larded his work here and there with ejaculations of horror and surprise.

These declarations of sentiment on the part of the author seem to be required by the majority of readers, in order to an interpretation of his purpose, as sixthly, seventhly, and eighthly were, in an old-fashioned sermon, to rouse the audience to a perception of the method made use of by the preacher.

But it has always seemed to me that those who need not such helps to their discriminating faculties, but read a work so thoroughly as to apprehend its whole scope and tendency, rather than hear what the author says it means, will regard the Elective Affinities as a work especially what is called moral in its outward effect, and religious even to piety in its spirit. The mental aberrations of the consorts from their plighted faith, though in the one case never indulged, and though in the other no veil of sophistry is cast over the weakness of passion, but all that is felt expressed with the openness of one who desires to legitimate what he feels, are punished by terrible griefs and a fatal catastrophe. Ottilia, that being of exquisite purity, with intellect and character so harmonized in feminine beauty, as they never before were found in any portrait of woman painted by the hand of man, perishes, on finding she has been breathed on by unhallowed passion, and led to err even by her ignorant wishes against what is held sacred. The only personage whom we do not pity is Edward, for he is the only one who stifles the voice of conscience.

There is indeed a sadness, as of an irresistible fatality, brooding over the whole. It seems as if only a ray of angelic truth could have enabled these men to walk wisely in this twilight, at first so soft and alluring, then deepening into blind horror.

But if no such ray came to prevent their earthly errors, it seems to point heavenward in the saintly sweetness of Ottilia. Her nature, too fair for vice, too finely wrought even for error, comes lonely, intense, and pale, like the evening star on the cold, wintry night. It tells of other worlds, where the meaning of such strange passages as this must be read to those faithful and pure like her, victims perishing in the green garlands of a spotless youth to atone for the unworthiness of others.

An unspeakable pathos is felt from the minutest trait of this character, and deepens with every new study of it. Not even in Shakespeare have I so felt the organizing power of genius. Through dead words I find the least gestures of this person, stamping themselves on my memory, betraying to the heart the secret of her life, which she herself, like all these divine beings, knew not. I feel myself familiarized with all beings of her order. I see not only what she was, but what she might have been, and live with her in yet untrodden realms.

Here is the glorious privilege of a form known only in the world of genius. There is on it no stain of usage or calculation to dull our sense of its immeasurable life. What in our daily walk, mid common faces and common places, fleets across us at moments from glances of the eye, or tones of the voice, is felt from the whole being of one of these children of genius.

This precious gem is set in a ring complete in its enamel. I cannot hope to express my sense of the beauty of this book as a work of art. I would not attempt it if I had elsewhere met any testimony to the same. The perfect picture, always before the mind, of the chateau, the moss hut, the park, the garden, the lake, with its boat and the landing beneath the platan trees; the gradual manner in which both localities and persons grow upon us, more living than life, inasmuch as we are, unconsciously, kept at our best temperature by the atmosphere of genius, and thereby more delicate in our perceptions than amid our customary fogs; the gentle unfolding of the central thought, as a flower in the morning sun; then the conclusion, rising like a cloud, first soft and white, but

darkening as it comes, till with a sudden wind it bursts
above our heads; the ease with which we every where find
points of view all different, yet all bearing on the same
circle, for, though we feel every hour new worlds, still
before our eye lie the same objects, new, yet the same,
unchangeable, yet always changing their aspects as we
proceed, till at last we find we ourselves have traversed
the circle, and know all we overlooked at first,—these
things are worthy of our highest admiration.

For myself, I never felt so completely that very thing
which genius should always make us feel—that I was in its
circle, and could not get out till its spell was done, and
its last spirit permitted to depart. I was not carried away,
instructed, delighted more than by other works, but I
was *there*, living there, whether as the platan tree, or
the architect, or any other observing part of the scene.
The personages live too intensely to let us live in them;
they draw around themselves circles within the circle;
we can only see them close, not be themselves.

Others, it would seem, on closing the book, exclaim,
"What an immoral book!" I well remember my own
thought, "It is a work of art!" At last I understood that
world within a world, the ripest fruit of human nature,
which is called art. With each perusal of the book my
surprise and delight at this wonderful fulfilment of design grew. I understood why Gœthe was well content
to be called Artist, and his works, works of Art, rather
than revelations. At this moment, remembering what I
then felt, I am inclined to class all my negations just
written on this paper as stuff, and to look upon myself,
for thinking them, with as much contempt as Mr. Carlyle, or Mrs. Austin, or Mrs. Jameson might do, to say
nothing of the German Gœtheans.

Yet that they were not without foundation I feel again
when I turn to the Iphigenia—a work beyond the possibility of negation; a work where a religious meaning not
only pierces but enfolds the whole; a work as admirable

in art, still higher in significance, more single in expression. . . .

If it be not possible to enhance the beauty with which such ideal figures as the Iphigenia and the Antigone appeared to the Greek mind, yet Gœthe has unfolded a part of the life of this being, unknown elsewhere in the records of literature. The character of the priestess, the full beauty of virgin womanhood, solitary, but tender, wise and innocent, sensitive and self-collected, sweet as spring, dignified as becomes the chosen servant of God, each gesture and word of deep and delicate significance,—where else is such a picture to be found?

It was not the courtier, nor the man of the world, nor the connoisseur, nor the friend of Mephistopheles, nor Wilhelm the Master, nor Egmont the generous, free liver, that saw Iphigenia in the world of spirits, but Gœthe, in his first-born glory; Gœthe, the poet; Gœthe, designed to be the brightest star in a new constellation. Let us not, in surveying his works and life, abide with him too much in the suburbs and outskirts of himself. Let us enter into his higher tendency, thank him for such angels as Iphigenia, whose simple truth mocks at all his wise "Beschrankungen," and hope the hour when, girt about with many such, he will confess, contrary to his opinion, given in his latest days, that it *is* well worth while to live seventy years, if only to find that they are nothing in the sight of God.

7. TO RALPH WALDO EMERSON,
October, 1841

(Text from Rusk, *The Letters of Ralph Waldo Emerson*, II, pp. 455–56.)

[Nothing, I am sure, could give us a more delicious sense of the oblique manner in which Transcendentalists conducted their personal relations than to learn that while Margaret Fuller was a guest in the Emerson household in October 1841, she and Emerson resolutely remained in their respective chambers and communicated by letter. Their postboy was Emerson's son, Waldo.

Emerson's Journals attest that Margaret was seeking to renew their sterile debate about "friendship." He mentions "these strange, cold-warm, attractive-repelling conversations with Margaret." We are tempted to remark that she was again mounting her assault upon him. Of course this device of letters "from room to room" did not melt in the slightest the now resolutely frozen Emerson.

In the first surviving epistle of this weird correspondence, Margaret tells Emerson:

I like to be in your library when you are out of it. It seems a sacred place. I came here to find a book, that I might feel more life and be worthy to sleep, but there is so much soul here I do not need a book. When I come to yourself, I cannot receive you, and you cannot give yourself; it does not profit. But when I cannot find you the beauty and permanence of your life come to me.

The manufactured perversity and calculated frustration here—a common New England trait—exhibit a secret joy that Transcendental philosophizing about the entire universe could not remove.]

My dear friend,

We shall never meet on these subjects while one atom of our proper individualities remains. Yet let me say a few words more on my side. The true love has no need of illusion: it is too deeply prophetic in its nature to be baffled or chilled, much less changed by the accidents of time. We are sure that what we love is living, though the ruins of old age have fallen upon the shrine. The "blank gray" upon the hallowed locks, the dimmed eye, the wasted cheek cannot deceive us. Neither can the diminution of vital fire and force, the scantiness of thought, the loss of grace, wit, fancy and springing enthusiasm, for it was none of these we loved, but the true self, that particular emanation from God which was made to correspond with that which we are, to teach it, to learn from it, to torture it, to enchant it, to deepen and at last to satisfy our wants. You go upon the idea that we must love most the most beauteous, but this is not so. We love most that which by working most powerfully on our peculiar nature awakens most deeply and constantly in us the idea of beauty. Where we have once seen clearly what is fit for us, if only a glance of the eye we cannot forget it, nor can any change in the form where we have seen it deceive us. We know that it will appear again and clothe the scene with new and greater beauty.

For the past year or two I begin to see a change in the forms of these my contemporaries who have filled my eye. It is a sight that makes one pensive, but awakens, I think, a deeper tenderness and even a higher hope than did these forms in the greatest perfection they ever attained. For they still only promised beauty not gave it, and now seeing the swift changes of time I feel what an illusion all ill, all imperfection is. As they fail to justify my expectation, it only rises the higher and they become dearer as the heralds of a great fulfilment. The princely crest is lowered, the proud glow of youth, its haughty smile and gleaming sweetness are fled, every languid motion assures me that this life will not complete the picture I had sketched, but I only postpone it for ages, and expect it on the same canvas yet.

The fact you repel of the mother and the child as seen in other nature does not repel, why should it in human nature? It is beautiful to see the red berry, the just blown rose and the rose bud on the same stalk as we sometimes do; nor are we displeased with the young blossoming scion that it grows up beside the aged tree; it borrows rather a charm from the neighborhood of that which it must sometimes resemble. But I might write a volume, and then should not have done. I seem to myself to say all when I say that the chivalric idea of love through disease, dungeons and death, mutilation on the battle field, and the odious changes effected by the enchanter's hate answers my idea far better than the stoical appreciation of the object beloved for what it positively presents. I would love in faith that could not change and face the inevitable shadows of old age happy in some occasion for fidelity. . . .

Waldo has brought me your page, and he looked so lovely as if he were the living word which should yet reveal to the world all that you do not feel ready to say. —I really did not mean to show you the letter to Cary but merely to gratify my fancy by having all the letters to these interesting persons under your seal. Do not regret having read it, for I do not care, since I can tell you I did not intend it; the only feeling was that what I had to say to you I should wish to say to yourself direct, and not to another, letting you see it. But just as I should not care for C. to show you the letter, so I do not now, for your having seen it. Do not fancy that I complain or grieve. I understand matters now, and always want you to withdraw when you feel like it; indeed, there is nothing I wish more than to be able to live with you, without disturbing you. This is the main stream of my feeling. I am satisfied and also feel our friendship will grow. But I am of a more lively and affectionate temper or rather more household and daily in my affection than you and have a thousand evanescent feelings and ebullitions like that in the letter. Cary has made a picture of the rock and the wave; if she had made the rock a noble enough figure it might stand for frontispiece to the chapter of my deepest life. For the moment the rock dashes back with a murmur, but it always returns. It is not now a murmur of sorrow but only the voice of a more flexible life. *I would not have it otherwise.* The genial flow of my desire may be checked for the moment, but it cannot long. I shall always burst out soon and burn up all the rubbish between you and me, and I shall always find you there true to yourself and deeply rooted as ever. My impatience is but the bubble on the stream; you know I want to be alone myself,—It is all right. As to the shadow I do not know myself what it is, but it rests on your aspect, and brings me near the second-sight as I look on you. Perhaps if we have Scotch mists enough I shall really see the tapestry of the coming time start into life, but, if I do, I shall not tell you, but with wise economy keep it for a poem which shall make ever sacred and illustrious the name of

Yours Margaret.

8. TO RALPH WALDO EMERSON, FROM CHICAGO, August 17, 1843

(Text from Rusk, *Letters,* III, pp. 200–1.)

[In the spring of 1843, Margaret's old friend and fellow-scholar in German, James Freeman Clarke (who re-

*sisted the impulse to fall in love with her) invited her
to accompany him and his sister on a trip to the "West."
At the time, this meant to her Chicago and its environs,
not the Wyoming of Francis Parkman.*

*Margaret took notes for a conventional "travel book";
but from Chicago she wrote to Emerson, out of a nos-
talgia she would yet more painfully experience, a Tran-
scendentalist's judgment upon the clodhoppers who were
settling the West, destroying the beauty that Emerson
had so revered in* Nature.]

. . . I must write to you this evening, my friend, as
a solace, though that is a way you do not like to love or
be loved.

O what can be so forlorn in its forlorn parts as this
travelling? the ceaseless packing and unpacking, the heartless, uncongenial intercourses, the cheerless hotel, the
many hours when you are too tired and your feelings
too much dissipated to settle to any pursuit, yet you
either have nothing to look at or are weary of looking.

This is my last evening in Chicago, (the *place of onions*
is the interpretation of the Indian name, and I can attest
there is some quality here fitted to draw tears and so can
two or three infants that are screaming in the gallery at
this instant). I have just done packing, Sarah is quite un-
well, and nobody comes in to claim my vacant hour.
But there are two of them (the hours c'est à dire), yet
before bed time, probably there will be some leave-
takings.

But I shall scarce leave friends behind me though, perhaps, no foes. I have not reached forth the hand, neither
has it been offered to me. I am silenced by these people,
they are so all life and no thought, any thing that might
fall from my lips would seem an impertinence. I move
about silently and look at them unnoticed.

Truly there is no place for me to live, I mean as regards being with men. I like not the petty intellectualities,

cant, and bloodless theory there at home, but this merely instinctive existence, to those who live it so "first rate" "off hand" and "go ahead," pleases me no better.

The country ah! that is another thing in these wide plains, with their endless flowing treasures one could breathe a breath, free as rapture, over these smooth green hills could stray no more burthened than the deer. But I have not been there all the time. You say, (for I have received your letter this afternoon,) that I did not write you of Rock River, but I had written of it to others who, I thought would show you the letters, and I don't like to write circulars. Those were fair days, grand sights, worth coming all this way and paying all this time for. But of details that must wait now till we meet.

At Milwaukie too I had an eye full, every day. From the lighthouse to look out over the lake, to see the thunder clouds gathering, reflected in that vast mirror, and the huge steamers looming up was very fine. Or to follow the margin of the lake beneath the tall bluff whose crumbling soil changed almost daily its bold and picturesque juts, to watch the color on the lake various as the prism with the varying depths lying in strata, an immense pallette, emerald, sapphire, amethyst. Or along the smiling river with it many ravines, there grow the most twisted old arbor vitae trees that ever were seen, and the waterfall—but I have not room to describe!

Here at Chicago every thing is flat as Holland. The place is made for trade, and used as such, let us be glad of any thing that fulfils its destiny.—Not without sadness even here have I taken my last drive over the prairie, my last walk along the shore, good bye is always sad; we know we have not taken from the places, from the persons all they were capable to give. . . .

9. TO RALPH WALDO EMERSON,
November 12, 1843

(Text from Rusk, *Letters*, III, pp. 220–21.)

[Immediately upon returning to Massachusetts, Margaret set to work on her "travel book." Meanwhile she produced a poem, "Triformis," which she insisted was offered her by an anonymous friend and which she asked Emerson to print in the Dial. *He must have realized the game, for with calculated cruelty he submitted it to "your enemy H." (Thoreau) and to Ellery Channing. Both found nothing of merit in it, which is not surprising, for while Margaret was editor of the* Dial, *she had stoutly resisted printing the works of Emerson's protégé, Henry Thoreau. Also she had never concealed her contempt for the poetry as well as the personality of her brother-in-law, the younger Ellery Channing. Margaret was justifiably angered, but kept her temper; and she here takes quiet revenge by holding Emerson to a standard of integrity superior to his own.]*

Thy letter, O best Waldo, displays the wonted glorious inconsistency, beginning as a hymn in praise of indolence, and ending with demands of work . . .

Don't expect any thing from the book about the West. I can't bear to be thus disappointing you all the time. No lives of Goethe, no romances.—My power of work is quite external. I can give lessons or do errands while there are minutes in the day, but I cannot think a thought, or write a line except under certain conditions. To have you in the world, doing something yourself, and ready to be pleased if I do any thing, I like—but don't expect. I cannot prom-

ise any thing. Often and long I am without any real
energy.— . . .

I must scold you about that little translation [i.e.
poem] on these grounds. When I had the care of the
Dial, I put in what those connected with me liked, even
when it did not well please myself, on this principle, that
I considered a magazine was meant to suit more than one
class of minds. As I should like to have writings from you,
Mr. Ripley, Mr. Parker, etc., so I should like to have
writings recommended by each of you. I thought it less
important that everything in it should be excellent, than
that it should represent with some fidelity the state of
mind among us as the name of "Dial" said was its intent. . . .

You go on a different principle; you would have everything in it good according to your taste, which is in my
opinion, though admirable as far as it goes, far too narrow in its range. This is *your* principle; very well! I ac-
quiesce, just as in our intercourse I do not expect you to
do what I consider justice to many things I prize. So if
I offered you anything for your Dial and you yourself did
not like it, I am willing you should reject it.

But if you are going to take any other person's judgment, beside your own, why should you not take mine?
Why do you set some other person to read and judge
that which pleased *me*, which you know I should have
put into the book?

I said I would scold you, however I do not mean to, but
simply state how discourteous this act seems to me. It is
good to catch sight of such a fact as this now and then,
we balance it against his fine speeches and get the average
of his view better than else his sweet smiles might let us.

I do not care for your *not liking* the piece, because,
when you wrote in your journal that I cared for talent as
well as genius, I accepted the words written in dispraise
as praise. I wish my tastes and sympathies still more expansive than they are, instead of more severe. Here we

differ. I know it, and am prepared for consequences, but this setting some other person to read and judge is quite another thing. . . .

10. SUMMER ON THE LAKES

(Text from the first edition, Boston, 1844.)

[Margaret Fuller completed her book of travel, largely a reworking of her journal, on May 23, 1844. Emerson acted as her agent with the firm of Little & Brown, which published it on June 5th. While composing it, she petitioned Harvard College to allow her to read in the library; her request being granted, she became the first woman ever to tread those precincts, to the astonishment of such undergraduates as Thomas Wentworth Higginson. The book yielded her no income; she received only a few copies to give to her friends.

The work has been oddly slighted, even by devotees of the "Margaret cult." The full text is a potpourri of a sort fashionable in the nineteenth century but tedious today. In this convention, reports on scenes alternate with random associations or with insertions of brazenly extraneous matter, especially with ad hoc poetic flights. Thus the real theme of the narrative—the trip itself—becomes miserably confused; the effect on a modern reader is that of an intolerable monstrosity. Henry Thoreau, although, as Emerson classified him, an "enemy" of Margaret Fuller, received from Summer much of the impetus for his similar compilation, A Week on the Concord and Merrimack Rivers, which likewise was a commercial failure and which also, for the same reasons, is heavy going today even for initiates in the "Henry cult."

By eliminating the digressions and most of the contrived pieces—even though Margaret's worshipers among

*the "Conversations" highly cherished these portions—and
by presenting what in substance is a remarkably sensitive
comment of a Transcendental New Englander upon the
boisterous rush of inland America in 1843, I have sought
to let the realistic Margaret Fuller reveal herself. After
all, Bronson Alcott said of her in 1839, she was "one of
the most intelligent of my contemporaries, having more
insight into character than most."]*

NIAGARA

Niagara, June 10, 1843

Since you are to share with me such footnotes as may
be made on the pages of my life during this summer's
wanderings, I should not be quite silent as to this magnificent prologue to the as yet unknown drama. Yet I, like
others, have little to say, where the spectacle is for once
great enough to fill the whole life and supersede thought,
giving us only its own presence. "It is good to be here,"
is the best, as the simplest, expression that occurs to the
mind.

We have been here eight days, and I am quite willing
to go away. So great a sight soon satisfies, making us content with itself and with what is less than itself. Our
desires, once realized, haunt us again less readily. Having
"lived one day," we would depart, and become worthy to
live another.

We have not been fortunate in weather, for there cannot be too much or too warm sunlight for this scene, and
the skies have been lowering, with cold, unkind winds.
My nerves, too much braced up by such an atmosphere, do
not well bear the continual stress of sight and sound. For
here there is no escape from the weight of perpetual creation; all other forms and motions come and go, the tide
rises and recedes, the wind, at its mightiest, moves in
gales and gusts, but here is really an incessant, an in-
defatigable motion. Awake or asleep, there is no escape,

still this rushing round you and through you. It is in this way I have most felt the grandeur—somewhat eternal, if not infinite.

At times a secondary music rises; the cataract seems to seize its own rhythm and sing it over again, so that the ear and soul are roused by a double vibration. This is some effect of the wind, causing echoes to the thundering anthem. It is very sublime, giving the effect of a spiritual repetition through all the spheres.

When I first came, I felt nothing but a quiet satisfaction. I found that drawing, the panorama, &c., had given me a clear notion of the position and proportions of all objects here; I knew where to look for everything, and everything looked as I thought it would.

Long ago, I was looking from a hillside with a friend at one of the finest sunsets that ever enriched this world. A little cowboy, trudging along, wondered what we could be gazing at. After spying about some time, he found it could only be the sunset, and looking, too, a moment, he said approvingly, "That sun looks well enough"; a speech worthy of Shakespeare's Cloten, or the infant Mercury, up to everything from the cradle, as you please to take it.

Even such a familiarity, worthy of Jonathan, our national hero, in a prince's palace, or "stumping," as he boasts to have done, "up the Vatican stairs, into the Pope's presence, in my old boots," I felt here; it looks really *well enough*, I felt, and was inclined, as you suggested, to give my approbation as to the one object in the world that would not disappoint.

But all great expression, which on a superficial survey seems so easy as well as so simple, furnishes after a while, to the faithful observer, its own standard by which to appreciate it. Daily these proportions widened and towered more and more upon my sight, and I got at last a proper foreground for these sublime distances. Before coming away, I think I really saw the full wonder of the scene. After a while it so drew me into itself as to inspire an undefined dread, such as I never knew before, such as may be felt when death is about to usher us into a new existence. The perpetual trampling of the waters seized my senses. I felt that no other sound, however near, could be heard, and would start and look behind me for a foe. I realized the identity of that mood of nature in which these waters were poured down with such absorbing force, with that in which the Indian was shaped on the same soil. For continually upon my mind came unsought and unwelcome images, such as never haunted it before, of naked savages stealing behind me with uplifted toma-hawks; again and again this illusion recurred, and even after I had thought it over, and tried to shake it off, I could not help starting and looking behind me.

As picture, the falls can only be seen from the British side. There they are seen in their veils, and at sufficient distance to appreciate the magical effects of these, and the light and shade. From the boat, as you cross, the effects and contrasts are more melodramatic. On the road back from the whirlpool, we saw them as a reduced picture with delight. But what I liked best was to sit on Table Rock, close to the great fall. There all power of observing details, all separate consciousness, was quite lost.

Once, just as I had seated myself there, a man came to take his first look. He walked close up to the fall, and after looking at it a moment, with an air as if thinking how he could best appropriate it to his own use, he spat into it.

This trait seemed wholly worthy of an age whose love of *utility* is such that the Prince Pückler-Muskau suggests the probability of men coming to put the bodies of their dead parents in the fields to fertilize them, and of a country such as Dickens has described; but these will not, I hope, be seen on the historic page to be truly the age or truly the America. A little leaven is leavening the mass for other bread.

The whirlpool I like very much. It is seen to advantage after the great falls; it is so sternly solemn. The river cannot look more imperturbable, almost sullen in its marble green, than it does just below the great fall; but the slight circles that mark the hidden vortex seem to whisper mysteries the thundering voice above could not proclaim —a meaning as untold as ever.

It is fearful, too, to know as you look that whatever has been swallowed by the cataract is like to rise suddenly to light here, whether uprooted tree or body of man or bird.

The rapids enchanted me far beyond what I expected; they are so swift that they cease to seem so; you can think only of their beauty. The fountain beyond the Moss Islands I discovered for myself, and thought it for some time an accidental beauty which it would not do to leave, lest I might never see it again. After I found it permanent, I returned many times to watch the play of its crest. In the little waterfall beyond, Nature seems, as she often does, to have made a study for some larger design. She delights in this—a sketch within a sketch, a dream within a dream. Wherever we see it, the lines of the great buttress in the fragment of stone, the hues of the waterfall copied in the flowers that star its bordering mosses, we are delighted; for all the lineaments become fluent, and we mold the scene in congenial thought with its genius.

People complain of the buildings at Niagara, and fear to see it further deformed. I cannot sympathize with such an apprehension: the spectacle is capable of swallowing up all such objects; they are not seen. . . .

And now farewell, Niagara. I have seen thee, and I think all who come here must in some sort see thee; thou are not to be got rid of as easily as the stars. I will be here again beneath some flooding July moon and sun. Owing to the absence of light, I have seen the rainbow only two or three times by day; the lunar bow not at all.

However, the imperial presence needs not its crown, though illustrated by it. . . .

LAKES HURON AND MICHIGAN

Coming up the river St. Clair, we saw Indians for the first time. They were camped out on the bank. It was twilight, and their blanketed forms, in listless groups or stealing along the bank, with a lounge and a stride so different in its wildness from the rudeness of the white settler, gave me the first feeling that I really approached the West.

The people on the boat were almost all New-Englanders, seeking their fortunes. They had brought with them their habits of calculation, their cautious manners, their love of polemics. It grieved me to hear these immigrants, who were to be the fathers of a new race, all, from the old man down to the little girl, talking, not of what they should do, but of what they should get in the new scene. It was to them a prospect, not of the unfolding of nobler energies, but of more ease and larger accumulation. It wearied me, too, to hear Trinity and Unity discussed in the poor, narrow, doctrinal way on these free waters; but that will soon cease; there is not time for this clash of opinion in the West where the clash of material interests is so noisy. They will need the spirit of religion more than ever to guide them, but will find less time than before for its doctrine. This change was to me, who am tired of the war of words on these subjects, and believe it only sows the wind to reap the whirlwind, refreshing, but I argue nothing from it; there is nothing real in the freedom of thought at the West—it is from the position of men's lives, not the state of their minds. So soon as they have time, unless they grow better meanwhile, they will cavil and criticise, and judge other men by their own standard, and outrage the law of love every way, just as they do with us. . . .

MANITOU ISLANDS

I come to the West prepared for the distaste I must experience at its mushroom growth. I know that where "go ahead" is the only motto, the village cannot grow in the gentle proportions that successive lives and the gradations of experience involuntarily give. In older countries the house of the son grew from that of the father, as naturally as new joints on a bough, and the cathedral crowned the whole as naturally as the leafy summit the tree. This cannot be here. The march of peaceful is scarce less wanton than that of warlike invasion. The old landmarks are broken down, and the land, for a season, bears none, except of the rudeness of conquest and the needs of the day, whose bivouac-fires blacken the sweetest forest glades. I have come prepared to see all this, to dislike it, but not with stupid narrowness to distrust or defame. On the contrary, while I will not be so obliging as to confound ugliness with beauty, discord with harmony, and laud and be contented with all I meet, when it conflicts with my best desires and tastes, I trust by reverent faith to woo the mighty meaning of the scene, perhaps to foresee the law by which a new order, a new poetry, is to be evoked from this chaos, and with a curiosity as ardent, but not so selfish, as that of Macbeth, to call up the apparitions of future kings from the strange ingredients of the witch's caldron. Thus I will not grieve that all the noble trees are gone already from this island to feed this caldron, but believe it will have Medea's virtue, and reproduce them in the form of new intellectual growths, since centuries cannot again adorn the land with such as have been removed. . . .

Chicago, June 20

. . . At first, the prairie seemed to speak of the very desolation of dulness. After sweeping over the vast mo-

notony of the lakes to come to this monotony of land,
with all around a limitless horizon,—to walk, and walk, and
run, but never climb, oh! it was too dreary for any but a
Hollander to bear. How the eye greeted the approach of a
sail, or the smoke of a steamboat; it seemed that anything
so animated must come from a better land, where mountains gave religion to the scene.

The only thing I liked at first to do was to trace with
slow and unexpecting step the narrow margin of the lake.
Sometimes a heavy swell gave it expression; at others, only
its varied coloring, which I found more admirable every
day, and which gave it an air of mirage instead of the
vastness of ocean. Then there was a grandeur in the feeling that I might continue that walk, if I had any seven-
leagued mode of conveyance to save fatigue, for hundreds
of miles without an obstacle and without a change.

But after I had ridden out, and seen the flowers, and
observed the sun set with that calmness seen only in
the prairies, and the cattle winding slowly to their homes
in the "island groves,"—most peaceful of sights,—I began
to love, because I began to know the scene, and shrank no
longer from "the encircling vastness."

It is always thus with the new form of life; we must
learn to look at it by its own standard. At first, no doubt,
my accustomed eye kept saying, if the mind did not,
"What! no distant mountains? What! no valleys?" But
after a while I would ascend the roof of the house where
we lived, and pass many hours, needing no sight but the
moon reigning in the heavens, or starlight falling upon
the lake, till all the lights were out in the island grove of
men beneath my feet, and felt nearer heaven that there
was nothing but this lovely, still reception on the earth;
no towering mountains, no deep tree-shadows, nothing
but plain earth and water bathed in light.

Sunset, as soon from that place, presented most generally, lowlying, flaky clouds, of the softest serenity.

One night a star "shot madly from its sphere," and it

had a fair chance to be seen, but that serenity could not
be astonished.

Yes! it was a peculiar beauty, that of those sunsets and
moonlights on the levels of Chicago, which Chamounix or
the Trosachs could not make me forget. . . .

ILLINOIS

In the afternoon of this day we reached the Rock River,
in whose neighborhood we proposed to make some stay,
and crossed at Dixon's Ferry.

This beautiful stream flows full and wide over a bed
of rocks, traversing a distance of near two hundred miles,
to reach the Mississippi. Great part of the country along
its banks is the finest region of Illinois, and the scene of
some of the latest romance of Indian warfare. To these
beautiful regions Black Hawk returned with his band, "to
pass the summer," when he drew upon himself the warfare in which he was finally vanquished. No wonder he
could not resist the longing, unwise though its indulgence
might be, to return in summer to the home of beauty.

Of Illinois, in general, it has often been remarked, that
it bears the character of country which has been inhabited
by a nation skilled like the English in all the ornamental
arts of life, especially in landscape-gardening. The villas
and castles seem to have been burnt, the enclosures taken
down, but the velvet lawns, the flower-gardens, the stately
parks, scattered at graceful intervals by the decorous hand
of art, the frequent deer, and the peaceful herd of cattle that make picture of the plain, all suggest more of
the masterly mind of man, than the prodigal, but careless,
motherly love of Nature. Especially is this true of the
Rock River country. The river flows sometimes through
these parks and lawns, then betwixt high bluffs, whose
grassy ridges are covered with fine trees, or broken with
crumbling stone, that easily assumes the forms of buttress,
arch, and clustered columns. Along the face of such crum-

bling rocks, swallows' nests are clustered, thick as cities, and eagles and deer do not disdain their summits. One morning, out in the boat along the base of these rocks, it was amusing, and affecting too, to see these swallows put their heads out to look at us. There was something very hospitable about it, as if man had never shown himself a tyrant near them. What a morning it was! Every sight is worth twice as much by the early morning light. We borrow something of the spirit of the hour to look upon them. . . .

There was a peculiar charm in coming here, where the choice of location, and the unobtrusive good taste of all the arrangements, showed such intelligent appreciation of the spirit of the scene, after seeing so many dwellings of the new settlers, which showed plainly that they had no thought beyond satisfying the grossest material wants. Sometimes they looked attractive, these little brown houses, the natural architecture of the country, in the edge of timber. But almost always, when you came near the slovenliness of the dwelling, and the rude way in which objects around it were treated, when so little care would have presented a charming whole, were very repulsive. Seeing the traces of the Indians, who chose the most beautiful sites for their dwellings, and whose habits do not break in on that aspect of Nature under which they were born, we feel as if they were the rightful lords of a beauty they forbore to deform. But most of these settlers do not see it at all; it breathes, it speaks in vain to those who are rushing into its sphere. Their progress is Gothic, not Roman, and their mode of cultivation will, in the course of twenty, perhaps ten years, obliterate the natural expression of the country.

This is inevitable, fatal; we must not complain, but look forward to a good result. Still, in travelling through this country, I could not but be struck with the force of a symbol. Wherever the hog comes, the rattlesnake disappears; the omnivorous traveller, safe in its stupidity, willingly and easily makes a meal of the most dangerous of reptiles, and one which the Indian looks on with a mystic awe. Even so the white settler pursues the Indian, and is victor in the chase. . . .

The great drawback upon the lives of these settlers, at present, is the unfitness of the women for their new lot. It has generally been the choice of the men, and the women follow, as women will, doing their best for affection's sake, but too often in heart-sickness and weariness. Beside, it frequently not being a choice or conviction of their own minds that it is best to be here, their part is the hardest, and they are least fitted for it. The men can find assistance in field labor, and recreations with the gun and fishing-rod. Their bodily strength is greater, and enables them to bear and enjoy both these forms of life.

The women can rarely find any aid in domestic labor. All its various and careful tasks must often be performed, sick, or well, by the mother and daughters, to whom a city education has imparted neither the strength nor the skill now demanded.

The wives of the poorer settlers, having more hard work to do than before, very frequently become slatterns; but the ladies accustomed to a refined neatness, feel that they cannot degrade themselves by its absence, and struggle under every disadvantage to keep up all the necessary routine of small arrangements.

With all these disadvantages for work, their resources for pleasure are fewer. When they can leave the housework, they have not learnt to ride, to drive, to row, alone. Their culture has too generally been that given to women to make them "the ornaments of society." They can dance, but not draw; talk French, but know nothing of the language of flowers; neither in childhood were allowed to cultivate them, lest they should tan their complexions.

Accustomed to the pavement of Broadway, they dare not tread the wild-wood paths for fear of rattlesnakes!

Seeing much of this joylessness, and inaptitude, both of body and mind, for a lot which would be full of blessings for those prepared for it, we could not but look with deep interest on the little girls, and hope they would grow up with the strength of body, dexterity, simple tastes, and resources that would fit them to enjoy and refine the Western farmer's life.

But they have a great deal to war with in the habits of thought acquired by their mothers from their own early life. Everywhere the fatal spirit of imitation, of reference to European standards, penetrates, and threatens to blight whatever of original growth might adorn the soil.

If the little girls grow up strong, resolute, able to exert their faculties, their mothers mourn over their want of fashionable delicacy. Are they gay, enterprising, ready to fly about in the various ways that teach them so much, these ladies lament that "they cannot go to school, where they might learn to be quiet." They lament the want of "education" for their daughters, as if the thousand needs which call out their young energies, and the language of nature around them, yielded no education.

Their grand ambition for their children is to send them to school in some Eastern city, the measure most likely to make them useless and unhappy at home. I earnestly hope that, ere-long, the existence of good schools near themselves, planned by persons of sufficient thought to meet the wants of the place and time, instead of copying New York or Boston, will correct this mania. Instruction the children want to enable them to profit by the great natural advantages of their position; but methods copied from the education of some English Lady Augusta are as ill suited to the daughter of an Illinois farmer, as satin shoes to climb the Indian mounds. An elegance she would diffuse around her, if her mind were opened to appreciate elegance; it might be of a kind new, original, enchanting, as different from that of the city belle as that of the prairie torch-flower from the shop-worn article that touches the cheek of that lady within her bonnet.

To a girl really skilled to make home beautiful and comfortable, with bodily strength to enjoy plenty of exercise, the woods, the streams, a few studies, music, and the sincere and familiar intercourse, far more easily to be met with here than elsewhere, would afford happiness enough. Her eyes would not grow dim, nor her cheeks sunken, in the absence of parties, morning visits, and milliners' shops.

As to music, I wish I could see in such places the guitar rather than the piano, and good vocal more than instrumental music.

The piano many carry with them, because it is the fashionable instrument in the Eastern cities. Even there, it is so merely from the habit of imitating Europe, for not one in a thousand is willing to give the labor requisite to insure any valuable use of the instrument.

But out here, where the ladies have so much less leisure, it is still less desirable. Add to this, they never know how to tune their own instruments, and as persons seldom visit them who can do so, these pianos are constantly out of tune, and would spoil the ear of one who began by having any.

The guitar, or some portable instrument which requires less practice, and could be kept in tune by themselves, would be far more desirable for most of these ladies. It would give all they want as a household companion to fill up the gaps of life, with a pleasant stimulus or solace, and be sufficient accompaniment to the voice in social meetings.

Singing in parts is the most delightful family amusement, and those who are constantly together can learn to sing in perfect accord. All the practice it needs, after some good elementary instruction, is such as meetings by summer twilight and evening firelight naturally suggest. And as music is a universal language, we cannot but think a fine Italian duet would be as much at home in the log cabin as one of Mrs. Gore's novels. . . .

CHICAGO

Chicago has become interesting to me, now that I knew it as the portal to so fair a scene. I had become interested in the land, in the people, and looked sorrowfully on the lake on which I must soon embark, to leave behind what I had just begun to enjoy.

Now was the time to see the lake. The July moon was near its full, and night after night it rose in a cloudless sky above this majestic sea. The heat was excessive, so that there was no enjoyment of life, except in the night; but then the air was of that delicious temperature worthy of orange-groves. However, they were not wanted;—nothing was, as that full light fell on faintly rippling waters, which then seemed boundless.

The most picturesque objects to be seen from Chicago on the inland side were the lines of Hoosier wagons. These rude farmers, the large first product of the soil, travel leisurely along, sleeping in their wagons by night, eating only what they bring with them. In the town they observe the same plan, and trouble no luxurious hotel for board and lodging. Here they look like foreign peasantry, and contrast well with the many Germans, Dutch, and Irish. In the country it is very pretty to see them prepared to "camp out" at night, their horses taken out of harness, and they lounging under the trees, enjoying the evening meal.

On the lake-side it is fine to see the great boats come panting in from their rapid and marvellous journey. Especially at night the motion of their lights is very majestic.

When the favorite boats, the "Great Western" and "Illinois," are going out, the town is thronged with people from the South and farther West, to go in them. These moonlight nights I hear the French rippling and fluttering familiarly amid the rude ups and downs of the Hoosier dialect.

At the hotel table were daily to be seen new faces, and new stories to be learned. And any one who has a large acquaintance may be pretty sure of meeting some of them here in the course of a few days.

At Chicago I read again *Philip Van Artevelde*, and certain passages in it will always be in my mind associated with the deep sound of the lake, as heard in the night. I used to read a short time at night, and then open the blind to look out. The moon would be full upon the lake, and the calm breath, pure light, and the deep voice harmonized well with the thought of the Flemish hero. When will this country have such a man? It is what she needs; no thin Idealist, no coarse Realist, but a man whose eye reads the heavens, while his feet step firmly on the ground, and his hands are strong and dexterous for the use of human implements. A man religious, virtuous, and—sagacious; a man of universal sympathies, but self-possessed; a man who knows the region of emotion, though he is not its slave; a man to whom this world is no mere spectacle, or fleeting shadow, but a great, solemn game, to be played with good heed, for its stakes are of eternal value, yet who, if his own play be true, heeds not what he loses by the falsehood of others;—a man who hives from the past, yet knows that its honey can but moderately avail him; whose comprehensive eye scans the present, neither infatuated by its golden lures, nor chilled by its many ventures; who possesses prescience, as the wise man must, but not so far as to be driven mad to-day by the gist which discerns to-morrow;—when there is such a man for America, the thought which urges her on will be expressed. . . .

WISCONSIN

While in the neighborhood of these lakes, we visited also a foreign settlement of great interest. Here were minds, it seemed, to "comprehend the trust" of their new life; and, if they can only stand true to them, will derive and bestow great benefits therefrom.

But sad and sickening to the enthusiast who comes to these shores, hoping the tranquil enjoyment of intellectual blessings, and the pure happiness of mutal love, must be a part of the scene that he encounters at first. He has escaped from the heartlessness of courts, to encounter the vulgarity of the mob; he has secured solitude, but it is a lonely, a deserted solitude. Amid the abundance of nature, he cannot, from petty, but insuperable obstacles, procure, for a long time, comforts or a home.

But let him come sufficiently armed with patience to learn the new spells which the new dragons require, (and this can only be done on the spot,) he will not finally be disappointed of the promised treasure; the mob will resolve itself into men, yet crude, but of good dispositions, and capable of good character; the solitude will become sufficiently enlivened, and home grow up at last from the rich sod. . . .

I feel about these foreigners very differently from what I do about Americans. American men and women are inexcusable if they do not bring up children so as to be fit for vicissitudes; the meaning of our star is, that here all men being free and equal, every man should be fitted for freedom and an independence by his own resources wherever the changeful wave of our mighty stream may take him. But the star of Europe brought a different horoscope, and to mix destinies breaks the thread of both. The Arabian horse will not plough well, nor can the plough-horse be rode to play the jereed. Yet a man is a man wherever he goes, and something precious cannot fail to be gained by one who knows how to abide by a resolution of any kind, and pay the cost without a murmur. . . .

11. TO RALPH WALDO EMERSON, July, 1844

(Text from Rusk, *Letters*, III, 252–54.)

[On June 3rd, just before copies of Summer were re-
leased, and as she was just beginning to work on Woman,
Emerson invited Margaret to stay in his house. She came
in July, for what would be her final sojourn in Concord.
While there she wrote this letter to her host—whether
again "from room to room" is not clear; obviously she was
putting on paper what she preferred not to speak. Horace
Greeley had just offered her a post on the New York
Tribune. Although there were still to be exchanges between Margaret and Emerson in the remaining years of
her life, the communications dwindled in number and
paled in intensity. In that sense, this letter may be read
as Margaret Fuller's farewell to Emerson—and to New
England. Her taunting of "my Druid" carries an unmis-
takable tone of exasperation, even a hint of derision.

The original letter concludes with a gnomic poem, too
trivial to be repeated entire, which heaps venomous scorn
on "the cold stone" and "cool replies." In it Margaret herself speaks:

> I must away
> Where the day
> With many-colored ray
> But now an aspect gave
> To the worlds, more fair
> Than they show in this cave
> Shut from the living air. . . .

As their close friendship comes to an end, she refuses to
be convinced "that life no better is than Death," imply-

*ing that such is the pall Emerson casts over his loves.
Emerson received this fanfaronade with his by now glacial
calm.]*

My dear Waldo,

Did you notice that, when you refused to go to walk
and declared the dark aspect of your mental fortunes, the
clouds that had been hanging lightly full of silver lustre,
grew dark too; bent heavily, and soon began to weep. It
was as miraculous a coincidence as many that have showed
the servitude of Nature to Saint or Prophet! In this instance, I fear me, it bodes no good to the hapless Africans
(not Afrites!) let me see how many millions, who will
be none the better for your silver tongue!

I always thought the saddest position in the world must
be that of some regal dame to whom husband, court,
kingdom, world look in vain for an heir! She is only supposed to eat, breathe, move, think, nay! live for this; the
book of her life is only perused for the sake of its appendix. Meanwhile she, perhaps, persists in living on as
if her life by itself were of any consequence, is the mother
of no prince or has even the impertinence to incumber
the kingdom with a parcel of princesses, girls who must be
"well-tochered" to make them of any value.

But what is this pathos compared to that perceptible
in the situation of a Jove, under the masculine obligations
of all sufficingness, who rubs his forehead in vain to induce the Minerva-bearing headache! Alas! his brain remains tranquil, his fancy daughterless! Nature keeps on
feeding him and putting him to sleep as if she thought
the oak was of consequence, whether it bear the mistle-
toe or not!

Heaven help thee, my Druid! if this blessed, brooding,
rainy day do not. It is a fine day for composition, were it
not in Concord. But I trow the fates which gave this place
Concord took away the animating influences of Discord.

Life here slumbers and steals on like the river. A very good place for a sage, but not for the lyrist or the orator. . . .

But Waldo, how can you expect the Muse *to come to you?* She hovers near, I have seen her several times, especially near night. Sometimes she looks in at your study windows when she can get a chance, for they are almost always shut. . . .

CHAPTER IV

NEW YORK, 1844–1846

1. WOMAN IN THE NINETEENTH CENTURY

(Text from the first edition, New York, 1845.)

*[Margaret Fuller's title to a place in the corpus of
American literature—in so far as anthologizers determine
it—is based on this one volume. The critical historian may
find (as I do) in her letters and in her* Tribune *reviews
a more enduring claim. These fragments are indeed poignant, frequently bold, even breathtaking; yet they do not
quite add up to a coherent or really consistent literary
personality. That they record a fascinating and anguished
intelligence is certainly indisputable; in this respect they
are more valuable testimonies to the literary consciousness
in America—at least in the America of her era—than is*
Woman in the Nineteenth Century, *memorable though
it may be.*

*The preface explains that she sketched the essential
argument of the book in an article for the* Dial, *published
in July 1843 (IV, 1–48), under the ungainly title "The
Great Lawsuit. Man versus Men. Woman versus Women."
(She entertained a notion of giving the book this title,
but was talked out of it, probably by Caroline Sturgis.)
The volume is a blown-up, I hesitate to say inflated, re-
statement of the essay. Like* Summer, *it is full of weari-
some digressions and excursions into fantasy and murky
dreams, and the thread of the discourse is frequently lost.*

Again, I believe that by abridging it I am presenting the central and substantive argument. Yet such amputations exercised upon any text of Margaret Fuller's are hazardous although motivated by the best of scholarly intentions. She wrote this book at breakneck speed, and to appreciate it fully, the reader must run an exhausting course beside the galloping filly.

By the autumn of 1844, Margaret was more than usually worn out as she started to refashion her Dial piece. Caroline Sturgis took her on a seven-week vacation at Fishkill Landing on the Hudson, and there, along with her customary amount of reading, Margaret set down the impassioned pages of this book, finishing her draft on November 15th. Two days later she wrote Emerson—he was already receding into an irrevocable past—that she was in the best health she had experienced for years, and that she was now prepared to confront the clangor of New York. Yet there was a last twinge of reluctance: "I shall feel my separation from almost all that has been companionable to me I suppose when fairly installed in my business life" (Rusk, Letters, III, 269).

In December, Emerson inquired of a correspondent whether the situation was any better with Margaret and added rhetorically, "The muses have feet, to be sure, but it is an odd arrangement that selects them for the treadmill."

Woman was published in New York City in February 1845, with the imprint of Greeley & McElrath, at 160 Nassau Street. It was enthusiastically reviewed in the Tribune on February 15th. Everywhere else—in the few places it was even noted—it was castigated for being immoral, hysterical, and absurd. It may therefore be said to have inaugurated Margaret Fuller's New York period, and to pertain to this era rather than to her New England apprenticeship. With its publication, the high priestess of Transcendentalism cut her ties with the provincial homeland; with it, she plunged into oceans uncharted.]

PREFACE

The following essay is a reproduction, modified and expanded, of an article published in the *Dial*, Boston, July 1843, under the title of "The Great Lawsuit—Man *versus* Men; Woman *versus* Women."

This article excited a good deal of sympathy and still more interest. It is in compliance with wishes expressed from many quarters that it is prepared for publication in its present form.

Objections having been made to the former title as not sufficiently easy to be understood, the present has been substituted as expressive of the main purpose of the essay; though by myself the other is preferred, partly for the reason others do not like it—that is, that it requires some thought to see what it means, and might thus prepare the reader to meet me on my own ground. Besides it offers a larger scope, and is in that way more just to my desire. I meant by that title to intimate the fact that while it is the destiny of Man in the course of the ages to ascertain and fulfill the law of his being, so that his life shall be seen as a whole to be that of an angel or messenger, the action of prejudices and passions which attend in the day the growth of the individual is continually obstructing the holy work that is to make the earth a part of heaven. By Man I mean both man and woman; these are the two halves of one thought. I lay no especial stress on the welfare of either. I believe that the development of the one cannot be effected without that of the other. My highest wish is that this truth should be distinctly and rationally apprehended, and the conditions of life and freedom recognized as the same for the daughters and the sons of time; twin exponents of a divine thought.

I solicit a sincere and patient attention from those who open the following pages at all. I solicit of women that they will lay it to heart to ascertain what is for them the liberty of law. It is for this and not for any, the largest, extension of partial privileges that I seek. I ask them, if interested by these suggestions, to search their own experience and intuitions for better, and fill up with fit materials the trenches that hedge them in. From men I ask a noble and earnest attention to anything that can be offered on this great and still obscure subject, such as I have met from many with whom I stand in private relations.

And may truth, unpolluted by prejudice, vanity, or selfishness, be granted daily more and more as the due of inheritance and only valuable conquest for us all!

November 1844

Frailty, thy name is Woman.

The Earth waits for her Queen.

The connection between these quotations may not be obvious but it is strict. Yet would any contradict us, if we made them applicable to the other side and began also,

Frailty, thy name is Man.

The Earth waits for its King?

Yet Man, if not yet fully installed in his powers, has given much earnest of his claims. Frail he is indeed—how frail, how impure! Yet often has the vein of gold displayed itself amid the baser ores, and Man has appeared before us in princely promise worthy of his future.

If oftentimes we see the prodigal son feeding on the husks in the fair field no more his own, anon we raise the eyelids, heavy from bitter tears, to behold in him the radiant apparition of genius and love, demanding not less than the all of goodness, power, and beauty. We see that in him the largest claim finds a due foundation. That claim is for no partial sway, no exclusive possession. He cannot be satisfied with any one gift of life, any one department of knowledge or telescopic peep at the heavens.

He feels himself called to understand and aid Nature, that she may through his intelligence be raised and interpreted; to be a student of and servant to the universe-spirit; and king of his planet, that as an angelic minister he may bring it into conscious harmony with the law of that spirit.

In clear, triumphant moments many times has rung through the spheres the prophecy of his jubilee; and those moments, though past in time, have been translated into eternity by thought; the bright signs they left hang in the heavens as single stars or constellations and already a thickly sown radiance consoles the wanderer in the darkest night. Other heroes since Hercules have fulfilled the zodiac of beneficent labors, and then given up their mortal part to the fire without a murmur; while no God dared deny that they should have their reward,

> *Siquis tamen, Hercule, siquis*
> *Forte Deo doliturus erit, data præmia nollet,*
> *Sed meruise dari sciet, invitus que probabit,*
> *Assensere Dei.*

Sages and lawgivers have bent their whole nature to the search for truth, and thought themselves happy if they could buy, with the sacrifice of all temporal ease and pleasure, one seed for the future Eden. Poets and priests have strung the lyre with the heartstrings, poured out their best blood upon the altar, which, reared anew from age to age, shall at last sustain the flame pure enough to rise to highest heaven. Shall we not name with as deep a benediction those who, if not so immediately or so consciously in connection with the eternal truth, yet led and fashioned by a divine instinct serve no less to develop and interpret the open secret of love passing into life, energy creating for the purpose of happiness; the artist whose hand, drawn by a pre-existent harmony to a certain medium, molds it to forms of life more highly and completely organized than are seen elsewhere, and by carrying out the intention of Nature reveals her meaning to those who are not yet

wise enough to divine it; the philosopher who listens steadily for laws and causes, and from those obvious infers
those yet unknown; the historian who in faith that all
events must have their reason and their aim records them,
and thus fills archives from which the youth of prophets
may be fed; the man of science dissecting the statements,
testing the facts, and demonstrating order, even where he
cannot its purpose?

Lives, too, which bear none of these names have yielded
tones of no less significance. The candlestick set in a low
place has given light as faithfully where it was needed as
that upon the hill. In close alleys, in dismal nooks, the
Word has been read as distinctly as when shown by angels
to holy men in the dark prison. Those who till a spot of
earth scarcely larger than is wanted for a grave have deserved that the sun should shine upon its sod till violets
answer.

So great has been from time to time the promise, that
in all ages men have said the gods themselves came down
to dwell with them; that the All-Creating wandered on
the earth to taste in a limited nature the sweetness of
virtue; that the All-Sustaining incarnated himself to guard
in space and time the destinies of this world; that heavenly
genius dwelt among the shepherds to sing to them and
teach them how to sing. Indeed,

Der stets den Hirten gnädig sich bewies.

"He has constantly shown himself favorable to shepherds."

And the dwellers in green pastures and natural students
of the stars were selected to hail first among men the holy
child, whose life and death were to present the type of
excellence which has sustained the heart of so large a portion of mankind in these later generations.

Such marks have been made by the footsteps of *man*
(still, alas, to be spoken of as the *ideal* man) wherever
he has passed through the wilderness of *men*, and whenever the pygmies stepped in one of those, they felt dilate

within the breast somewhat that promised nobler stature
and purer blood. They were impelled to forsake their evil
ways of decrepit skepticism and covetousness of corrupti-
ble possessions. Convictions flowed in upon them. They,
too, raised the cry: God is living now, today; and all beings
are brothers, for they are his children. Simple words
enough, yet which only angelic natures can use or hear in
their full, free sense.

These were the triumphant moments; but soon the
lower nature took its turn, and the era of a truly human
life was postponed.

Thus is Man still a stranger in his inheritance, still a
pleader, still a pilgrim. Yet his happiness is secure in the
end. And now no more a glimmering consciousness but
assurance begins to be felt and spoken, that the highest
ideal Man can form of his own powers is that which he
is destined to attain. Whatever the soul knows how to
seek, it cannot fail to obtain. This is the Law and the
Prophets. Knock and it shall be opened; seek and ye shall
find. It is demonstrated; it is a maxim. Man no longer
paints his proper nature in some form, and says, "Prome-
theus had it; it is God-like"; but "Man must have it; it is
human." However disputed by many, however ignorantly
used or falsified by those who do receive it, the fact of a
universal, unceasing revelation has been too clearly stated
in words to be lost sight of in thought; and sermons
preached from the text, "Be ye perfect," are the only
sermons of a pervasive and deep-searching influence.

But among those who meditate upon this text there is a
great difference of view as to the way in which perfection
shall be sought.

"Through the intellect," say some. "Gather from every
growth of life its seed of thought; look behind every symbol for its law; if thou canst *see* clearly, the rest will
follow."

"Through the life," say others. "Do the best thou know-
est today. Shrink not from frequent error in this gradual,

fragmentary state. Follow thy light for as much as it will
show thee; be faithful as far as thou canst, in hope that
faith presently will lead to sight. Help others without
blaming their need of thy help. Love much, and be for-
given."

"It needs not intellect, needs not experience," says a
third. "If you took the true way, your destiny would be
accomplished in a purer and more natural order. You
would not learn through facts of thought or action, but
express through them the certainties of wisdom. In quiet-
ness yield thy soul to the causal soul. Do not disturb thy
apprenticeship by premature effort; neither check the tide
of instruction by methods of thy own. Be still; seek not,
but wait in obedience. Thy commission will be given."

Could we indeed say what we want, could we give a
description of the child that is lost, he would be found.
As soon as the soul can affirm clearly that a certain demon-
stration is wanted, it is at hand. When the Jewish prophet
described the Lamb as the expression of what was required
by the coming era, the time drew nigh. But we say not,
see not as yet clearly what we would. Those who call for
a more triumphant expression of love, a love that cannot
be crucified, show not a perfect sense of what has already
been given. Love has already been expressed that made all
things new, that gave the worm its place and ministry as
well as the eagle; a love to which it was alike to descend
into the depths of hell, or to sit at the right hand of the
Father.

Yet no doubt a new manifestation is at hand, a new
hour in the day of Man. We cannot expect to see any one
sample of completed being, when the mass of men still lie
engaged in the sod, or use the freedom of their limbs only
with wolfish energy. The tree cannot come to flower till
its root be free from the cankering worm, and its whole
growth open to air and light. While any one is base, none
can be entirely free and noble. Yet something new shall

presently be shown of the life of man, for hearts crave, if minds do not know how to ask it. . . .

It should be remarked that as the principle of liberty is better understood, and more nobly interpreted, a broader protest is made in behalf of Woman. As men become aware that few men have had a fair chance, they are inclined to say that no women have had a fair chance. The French Revolution, that strangely disguised angel, bore witness in favor of Woman, but interpreted her claims no less ignorantly than those of Man. Its idea of happiness did not rise beyond outward enjoyment, unobstructed by the tyranny of others. The title it gave was *citoyen, citoyenne*; and it is not unimportant to Woman that even this species of equality was awarded her. Before, she could be condemned to perish on the scaffold for treason, not as a citizen but as a subject. The right with which this title then invested a human being was that of bloodshed and license. The Goddess of Liberty was impure. As we read the poem addressed to her not long since by Béranger, we can scarcely refrain from tears as painful as the tears of blood that flowed when "such crimes were committed in her name." Yes! Man, born to purify and animate the unintelligent and the cold, can in his madness degrade and pollute no less the fair and the chaste. Yet truth was prophesied in the ravings of that hideous fever caused by long ignorance and abuse. Europe is conning a valued lesson from the bloodstained page. The same tendencies further unfolded will bear good fruit in this country.

Yet by men in this country, as by the Jews when Moses was leading them to the promised land, everything has been done that inherited depravity could do to hinder the promise of Heaven from its fulfillment. The cross, here as elsewhere, has been planted only to be blasphemed by cruelty and fraud. The name of the Prince of Peace has been profaned by all kinds of injustice toward the Gentile whom he said he came to save. But I need not speak of what has been done toward the Red Man, the Black Man. Those deeds are the scoff of the world; and they have been accompanied by such pious words that the gentlest would not dare to intercede with, "Father, forgive them, for they know not what they do."

Here as elsewhere the gain of creation consists always in the growth of individual minds, which live and aspire as flowers bloom and birds sing in the midst of morasses; and in the continual development of that thought, the thought of human destiny, which is given to eternity adequately to express, and which ages of failure only seemingly impede. Only seemingly; and whatever seems to the contrary, this country is as surely destined to elucidate a great moral law as Europe was to promote the mental culture of Man. . . .

This law cannot fail of universal recognition. Accursed be he who willingly saddens an immortal spirit—doomed to infamy in later, wiser ages, doomed in future stages of his own being to deadly penance only short of death. Accursed be he who sins in ignorance, if that ignorance be caused by sloth.

We sicken no less at the pomp than the strife of words. We feel that never were lungs so puffed with the wind of declamation on moral and religious subjects as now. We are tempted to implore these "word-heroes," these word-Catos, word-Christs, to beware of cant* above all things; to remember that hypocrisy is the most hopeless as well as the meanest of crimes, and that those must surely be polluted by it who do not reserve a part of their morality and religion for private use. Landor says that he cannot have a great deal of mind who cannot afford

* Dr. Johnson's one piece of advice should be written on every door: "Clear your mind of cant." But Byron, to whom it was so acceptable, in clearing away the noxious vine shook down the building. Sterling's emendation is worthy of honor: "Realize your cant, not cast it off." [M.F.'s note]

to let the larger part of it lie fallow; and what is true of genius is not less so of virtue. The tongue is a valuable member, but should appropriate but a small part of the vital juices that are needful all over the body. We feel that the mind may "grow black and rancid in the smoke" even "of altars." We start up from the harangue to go into our closet and shut the door. There inquires the spirit, "Is this rhetoric the bloom of healthy blood, or a false pigment artfully laid on?" And yet again we know where is so much smoke, must be some fire; with so much talk about virtue and freedom, must be mingled some desire for them; that it cannot be in vain that such have become the common topics of conversation among men rather than schemes for tyranny and plunder, that the very newspapers see it best to proclaim themselves "Pilgrims," "Puritans," "Heralds of Holiness." The king that maintains so costly a retinue cannot be a mere boast or Barabbas fiction. We have waited here long in the dust, we are tired and hungry, but the triumphal procession must appear at last.

Of all its banners, none has been more steadily upheld, and under none have more valor and willingness for real sacrifices been shown, than that of the champions of the enslaved African. And this band it is which, partly from a natural following out of principles, partly because many women have been prominent in that cause, makes just now the warmest appeal in behalf of Woman.

Though there has been a growing liberality on this subject, yet society at large is not so prepared for the demands of this party, but that its members are and will be for some time coldly regarded as the Jacobins of their day.

"Is it not enough," cries the irritated trader, "that you have done all you could to break up the national union and thus destroy the prosperity of our country, but now you must be trying to break up family union, to take my wife away from the cradle and the kitchen-hearth to vote at polls and preach from a pulpit? Of course, if she does such things, she cannot attend to those of her own sphere. She is happy enough as she is. She has more leisure than I have—every means of improvement, every indulgence."

"Have you asked her whether she was satisfied with these *indulgences?*"

"No, but I know she is. She is too amiable to desire what would make me unhappy, and too judicious to wish to step beyond the sphere of her sex. I will never consent to have our peace disturbed by any such discussions."

" 'Consent—you?' It is not consent from you that is in question—it is assent from your wife."

"Am not I the head of my house?"

"You are not the head of your wife. God has given her a mind of her own."

"I am the head, and she the heart."

"God grant you play true to one another, then! I suppose I am to be grateful that you did not say she was only the hand. If the head represses no natural pulse of the heart, there can be no question as to your giving your consent. Both will be of one accord, and there needs but to present any question to get a full and true answer. There is no need of precaution, of indulgence, or consent. But our doubt is whether the heart *does* consent with the head, or only obeys its decrees with a passiveness that precludes the exercise of its natural powers, or a repugnance that turns sweet qualities to bitter, or a doubt that lays waste the fair occasions of life. It is to ascertain the truth that we propose some liberating measures."

Thus vaguely are these questions proposed and discussed at present. But their being proposed at all implies much thought and suggests more. Many women are considering within themselves what they need that they have not, and what they can have if they find they need it. Many men are considering whether women are capable of being and having more than they are and have, *and* whether, if so, it will be best to consent to improvement in their condition. . . .

But to return to the historical progress of this matter. Knowing that there exists in the minds of men a tone of feeling toward women as toward slaves, such as is expressed in the common phrase, "Tell that to women and children"; that the infinite soul can only work through them in already ascertained limits; that the gift of reason, Man's highest prerogative, is allotted to them in much lower degree; that they must be kept from mischief and melancholy by being constantly engaged in active labor, which is to be furnished and directed by those better able to think, &c., &c.—we need not multiply instances, for who can review the experience of last week without recalling words which imply, whether in jest or earnest, these views or views like these—knowing this, can we wonder that many reformers think that measures are not likely to be taken in behalf of women, unless their wishes could be publicly represented by women?

"That can never be necessary," cry the other side. "All men are privately influenced by women; each has his wife, sister, or female friends, and is too much biased by these relations to fail of representing their interests; and if this is not enough, let them propose and enforce their wishes with the pen. The beauty of home would be destroyed, the delicacy of the sex be violated, the dignity of halls of legislation degraded by an attempt to introduce them there. Such duties are inconsistent with those of a mother"; and then we have ludicrous pictures of ladies in hysterics at the polls, and senate chambers filled with cradles.

But if in reply we admit as truth that Woman seems destined by nature rather for the inner circle, we must add that the arrangements of civilized life have not been as yet such as to secure it to her. Her circle, if the duller, is not the quieter. If kept from "excitement," she is not from drudgery. Not only the Indian squaw carries the burdens of the camp, but the favorites of Louis XIV accompany him in his journeys, and the washerwoman stands at her tub and carries home her work at all seasons and in all states of health. Those who think the physical circumstances of Woman would make a part in the affairs of national government unsuitable are by no means those who think it impossible for Negresses to endure field work even during pregnancy, or for seamstresses to go through their killing labors.

As to the use of the pen, there was quite as much opposition to Woman's possessing herself of that help to free agency as there is now to her seizing on the rostrum or the desk; and she is likely to draw, from a permission to plead her cause that way, opposite inferences to what might be wished by those who now grant it.

As to the possibility of her filling with grace and dignity any such position, we should think those who had seen the great actresses and heard the Quaker preachers of modern times would not doubt that Woman can express publicly the fullness of thought and creation without losing any of the peculiar beauty of her sex. What can pollute and tarnish is to act thus from any motive except that something needs to be said or done. Woman could take part in the processions, the songs, the dances of old religion; no one fancied her delicacy was impaired by appearing in public for such a cause.

As to her home, she is not likely to leave it more than she now does for balls, theaters, meetings for promoting missions, revival meetings, and others to which she flies in hope of an animation for her existence commensurate with what she sees enjoyed by men. Governors of ladies' fairs are no less engrossed by such a charge than the governor of a state by his; presidents of Washingtonian societies no less away from home than presidents of conventions. If men look straitly to it, they will find that unless their lives are domestic, those of the women will not be. A house is no home unless it contain food and fire for the mind as well as for the body. The female Greek of our day is as much in the street as the male to cry, "What news?" We doubt not it was the same in Athens of old. The women, shut out from the market-place, made up for it at the religious festivals. For human beings are not so constituted that they can live without expansion. If they do not get it in one way, they must in another or perish.

As to men's representing women fairly at present, while we hear from men who owe to their wives not only all that is comfortable or graceful but all that is wise in the arrangement of their lives the frequent remark, "You cannot reason with a woman"—when from those of delicacy, nobleness, and poetic culture falls the contemptuous phrase "women and children," and that in no light sally of the hour, but in works intended to give a permanent statement of the best experiences—when not one man in the million, shall I say? no, not in the hundred million, can rise above the belief that Woman was made *for Man* —when such traits as these are daily forced upon the attention, can we feel that Man will always do justice to the interests of Woman? Can we think that he takes a sufficiently discerning and religious view of her office and destiny *ever* to do her justice, except when prompted by sentiment—accidentally or transiently, that is, for the sentiment will vary according to the relations in which he is placed? The lover, the poet, the artist are likely to view her nobly. The father and the philosopher have some chance of liberality; the man of the world, the legislator for expediency none.

Under these circumstances, without attaching importance in themselves to the changes demanded by the champions of Woman, we hail them as signs of the times. We would have every arbitrary barrier thrown down. We would have every path laid open to Woman as freely as to Man. Were this done and a slight temporary fer-

mentation allowed to subside, we should see crystalliza-
tions more pure and of more various beauty. We believe
the divine energy would pervade nature to a degree
unknown in the history of former ages, and that no dis-
cordant collision but a ravishing harmony of the spheres
would ensue.

Yet then and only then will mankind be ripe for this,
when inward and outward freedom for Woman as much
as for Man shall be acknowledged as a *right*, not yielded
as a concession. As the friend of the Negro assumes that
one man cannot by right hold another in bondage, so
should the friend of Woman assume that Man cannot
by right lay even well-meant restrictions on Woman. If
the Negro be a soul, if the woman be a soul, appareled
in flesh, to one Master only are they accountable. There is
but one law for souls, and if there is to be an interpreter of
it, he must come not as man or son of man, but as son
of God.

Were thought and feeling once so far elevated that
Man should esteem himself the brother and friend,
but nowise the lord and tutor, of Woman—were he really
bound with her in equal worship—arrangements as to function and employment would be of no consequence. What
Woman needs is not as a woman to act or rule, but as
a nature to grow, as an intellect to discern, as a soul to
live freely and unimpeded to unfold such powers as were
given her when we left our common home. If fewer talents
were given her, yet if allowed the free and full employment of these, so that she may render back to the giver
his own with usury, she will not complain; nay, I dare
to say she will bless and rejoice in her earthly birthplace,
her earthly lot. Let us consider what obstructions impede
this good era, and what signs give reason to hope that it
draws near.

I was talking on this subject with Miranda, a woman,
who, if any in the world could, might speak without heat
and bitterness of the position of her sex. Her father was

a man who cherished no sentimental reverence for Woman, but a firm belief in the equality of the sexes. She was his eldest child, and came to him at an age when he needed a companion. From the time she could speak and go alone, he addressed her not as a plaything but as a living mind. Among the few verses he ever wrote was a copy addressed to this child, when the first locks were cut from her head; and the reverence expressed on this occasion for that cherished head, he never belied. It was to him the temple of immortal intellect. He respected his child, however, too much to be an indulgent parent. He called on her for clear judgment, for courage, for honor and fidelity; in short, for such virtues as he knew. In so far as he possessed the keys to the wonders of this universe, he allowed free use of them to her, and by the incentive of a high expectation he forbade, so far as possible, that she should let the privilege lie idle.

Thus this child was early led to feel herself a child of the spirit. She took her place easily not only in the world of organized being, but in the world of mind. A dignified sense of self-dependence was given as all her portion, and she found it a sure anchor. Herself securely anchored, her relations with others were established with equal security. She was fortunate in a total absence of those charms which might have drawn to her bewildering flatteries, and in a strong electric nature which repelled those who did not belong to her and attracted those who did. With men and women her relations were noble—affectionate without passion, intellectual without coldness. The world was free to her, and she lived freely in it. Outward adversity came and inward conflict, but that faith and self-respect had early been awakened which must always lead at last to an outward serenity and an inward peace.

Of Miranda I had always thought as an example, that the restraints upon the sex were insuperable only to those who think them so, or who noisily strive to break them. She had taken a course of her own, and no man stood in her way. Many of her acts had been unusual, but excited no uproar. Few helped but none checked her; and the many men who knew her mind and her life showed to her confidence as to a brother, gentleness as to a sister. And not only refined, but very coarse men approved and aided one in whom they saw resolution and clearness of design. Her mind was often the leading one, always effective.

When I talked with her upon these matters and had said very much what I have written, she smilingly replied: "And yet we must admit that I have been fortunate, and this should not be. My good father's early trust gave the first bias, and the rest followed of course. It is true that I have had less outward aid in after years than most women; but that is of little consequence. Religion was early awakened in my soul—a sense that what the soul is capable to ask it must attain, and that though I might be aided and instructed by others, I must depend on myself as the only constant friend. This self-dependence, which was honored in me, is deprecated as a fault in most women. They are taught to learn their rule from without, not to unfold it from within.

"This is the fault of Man, who is still vain, and wishes to be more important to Woman than by right he should be."

"Men have not shown this disposition toward you," I said.

"No, because the position I early was enabled to take was one of self-reliance. And were all women as sure of their wants as I was, the result would be the same. But they are so overloaded with precepts by guardians who think that nothing is so much to be dreaded for a woman as originality of thought or character, that their minds are impeded by doubts till they lose their chance of fair, free proportions. The difficulty is to get them to the point from which they shall naturally develop self-respect and learn self-help.

"Once I thought that men would help to forward this state of things more than I do now. I saw so many of them wretched in the connections they had formed in weakness and vanity. They seemed so glad to esteem women whenever they could.

"'The soft arms of affection,' said one of the most discerning spirits, 'will not suffice for me, unless on them I see the steel bracelets of strength.'

"But early I perceived that men never in any extreme of despair wished to be women. On the contrary, they were ever ready to taunt one another at any sign of weakness with,

Art thou not like the women, who—

The passage ends various ways, according to the occasion and rhetoric of the speaker. When they admired any woman, they were inclined to speak of her as 'above her sex.' Silently I observed this, and feared it argued a rooted skepticism which for ages had been fastening on the heart and which only an age of miracles could eradicate. Ever I have been treated with great sincerity; and I look upon it as a signal instance of this, that an intimate friend of the other sex said in a fervent moment that I 'deserved in some star to be a man.' He was much surprised when I disclosed my view of my position and hopes, when I declared my faith that the feminine side, the side of love, of beauty, of holiness, was now to have its full chance, and that if either were better, it was better now to be a woman; for even the slightest achievement of good was furthering an especial work of our time. He smiled incredulously. 'She makes the best she can of it,' thought he. 'Let Jews believe the pride of Jewry, but I am of the better sort, and know better.'

"Another used as highest praise in speaking of a character in literature, the words 'a manly woman.'

"So in the noble passage of Ben Jonson:

> I meant the day-star should not brighter ride,
>   Nor shed like influence from its lucent seat;
> I meant she should be courteous, facile, sweet,
>   Free from that solemn vice of greatness, pride;
> I meant each softest virtue there should meet,
>   Fit in that softer bosom to abide,
> Only a learned and a *manly* soul
>   I purposed her, that should with even powers
> The rock, the spindle, and the shears control
>   Of destiny, and spin her own free hours."

"Methinks," said I, "you are too fastidious in objecting to this. Jonson in using the word 'manly' only meant to heighten the picture of this, the true, the intelligent fate with one of the deeper colors."

"And yet," said she, "so invariable is the use of this word when a heroic quality is to be described, and I feel so sure that persistence and courage are the most womanly no less than the most manly qualities, that I would exchange these words for others of a larger sense, at the risk of marring the fine tissue of the verse. Read, 'A heavenward and instructed soul,' and I should be satisfied. Let it not be said, wherever there is energy or creative genius, 'She has a masculine mind.'" . . .

It is not the transient breath of poetic incense that women want; each can receive that from a lover. It is not lifelong sway; it needs but to become a coquette, a shrew, or a good cook to be sure of that. It is not money nor notoriety nor the badges of authority which men have appropriated to themselves. If demands made in their behalf lay stress on any of these particulars, those who make them have not searched deeply into the need. The want is for that which at once includes these and precludes them; which would not be forbidden power, lest there be temptation to steal and misuse it; which would not have the mind perverted by flattery from a worthiness of esteem; it is for that which is the birthright of every being capable of receiving it—the freedom, the religious, the intelligent freedom of the universe to use its means, to learn its secret as far as Nature has enabled them, with God alone for their guide and their judge.

Ye cannot believe it, men; but the only reason why women ever assume what is more appropriate to you, is because you prevent them from finding out what is fit for themselves. Were they free, were they wise fully to develop the strength and beauty of Woman; they would never wish to be men or manlike. The well-instructed moon flies not from her orbit to seize on the glories of her partner. No, for she knows that one law rules, one heaven contains, one universe replies to them alike. It is with women as with the slave:

> *Vor dem Sklaven, wenn er die Kette bricht,*
> *Vor dem freien Menschen erzittert nicht.*

("Tremble not before the free man, but before the slave who has chains to break.")

In slavery, acknowledged slavery, women are on a par with men. Each is a worktool, an article of property—no more! In perfect freedom, such as is painted in Olympus, in Swedenborg's angelic state, in the heaven where there is no marrying nor giving in marriage, each is a purified intelligence, an enfranchised soul—no less.

> *Jene himmlische Gestalten*
> *Sie fragen nicht nach Mann und Weib,*
> *Und keine kleider, keine Falten*
> *Umgeben den verklarten Leib.*

The child who sang this was a prophetic form expressive of the longing for a state of perfect freedom, pure love. She could not remain here, but was translated to another air. And it may be that the air of this earth will never be so tempered that such can bear it long. But while they stay, they must bear testimony to the truth they are constituted to demand.

That an era approaches which shall approximate nearer to such a temper than any has yet done, there are many tokens; indeed so many that only a few of the most prominent can here be enumerated.

The reigns of Elizabeth of England and Isabella of Castile foreboded this era. They expressed the beginning of the new state while they forwarded its progress. These were strong characters and in harmony with the wants of their time. One showed that this strength did not unfit a woman for the duties of a wife and a mother; the other, that it could enable her to live and die alone, a wide energetic life, a courageous death. Elizabeth is certainly no pleasing example. In rising above the weakness, she did not lay aside the foibles ascribed to her sex; but her strength must be respected now as it was in her own time.

Mary Stuart and Elizabeth seem types, molded by the spirit of the time and placed upon an elevated platform, to show to the coming ages Woman such as the conduct and wishes of Man in general is likely to make her. The first shows Woman lovely even to allurement; quick in apprehension and weak in judgment; with grace and dignity of sentiment, but no principle; credulous and indiscreet, yet artful; capable of sudden greatness or of crime, but not of a steadfast wisdom, nor self-restraining virtue. The second reveals Woman half-emancipated and jealous of her freedom, such as she has figured before or since in many a combative attitude; mannish, not equally manly; strong and prudent more than great or wise; able to control vanity, and the wish to rule through coquetry and passion, but not to resign these dear deceits from the very foundation, as unworthy a being capable of truth and nobleness. Elizabeth, taught by adversity, put on her virtues as armor, more than produced them in a natural order from her soul. The time and her position called on her to act the wise sovereign and she was proud that she could do so, but her tastes and inclinations would have led her to act the weak woman. She was without magnanimity of any kind.

We may accept as an omen for ourselves that it was Isabella who furnished Columbus with the means of coming hither. This land must pay back its debt to Woman, without whose aid it would not have been brought into alliance with the civilized world. . . .

. . . Centuries have passed since, but civilized Europe is still in a transition state about marriage; not only in practice but in thought. It is idle to speak with contempt of the nations where polygamy is an institution or seraglios a custom, while practices far more debasing haunt, well-nigh fill, every city and every town, and so far as union of one with one is believed to be the only pure form of marriage, a great majority of societies and individuals are still doubtful whether the earthly bond must be a meeting of souls, or only supposes a contract of convenience and utility. Were Woman established in the rights of an immortal being, this could not be. She would not in some countries be given away by her father, with scarcely more respect for her feelings than is shown by the Indian chief who sells his daughter for a horse, and beats her if she runs away from her new home. Nor in societies where her choice is left free, would she be perverted by the current of opinion that seizes her, into the belief that she must marry, if it be only to find a protector and a home of her own. Neither would Man, if he thought the connection of permanent importance, form it so lightly. He would not deem it a trifle that he was to enter into the closest relations with another soul, which, if not eternal in themselves, must eternally affect his growth. Neither did he believe Woman capable of friendship, would he by rash haste lose the chance of finding a friend in the person who might probably live half a century by his side. Did love to his mind stretch forth into infinity, he would not miss his chance of its revelations, that he might the sooner rest from his weariness by a bright fireside, and secure a sweet and graceful attendant "devoted to him alone." Were he a step higher, he would not carelessly enter into a relation where he might not be able to do the duty of a friend, as well as a protector from external ill, to the other party, and have a being in his power pining for sympathy, intelligence, and aid that he could not give.

What deep communion, what real intercourse is implied in sharing the joys and cares of parentage, when any degree of equality is admitted between the parties! It is true that in a majority of instances the man looks upon his wife as an adopted child, and places her to the other children in the relation of nurse or governess rather than that of parent. Her influence with them is sure; but she misses the education which should enlighten that influence, by being thus treated. It is the order of nature that children should complete the education, moral and mental, of parents by making them think what is needed for the best culture of human beings, and conquer all faults and impulses that interfere with their giving this to these dear objects who represent the world to them. Father and mother should assist one another to learn what is required for this sublime priesthood of Nature. But for this a religious recognition of equality is required.

Where this thought of equality begins to diffuse itself, it is shown in four ways.

First: The household partnership. In our country the woman looks for a "smart but kind" husband; the man for a "capable, sweet-tempered" wife. The man furnishes the house; the woman regulates it. Their relation is one of mutual esteem, mutual dependence. Their talk is of business; their affection shows itself by practical kindness. They know that life goes more smoothly and cheerfully to each for the other's aid; they are grateful and content. The wife praises her husband as a "good provider"; the husband, in return, compliments her as a "capital house-keeper." This relation is good so far as it goes.

Next comes a closer tie, which takes the form either of mutual idolatry or of intellectual companionship. The first, we suppose, is to no one a pleasing subject of con-templation. The parties weaken and narrow one another; they lock the gate against all the glories of the universe that they may live in a cell together. To themselves they seem the only wise; to all others steeped in infatuation; the gods smile as they look forward to the crisis of cure; to men, the woman seems an unlovely siren; to women, the man an effeminate boy.

The other form, of intellectual companionship, has become more and more frequent. Men engaged in public life, literary men, and artists have often found in their wives companions and confidantes in thought no less than in feeling. And as the intellectual development of Woman has spread wider and risen higher, they have not un-frequently shared the same employment; as in the case of Roland and his wife, who were friends in the house-hold and in the nation's councils, read, regulated home affairs, or prepared public documents together indif-ferently. It is very pleasant, in letters begun by Roland and finished by his wife, to see the harmony of mind and the difference of nature; one thought but various ways of treating it.

This is one of the best instances of a marriage of friendship. It was only friendship, whose basis was esteem; probably neither party knew love except by name. Roland was a good man, worthy to esteem and be esteemed; his wife as deserving of admiration as able to do without it.

Madame Roland is the fairest specimen we yet have of her class; as clear to discern her aim, as valiant to pursue it as Spenser's Britomart; austerely set apart from all that did not belong to her whether as Woman or as

mind. She is an antetype of a class to which the coming
time will afford a field—the Spartan matron brought by
the culture of the age of books to intellectual consciousness and expansion. Self-sufficingness, strength, and, clear-
sightedness were in her combined with a power of deep
and calm affection. She, too, would have given a son or
husband the device for his shield: "Return with it or
upon it"; and this not because she loved little, but much.
The page of her life is one of unsullied dignity. Her
appeal to posterity is one against the injustice of those
who committed such crimes in the name of Liberty. She
makes it in behalf of herself and her husband. I would
put beside it on the shelf a little volume, containing a
similar appeal from the verdict of contemporaries to that
of mankind made by Godwin in behalf of his wife, the
celebrated, the by most men detested Mary Wollstonecraft. In his view it was an appeal from the injustice of
those who did such wrong in the name of virtue. Were
this little book interesting for no other cause, it would
be so for the generous affection evinced under the peculiar
circumstances. This man had courage to love and honor
this woman in the face of the world's sentence and of
all that was repulsive in her own past history. He believed
he saw of what soul she was, and that the impulses she
had struggled to act out were noble, though the opinions
to which they had led might not be thoroughly weighed.
He loved her, and he defended her for the meaning and
tendency of her inner life. It was a good fact.

Mary Wollstonecraft, like Madame Dudevant (commonly known as George Sand) in our day, was a woman
whose existence better proved the need of some new interpretation of Woman's Rights than anything she wrote.
Such beings as these, rich in genius, of most tender
sympathies, capable of high virtue and a chastened harmony, ought not to find themselves by birth in a place
so narrow that in breaking bonds they become outlaws.
Were there as much room in the world for such as in

Spenser's poem for Britomart, they would not run their heads so wildly against the walls, but prize their shelter rather. They find their way at last to light and air, but the world will not take off the brand it has set upon them. The champion of the Rights of Woman found in Godwin one who would plead that cause like a brother. He who delineated with such purity of traits the form of Woman in the Marguerite of whom the weak St. Leon could never learn to be worthy—a pearl indeed whose price was above rubies—was not false in life to the faith by which he had hallowed his romance. He acted as he wrote, like a brother. This form of appeal rarely fails to touch the basest man: "Are you acting toward other women in the way you would have men act toward your sister?" George Sand smokes, wears male attire, wishes to be addressed as "*Mon frère*"—perhaps if she found those who were as brothers indeed, she would not care whether she were brother or sister. We rejoice to see that she, who expresses such a painful contempt for men in most of her works as shows she must have known great wrong from them, depicts in *La Roche Mauprat* a man raised by the workings of love from the depths of savage sensualism to a moral and intellectual life. It was love for a pure object, for a steadfast woman, one of those who the Italian said could make the "stair to heaven."

This author, beginning like the many in assault upon bad institutions, and external ills, yet deepening the experience through comparative freedom, sees at last that the only efficient remedy must come from individual character. These bad institutions indeed, it may always be replied, prevent individuals from forming good character, therefore we must remove them. Agreed; yet keep steadily the higher aim in view. Could you clear away all the bad forms of society, it is vain unless the individual begin to be ready for better. There must be a parallel movement in these two branches of life. And all the rules left by

Moses availed less to further the best life than the living example of one Messiah.

Still the mind of the age struggles confusedly with these problems, better discerning as yet the ill it can no longer bear than the good by which it may supersede it. But women like Sand will speak now and cannot be silenced; their characters and their eloquence alike foretell an era when such as they shall easier learn to lead true lives. But though such forebode, not such shall be parents of it. Those who would reform the world must show that they do not speak in the heat of wild impulse; their lives must be unstained by passionate error; they must be severe lawgivers to themselves. They must be religious students of the divine purpose with regard to man, if they would not confound the fancies of a day with the requisitions of eternal good. Their liberty must be the liberty of law and knowledge. But as to the transgressions against custom which have caused such outcry against those of noble intention, it may be observed that the resolve of Héloïse to be only the mistress of Abélard, was that of one who saw in practice around her the contract of marriage made the seal of degradation. Shelley feared not to be fettered unless so to be was to be false. Wherever abuses are seen, the timid will suffer; the bold will protest. But society has a right to outlaw them till she has revised her law; and this she must be taught to do by one who speaks with authority, not in anger or haste. . . .

The fourth and highest grade of marriage union is the religious, which may be expressed as pilgrimage toward a common shrine. This includes the others: home sympathies and household wisdom, for these pilgrims must know how to assist each other along the dusty way; intellectual communion, for how sad it would be on such a journey to have a companion to whom you could not communicate your thoughts and aspirations as they sprang to life; who would have no feeling for the prospects that open more and more glorious as we advance; who would never see the flowers that may be gathered by the most industrious traveler! It must include all these. . . .

But to return to the thread of my subject.

Another sign of the times is furnished by the triumphs of Female Authorship. These have been great and are constantly increasing. Women have taken possession of so many provinces for which men had pronounced them unfit, that though these still declare there are some inaccessible to them, it is difficult to say just _where_ they must stop.

The shining names of famous women have cast light upon the path of the sex, and many obstructions have been removed. When a Montagu could learn better than her brother and use her lore afterward to such purpose as an observer, it seemed amiss to hinder women from preparing themselves to see, or from seeing all they could when prepared. Since Somerville has achieved so much, will any young girl be prevented from seeking a knowledge of the physical sciences if she wishes it? De Staël's name was not so clear of offense; she could not forget the Woman in the thought; while she was instructing you as a mind, she wished to be admired as a Woman; sentimental tears often dimmed the eagle glance. Her intellect, too, with all its splendor, trained in a drawing-room, fed on flattery, was tainted and flawed; yet its beams make the obscurest schoolhouse in New England warmer and lighter to the little rugged girls who are gathered together on its wooden bench. They may never through life hear her name, but she is not the less their benefactress.

The influence has been such that the aim certainly is now, in arranging school instruction for girls, to give them as fair a field as boys. As yet, indeed, these arrangements are made with little judgment or reflection; just as the tutors of Lady Jane Grey and other distinguished women of her time taught them Latin and Greek, because they knew nothing else themselves, so now the improvement in the education of girls is to be made by giving them young men as teachers, who only teach what has been taught themselves at college, while methods and topics need revision for these new subjects, which could better be made by those who had experienced the same wants. Women are often at the head of these institutions; but they have as yet seldom been thinking women, capable of organizing a new whole for the wants of the time, and choosing persons to officiate in the departments. And when some portion of instruction of a good sort is got from the school, the far greater proportion which is infused from the general atmosphere of society contradicts its purport. Yet books and a little elementary instruction are not furnished in vain. Women are better aware how great and rich the universe is, not so easily blinded by narrowness or partial views of a home circle. "Her mother did so before her" is no longer a sufficient excuse. Indeed it was never received as an excuse to mitigate the severity of censure, but was adduced as a reason, rather, why there should be no effort made for reformation.

Whether much or little has been done, or will be done—whether women will add to the talent of narration the power of systematizing—whether they will carve marble as well as draw and paint—is not important. But that it should be acknowledged that they have intellect which needs developing—that they should not be considered complete if beings of affection and habit alone—is important.

Yet even this acknowledgment, rather conquered by Woman than proffered by Man, has been sullied by the usual selfishness. Too much is said of women being better educated that they may become better companions and mothers *for men.* They should be fit for such companionship, and we have mentioned with satisfaction instances where it has been established. Earth knows no fairer, holier relation than that of a mother. It is one which rightly understood must both promote and require the highest attainments. But a being of infinite scope must not be treated with an exclusive view to any one relation. Give the soul free course, let the organization both of body and mind be freely developed, and the being will be fit for any and every relation to which it may be called. The intellect, no more than the sense of hearing, is to be cultivated merely that Woman may be a more valuable companion to Man, but because the Power who gave a power by its mere existence signifies that it must be brought out toward perfection.

In this regard of self-dependence, and a greater simplicity and fullness of being, we must hail as a preliminary the increase of the class contemptuously designated as "old maids."

We cannot wonder at the aversion with which old bachelors and old maids have been regarded. Marriage is the natural means of forming a sphere, of taking root in the earth; it requires more strength to do this without such an opening; very many have failed, and their imperfections have been in everyone's way. They have been more partial, more harsh, more officious and impertinent than those compelled by severer friction to render themselves endurable. Those who have a more full experience of the instincts have a distrust as to whether the unmarried can be thoroughly human and humane, such as is hinted in the saying, "Old maids' and bachelors' children are well cared for," which derides at once their ignorance and their presumption.

Yet the business of society has become so complex that it could now scarcely be carried on without the presence of these despised auxiliaries; and detachments from the army of aunts and uncles are wanted to stop gaps in every hedge. They rove about, mental and moral Ishmaelites, pitching their tents amid the fixed and ornamented homes of men.

In a striking variety of forms, genius of late, both at home and abroad, has paid its tribute to the character of the aunt and the uncle, recognizing in these personages the spiritual parents who have supplied defects in the treatment of the busy or careless actual parents.

They also gain a wider, if not so deep experience. Those who are not intimately and permanently linked with others are thrown upon themselves; and if they do not there find peace and incessant life, there is none to flatter them that they are not very poor and very mean.

A position which so constantly admonishes may be of inestimable benefit. The person may gain, undistracted by other relationships, a closer communion with the one. Such a use is made of it by saints and sibyls. Or she may be one of the lay sisters of charity, a canoness bound by an inward vow—or the useful drudge of all men, the Martha, much sought, little prized—or the intellectual interpreter of the varied life she sees; the Urania of a half-formed world's twilight.

Or she may combine all these. Not "needing to care that she may please a husband," a frail and limited being, her thoughts may turn to the center, and she may, by steadfast contemplation entering into the secret of truth and love, use it for the good of all men instead of a chosen few, and interpret through it all the forms of life. It is possible, perhaps, to be at once a priestly servant and a loving muse.

Saints and geniuses have often chosen a lonely position, in the faith that if, undisturbed by the pressure of near ties, they would give themselves up to the inspiring spirit, it would enable them to understand and reproduce life better than actual experience could.

How many "old maids" take this high stand we cannot say: it is an unhappy fact that too many who have come before the eye are gossips rather, and not always good-natured gossips. But if these abuse, and none make the best of their vocation, yet it has not failed to produce some good results. It has been seen by others, if not by themselves, that beings, likely to be left alone, need to be fortified and furnished within themselves; and education and thought have tended more and more to regard these beings as related to absolute Being, as well as to others. It has been seen that as the breaking of no bond ought to destroy a man, so ought the missing of none to hinder him from growing. And thus a circumstance of the time which springs rather from its luxury than its purity, has helped to place women on the true platform.

Perhaps the next generation, looking deeper into this matter, will find that contempt is put upon old maids or old women at all, merely because they do not use the elixir which would keep them always young. Under its influence, a gem brightens yearly which is only seen to more advantage through the fissures Time makes in the casket. No one thinks of Michelangelo's "Persican Sibyl" or St. Theresa or Tasso's Leonora or the Greek Electra as an old maid, more than of Michelangelo or Canova as old bachelors, though all had reached the period in life's course appointed to take that degree.

See a common woman at forty; scarcely has she the remains of beauty, of any soft poetic grace which gave her attraction as Woman, which kindled the hearts of those who looked on her to sparkling thoughts, or diffused round her a roseate air of gentle love. See her who was indeed a lovely girl in the coarse, full-blown dahlia flower of what is commonly matron-beauty, "fat, fair, and forty," showily dressed, and with manners as broad and full as her frill or satin cloak. People observe, "How well she is preserved!" "She is a fine woman still," they say. This woman, whether as a duchess in diamonds or one of our city dames in mosaics, charms the poet's heart no more, and would look much out of place kneeling before the Madonna. She "does well the honors of her house"—"leads society"—is in short always spoken and thought of upholstery-wise.

Or see that careworn face from which every soft line is blotted—those faded eyes from which lonely tears have driven the flashes of fancy, the mild white beam of a tender enthusiasm. This woman is not so ornamental to a tea party; yet she would please better in picture. Yet surely she, no more than the other, looks as a human being should at the end of forty years. Forty years! Have they bound those brows with no garland? Shed in the lamp no drop of ambrosial oil? . . .

The electrical, the magnetic element in Woman has not been fairly brought out at any period. Everything might be expected from it; she has far more of it than Man. This is commonly expressed by saying that her intuitions are more rapid and more correct. You will often see men of high intellect absolutely stupid in regard to the atmospheric changes, the fine invisible links which connect the forms of life around them, while common women, if pure and modest so that a vulgar self do not overshadow the mental eye, will seize and delineate these with unerring discrimination.

Women who combine this organization with creative genius are very commonly unhappy at present. They see too much to act in conformity with those around them, and their quick impulses seem folly to those who do not discern the motives. This is a usual effect of the apparition of genius whether in Man or Woman, but is more frequent with regard to the latter, because a harmony, an obvious order and self-restraining decorum, is most expected from her.

Then women of genius, even more than men, are likely to be enslaved by an impassioned sensibility. The world repels them more rudely, and they are of weaker bodily frame.

Those who seem overladen with electricity frighten those around them. "When she merely enters the room, I am what the French call *hérissé*," said a man of petty feelings and worldly character of such a woman, whose

depth of eye and powerful motion announced the con-
ductor of the mysterious fluid.

Woe to such a woman who finds herself linked to such
a man in bonds too close! It is the cruelest of errors.
He will detest her with all the bitterness of wounded
self-love. He will take the whole prejudice of manhood
upon himself, and to the utmost of his power imprison
and torture her by its imperious rigors.

Yet allow room enough, and the electric fluid will be
found to invigorate and embellish, not destroy life. Such
women are the great actresses, the songsters. Such traits
we read in a late searching, though too French, analysis
of the character of Mademoiselle Rachel by a modern La
Rochefoucauld. The Greeks thus represent the muses;
they have not the golden serenity of Apollo; they are
*over*flowed with thought; there is something tragic in their
air. Such are the Sibyls of Guercino; the eye is overfull
of expression, dilated and lustrous; it seems to have drawn
the whole being into it.

Sickness is the frequent result of this overcharged existence. To this region, however misunderstood or interpreted with presumptuous carelessness, belong the phenomena of magnetism, or mesmerism as it is now often
called, where the trance of the Ecstatica purports to be
produced by the agency of one human being on another,
instead of as in her case direct from the spirit.

The worldling has his sneer at this as at the services of
religion. "The churches can always be filled with women"
—"Show me a man in one of your magnetic states, and
I will believe."

Women are, indeed, the easy victims both of priestcraft
and self-delusion; but this would not be, if the intellect
was developed in proportion to the other powers. They
would then have a regulator and be more in equipoise, yet
must retain the same nervous susceptibility while their
physical structure is such as it is.

It is with just that hope that we welcome everything

that tends to strengthen the fiber and develop the nature
on more sides. When the intellect and affections are in
harmony; when intellectual consciousness is calm and
deep; inspiration will not be confounded with fancy. Then,

> . . . she who advances
> With rapturous, lyrical glances,
> Singing the song of the earth, singing
> Its hymn to the Gods,

will not be pitied as a madwoman nor shrunk from as
unnatural. . . .

In our own country women are in many respects better
situated than men. Good books are allowed, with more
time to read them. They are not so early forced into the
bustle of life, nor so weighed down by demands for
outward success. The perpetual changes incident to our
society make the blood circulate freely through the body
politic, and if not favorable at present to the grace and
bloom of life, they are so to activity, resource, and would
be to reflection, but for a low materialist tendency from
which the women are generally exempt in themselves,
though its existence among the men has a tendency to
repress their impulses and make them doubt their instincts, thus often paralyzing their action during the best
years.

But they have time to think, and no traditions chain
them and few conventionalities, compared with what must
be met in other nations. There is no reason why they
should not discover that the secrets of nature are open,
the revelations of the spirit waiting for whoever will seek
them. When the mind is once awakened to this consciousness, it will not be restrained by the habits of the past,
but fly to seek the seeds of a heavenly future.

Their employments are more favorable to meditation
than those of men.

Woman is not addressed religiously here more than

elsewhere. She is told that she should be worthy to be the mother of a Washington or the companion of some good man. But in many, many instances, she has already learned that all bribes have the same flaw; that truth and good are to be sought solely for their own sakes. And already an ideal sweetness floats over many forms, shines in many eyes.

Already deep questions are put by young girls on the great theme: What shall I do to enter upon the eternal life?

Men are very courteous to them. They praise them often, check them seldom. There is chivalry in the feeling toward the "ladies," which gives them the best seats in the stage-coach, frequent admission not only to lectures of all sorts but to courts of justice, halls of legislature, reform conventions. The newspaper editor "would be better pleased that the Lady's Book should be filled up exclusively by ladies. It would then indeed be a true gem, worthy to be presented by young men to the mistress of their affections." Can gallantry go further? . . .

There are two aspects of Woman's nature, represented by the ancients as Muse and Minerva. It is the former to which the writer in the *Pathfinder* looks. It is the latter which Wordsworth has in mind when he says,

> With a placid brow,
> Which woman ne'er should forfeit, keep thy vow.

The especial genius of Woman I believe to be electrical in movement, intuitive in function, spiritual in tendency. She excels not so easily in classification or recreation, as in an instinctive seizure of causes, and a simple breathing out of what she receives that has the singleness of life, rather than the selecting and energizing of art.

More native is it to her to be the living model of the artist than to set apart from herself any one form in objective reality; more native to inspire and receive the poem than to create it. In so far as soul is in her completely developed, all soul is the same; but in so far as it is modified in her as Woman, it flows, it breathes, it sings, rather than deposits soil or finishes work; and that which is especially feminine flushes in blossom the face of earth, and pervades like air and water all this seeming solid globe, daily renewing and purifying its life. Such may be the especially feminine element spoken of as Femality. But it is no more the order of nature that it should be incarnated pure in any form, than that the masculine energy should exist unmingled with it in any form.

Male and female represent the two sides of the great radical dualism. But in fact they are perpetually passing into one another. Fluid hardens to solid, solid rushes to fluid. There is no wholly masculine man, no purely feminine woman.

History jeers at the attempts of physiologists to bind great original laws by the forms which flow from them. They make a rule; they say from observation what can and cannot be. In vain! Nature provides exceptions to every rule. She sends women to battle, and sets Hercules spinning; she enables women to bear immense burdens, cold, and frost; she enables the man who feels maternal love to nourish his infant like a mother. Of late she plays still gayer pranks. Not only she deprives organizations but organs of a necessary end. She enables people to read with the top of the head and see with the pit of the stomach. Presently she will make a female Newton and a male siren.

Man partakes of the feminine in the Apollo; Woman of the masculine as Minerva.

What I mean by the Muse is that unimpeded clearness of the intuitive powers, which a perfectly truthful adherence to every admonition of the higher instincts would bring to a finely organized human being. It may appear as prophecy or as poesy. It enabled Cassandra to foresee

the results of actions passing round her; the Seeress to
behold the true character of the person through the mask
of his customary life. (Sometimes she saw a feminine
form behind the man, sometimes the reverse.) It enabled
the daughter of Linnaeus to see the soul of the flower
exhaling from the flower.* It gave a man, but a poet-man,
the power of which he thus speaks: "Often in my contemplation of nature, radiant intimations and as it were
sheaves of light appear before me as to the facts of cos-
mogony, in which my mind has perhaps taken especial
part." He wisely adds, "But it is necessary with earnestness
to verify the knowledge we gain by these flashes of light."
And none should forget this. Sight must be verified by
light before it can deserve the honors of piety and genius.
Yet sight comes first, and of this sight of the world of
causes, this approximation to the region of primitive motions, women I hold to be especially capable. Even without
equal freedom with the other sex, they have already
shown themselves so; and should these faculties have free
play, I believe they will open new, deeper, and purer
sources of joyous inspiration than have as yet refreshed
the earth.

Let us be wise, and not impede the soul. Let her work
as she will. Let us have one creative energy, one incessant
revelation. Let it take what form it will, and let us not
bind it by the past to man or woman, black or white.
Jove sprang from Rhea, Pallas from Jove. So let it be.

If it has been the tendency of these remarks to call
Woman rather to the Minerva side—if I, unlike the more
generous writer, have spoken from society no less than the
soul—let it be pardoned! It is love that has caused this—

---

* The daughter of Linnaeus states that while looking stead-
fastly at the red lily, she saw its spirit hovering above it as a red
flame. It is true this, like many fair spirit-stories, may be explained away as an optical illusion, but its poetic beauty and
meaning would even then make it valuable as an illustration of
the spiritual fact. [M.F.'s note]

love for many incarcerated souls that might be freed could the idea of religious self-dependence be established in them, could the weakening habit of dependence on others be broken up.

Proclus teaches that every life has in its sphere a totality or wholeness of the animating powers of the other spheres, having only as its own characteristic a predominance of some one power. Thus Jupiter comprises within himself the other twelve powers, which stand thus: the first triad is *demiurgic* or *fabricative*, that is, Jupiter, Neptune, Vulcan; the second, *defensive*, Vesta, Minerva, Mars; the third, *vivific*, Ceres, Juno, Diana; and the fourth, *elevating* and *harmonic*, Mercury, Venus, Apollo. In the sphere of Jupiter, energy is predominant—with Venus, beauty; but each comprehends and apprehends all the others.

When the same community of life and consciousness of mind begin among men, humanity will have positively and finally subjugated its brute elements and Titanic childhood; criticism will have perished; arbitrary limits and ignorant censure be impossible; all will have entered upon the liberty of law and the harmony of common growth.

Then Apollo will sing to his lyre what Vulcan forges on the anvil, and the Muse weave anew the tapestries of Minerva.

It is therefore only in the present crisis that the preference is given to Minerva. The power of continence must establish the legitimacy of freedom, the power of self-poise the perfection of motion.

Every relation, every gradation of nature is incalculably precious, but only to the soul which is poised upon itself and to whom no loss, no change, can bring dull discord, for it is in harmony with the central soul.

If any individual live too much in relations, so that he becomes a stranger to the resources of his own nature, he falls after a while into a distraction, or imbecility, from which he can only be cured by a time of isolation which gives the renovating fountains time to rise up. With a society it is the same. Many minds, deprived of the traditionary or instinctive means of passing a cheerful existence, must find help in self-impulse or perish. It is therefore that, while any elevation in the view of union is to be hailed with joy, we shall not decline celibacy as the great fact of the time. It is one from which no vow, no arrangement can at present save a thinking mind. For now the rowers are pausing on their oars; they wait a change before they can pull together. All tends to illustrate the thought of a wise contemporary. Union is only possible to those who are units. To be fit for relations in time, souls, whether of Man or Woman, must be able to do without them in the spirit.

It is therefore that I would have Woman lay aside all thought, such as she habitually cherishes, of being taught and led by men. I would have her, like the Indian girl, dedicate herself to the Sun, the Sun of Truth, and go nowhere if his beams did not make clear the path. I would have her free from compromise, from complaisance, from helplessness, because I would have her good enough and strong enough to love one and all beings, from the fullness, not the poverty of being. . . .

O men! I speak not to you. It is true that your wickedness (for you must not deny that at least nine thousand out of the ten fall through the vanity you have systematically flattered, or the promises you have treacherously broken); yes, it is true that your wickedness is its own punishment. Your forms degraded and your eyes clouded by secret sin; natural harmony broken and fineness of perception destroyed in your mental and bodily organization; God and love shut out from your hearts by the foul visitants you have permitted there; incapable of pure marriage; incapable of pure parentage; incapable of worship; O wretched men, your sin is its own punishment! You have lost the world in losing yourselves. Who ruins another has admitted the worm to the root of his own tree, and the fuller ye fill the cup of evil, the deeper must be your own bitter draft. But I speak not to you—you need to teach and warn one another. And more than one voice rises in earnestness. And all that *women* say to the heart that has once chosen the evil path is considered prudery or ignorance or perhaps a feebleness of nature which exempts from similar temptations.

But to you women, American women, a few words may not be addressed in vain. One here and there may listen.

You know how it was in the Oriental clime. One man, if wealth permitted, had several wives and many handmaidens. The chastity and equality of genuine marriage, with the "thousand decencies that flow" from its communion, the precious virtues that gradually may be matured within its enclosure, were unknown.

But this man did not wrong according to his light. What he did, he might publish to God and Man; it was not a wicked secret that hid in vile lurking-places and dens, like the banquets of beasts of prey. Those women were not lost, not polluted in their own eyes nor those of others. If they were not in a state of knowledge and virtue, they were at least in one of comparative innocence.

You know how it was with the natives of this continent. A chief had many wives whom he maintained and who did his household work; those women were but servants, still they enjoyed the respect of others and their own. They lived together in peace. They knew that a sin against what was in their nation esteemed virtue would be as strictly punished in Man as in Woman.

Now pass to the countries where marriage is between one and one. I will not speak of the pagan nations, but come to those which own the Christian rule. We all know what that enjoins; there is a standard to appeal to.

See now not the mass of the people, for we all know that it is a proverb and a bitter jest to speak of the "downtrodden million." We know that down to our own time a principle never had so fair a chance to pervade the mass of the people, but that we must solicit its illustration from select examples.

Take the Paladin, take the Poet. Did *they* believe purity more impossible to Man than to Woman? Did they wish Woman to believe that Man was less amenable to higher motives—that pure aspirations would not guard him against bad passions—that honorable employments and temperate habits would not keep him free from slavery to the body? Oh, no! Love was to them a part of heaven, and they could not even wish to receive its happiness unless assured of being worthy of it. Its highest happiness to them was that it made them wish to be worthy. They courted probation. They wished not the title of knight till the banner had been upheld in the heats of battle amid the rout of cowards.

I ask of you, young girls—I do not mean *you* whose heart is that of an old coxcomb, though your locks have not yet lost their sunny tinge. Not of you whose whole character is tainted with vanity inherited or taught, who have early learned the love of coquettish excitement and whose eyes rove restlessly in search of a "conquest" or a "beau"; you who are ashamed *not* to be seen by others as the mark of the most contemptuous flattery or injurious desire. To such I do not speak. But to thee, maiden, who if not so fair, art yet of that unpolluted nature which Milton saw when he dreamed of Comus and the Paradise. Thou child of an unprofaned wedlock, brought up amid the teachings of the woods and fields, kept fancy-free by useful employment and a free flight into the heaven of thought, loving to please only those whom thou wouldst not be ashamed to love; I ask of thee, whose cheek has not forgotten its blush nor thy heart its larklike hopes, if he whom thou mayest hope the Father will send thee as the companion of life's toils and joys, is not to thy thought pure? Is not manliness to thy thought purity, *not* lawlessness? Can his lips speak falsely? Can he do in secret what he could not avow to the mother that bore him? Oh, say, dost thou not look for a heart free, open as thine own, all whose thoughts may be avowed, incapable of wronging the innocent or still further degrading the fallen —a man in short in whom brute nature is entirely subject to the impulses of his better self?

Yes! It was thus that thou didst hope; for I have many, many times seen the image of a future life, of a destined spouse, painted on the tablets of a virgin heart.

It might be that she was not true to these hopes. She was taken into what is called the "world," froth and scum as it mostly is on the social caldron. There, she saw fair Woman carried in the waltz close to the heart of a being who appeared to her a Satyr. Being warned by a male friend that he was in fact of that class and not fit for such familiar nearness to a chaste being, the advised replied that "women should know nothing about such things." She saw one fairer given in wedlock to a man of the same class. "Papa and mamma said that 'all men were faulty at some time in their lives; they had a great many temptations.' Frederick would be so happy at home; he would not want to do wrong." She turned to the married women; they, O tenfold horror, laughed at her supposing "men were like women." Sometimes I say she was not true, and either sadly accommodated herself to "Woman's lot" or acquired a taste for satyr society, like some of the Nymphs and all the Bacchanals of old. But to those who could not and would not accept a mess of pottage or a Circe cup in lieu of their birthright, and to these others who have yet their choice to make, I say, courage! I have some words of cheer for you. A man, himself of unbroken purity, reported to me the words of a foreign artist that the "world would never be better till men subjected themselves to the same laws they had imposed on women"; that artist, he added, was true to the thought. The same was true of Canova, the same of Beethoven. "Like each other demigod, they kept themselves free from stain"; and Michelangelo, looking over here from the loneliness of his century, might meet some eyes that need not shun his glance. . . .

To return—attention has been awakened among men to the stains of celibacy and the profanations of marriage. They begin to write about it and lecture about it. It is the tendency now to endeavor to help the erring by showing them the physical law. This is wise and excellent; but forget not the better half. Cold bathing and exercise will not suffice to keep a life pure, without an inward baptism and noble, exhilarating employment for the thoughts and the passions. Early marriages are desirable, but if (and the world is now so out of joint that there are a hundred thousand chances to one against it) a man does not early or at all find the person to whom he can be united in the marriage of souls, will you give him in the marriage *de convenance?* Or if not married, can you find no way for him to lead a virtuous and happy life? Think of it well, ye who think yourselves better than pagans, for many of *them* knew this sure way.*

To you, women of America, it is more especially my business to address myself on this subject, and my advice may be classed under three heads:

Clear your souls from the taint of vanity.

Do not rejoice in conquests, either that your power to

* The Persian sacred books, the *Desatir*, describe the great and holy prince Ky Khosrou as being an "angel, and the son of an angel," one to whom the Supreme says: "Thou art not absent from before me for one twinkling of an eye. I am never out of thy heart. And I am contained in nothing but in thy heart, and in a heart like thy heart. And I am nearer unto thee than thou art to thyself." This prince had in his Golden Seraglio three ladies of surpassing beauty, and all four in this royal monastery passed their lives, and left the world as virgins.

The Persian people had no skepticism when the history of such a mind was narrated. [M.F.'s note]

allure may be seen by other women, or for the pleasure
of rousing passionate feelings that gratify your love of
excitement.

It must happen no doubt that frank and generous
women will excite love they do not reciprocate, but in
nine cases out of ten, the woman has half consciously done
much to excite. In this case she shall not be held guiltless,
either as to the unhappiness or injury of the lover. Pure
love inspired by a worthy object must ennoble and bless,
whether mutual or not; but that which is excited by coquettish attraction of any grade of refinement, must cause
bitterness and doubt as to the reality of human goodness,
so soon as the flush of passion is over. And that you may
avoid all taste for these false pleasures,

> Steep the soul
> In one pure love, and it will last thee long.

The love of truth, the love of excellence, whether you
clothe them in the person of a special object or not, will
have power to save you from following Duessa, and lead
you in the green glades where Una's feet have trod. . . .

A little while since I was at one of the most fashionable places of public resort. I saw there many women,
dressed without regard to the season or the demands of
the place in apery, or as it looked in mockery, of European fashions. I saw their eyes restlessly courting attention. I saw the way in which it was paid; the style of devotion, almost an open sneer, which it pleased those ladies
to receive from men whose expression marked their own
low position in the moral and intellectual world. Those
women went to their pillows with their heads full of folly,
their hearts of jealousy or gratified vanity; those men, with
the low opinion they already entertained of Woman confirmed. These were American *ladies*; that is, they were of
that class who have wealth and leisure to make full use of
the day and confer benefits on others. They were of that

class whom the possession of external advantages makes of pernicious example to many, if these advantages be misused.

Soon after I met a circle of women stamped by society as among the most degraded of their sex. "How," it was asked of them, "did you come here?" for by the society that I saw in the former place they were shut up in a prison. The causes were not difficult to trace: love of dress, love of flattery, love of excitement. They had not dresses like the other ladies, so they stole them; they could not pay for flattery by distinctions and the dower of a worldly marriage, so they paid by the profanation of their persons. In excitement, more and more madly sought from day to day, they drowned the voice of conscience.

Now I ask you, my sisters, if the women at the fashionable house be not answerable for those women being in the prison?

As to position in the world of souls, we may suppose the women of the prison stood fairest, both because they had misused less light, and because loneliness and sorrow had brought some of them to feel the need of better life, nearer truth and good. This was no merit in them, being an effect of circumstance, but it was hopeful. But you, my friends (and some of you I have already met), consecrate yourselves without waiting for reproof, in free love and unbroken energy, to win and to diffuse a better life. Offer beauty, talents, riches on the altar; thus shall ye keep spotless your own hearts and be visibly or invisibly the angels to others.

I would urge upon those women who have not yet considered this subject to do so. Do not forget the unfortunates who dare not cross your guarded way. If it does not suit you to act with those who have organized measures of reform, then hold not yourself excused from acting in private. Seek out these degraded women, give them tender sympathy, counsel, employment. Take the place of mothers, such as might have saved them originally.

If you can do little for those already under the ban of the world—and the best-considered efforts have often failed from a want of strength in those unhappy ones to bear up against the sting of shame and the prejudices of the world, which makes them seek oblivion again in their old excitements—you will at least leave a sense of love and justice in their hearts that will prevent their becoming utterly embittered and corrupt. And you may learn the means of prevention for those yet uninjured. These will be found in a diffusion of mental culture, simple tastes, best taught by your example, a genuine self-respect, and above all, what the influence of Man tends to hide from Woman, the love and fear of a divine, in preference to a human tribunal.

But suppose you save many who would have lost their bodily innocence (for as to mental, the loss of that is incalculably more general) through mere vanity and folly; there still remain many, the prey and spoil of the brute passions of Man; for the stories frequent in our newspapers outshame antiquity and vie with the horrors of war.

As to this, it must be considered that as the vanity and proneness to seduction of the imprisoned women represented a general degradation in their sex, so do these acts a still more general and worse in the male. Where so many are weak, it is natural there should be many lost; where legislators admit that ten thousand prostitutes are a fair proportion to one city, and husbands tell their wives that it is folly to expect chastity from men, it is inevitable that there should be many monsters of vice. . . .

And now I have designated in outline, if not in fullness, the stream which is ever flowing from the heights of my thought.

In the earlier tract I was told I did not make my meaning sufficiently clear. In this I have consequently tried to illustrate it in various ways, and may have been guilty of much repetition. Yet as I am anxious to leave no room for doubt, I shall venture to retrace once more the scope of my design in points, as was done in old-fashioned sermons.

Man is a being of twofold relations, to nature beneath and intelligences above him. The earth is his school, if not his birthplace; God his object; life and thought his means of interpreting nature and aspiring to God.

Only a fraction of this purpose is accomplished in the life of any one man. Its entire accomplishment is to be hoped only from the sum of the lives of men, or Man considered as a whole.

As this whole has one soul and one body, any injury or obstruction to a part or to the meanest member affects the whole. Man can never be perfectly happy or virtuous till all men are so.

To address Man wisely, you must not forget that his life is partly animal, subject to the same laws with Nature.

But you cannot address him wisely unless you consider him still more as soul, and appreciate the conditions and destiny of soul.

The growth of Man is twofold, masculine and feminine.

So far as these two methods can be distinguished, they are so as

Energy and Harmony;
Power and Beauty;
Intellect and Love;

or by some such rude classification; for we have not language primitive and pure enough to express such ideas with precision.

These two sides are supposed to be expressed in Man and Woman, that is, as the more and the less, for the faculties have not been given pure to either, but only in preponderance. There are also exceptions in great number, such as men of far more beauty than power, and the reverse. But as a general rule it seems to have been the intention to give a preponderance on the one side that is called masculine, and on the other, one that is called feminine.

There cannot be a doubt that if these two developments were in perfect harmony, they would correspond to and fulfill one another, like hemispheres or the tenor and bass in music.

But there is no perfect harmony in human nature; and the two parts answer one another only now and then; or if there be a persistent consonance, it can only be traced at long intervals, instead of discoursing an obvious melody.

What is the cause of this?

Man in the order of time was developed first; as energy comes before harmony; power before beauty.

Woman was therefore under his care as an elder. He might have been her guardian and teacher.

But as human nature goes not straight forward, but by excessive action and then reaction in an undulated course, he misunderstood and abused his advantages, and became her temporal master instead of her spiritual sire.

On himself came the punishment. He educated Woman more as a servant than a daughter, and found himself a king without a queen.

The children of this unequal union showed unequal natures, and more and more men seemed sons of the handmaid rather than princess.

At last there were so many Ishmaelites that the rest grew frightened and indignant. They laid the blame on Hagar, and drove her forth into the wilderness.

But there were none the fewer Ishmaelites for that.

At last men became a little wiser, and saw that the infant Moses was in every case saved by the pure instincts of Woman's breast. For as too much adversity is better for the moral nature than too much prosperity, Woman in this respect dwindled less than Man, though in other respects still a child in leading-strings.

So Man did her more and more justice, and grew more and more kind.

But yet—his habits and his will corrupted by the past— he did not clearly see that Woman was half himself; that her interests were identical with his; and that by the law of their common being he could never reach his true proportions while she remained in any wise shorn of hers.

And so it has gone on to our day; both ideas developing, but more slowly than they would under a clearer recognition of truth and justice, which would have permitted the sexes their due influence on one another and mutual improvement from more dignified relations.

Wherever there was pure love, the natural influences were for the time restored.

Wherever the poet or artist gave free course to his genius, he saw the truth and expressed it in worthy forms, for these men especially share and need the feminine principle. The divine birds need to be brooded into life and song by mothers.

Wherever religion (I mean the thirst for truth and good, not the love of sect and dogma) had its course, the original design was apprehended in its simplicity, and the dove presaged sweetly from Dodona's oak.

I have aimed to show that no age was left entirely without a witness of the equality of the sexes in function, duty, and hope.

Also that when there was unwillingness or ignorance which prevented this being acted upon, women had not the less power for their want of light and noble freedom. But it was power which hurt alike them and those against whom they made use of the arms of the servile—cunning, blandishment, and unreasonable emotion.

That now the time has come when a clearer vision and better action are possible—when Man and Woman may regard one another as brother and sister, the pillars of one porch, the priests of one worship.

I have believed and intimated that this hope would receive an ampler fruition than ever before in our own land.

And it will do so if this land carry out the principles from which sprang our national life.

I believe that at present women are the best helpers of one another.

Let them think, let them act, till they know what they need.

We only ask of men to remove arbitrary barriers. Some would like to do more. But I believe it needs that Woman show herself in her native dignity to teach them how to aid her; their minds are so encumbered by tradition.

When Lord Edward Fitzgerald traveled with the Indians, his manly heart obliged him at once to take the packs from the squaws and carry them. But we do not read that the red men followed his example, though they are ready enough to carry the pack of the white woman, because she seems to them a superior being.

Let Woman appear in the mild majesty of Ceres, and rudest churls will be willing to learn from her.

You ask: what use will she make of liberty, when she has so long been sustained and restrained?

I answer: in the first place this will not be suddenly given. I read yesterday a debate of this year on the subject of enlarging women's rights over property. It was a leaf from the classbook that is preparing for the needed instruction. The men learned visibly as they spoke. The champions of Woman saw the fallacy of arguments on the opposite side, and were startled by their own convictions. With their wives at home, and the readers of the paper, it was the same. And so the stream flows on; thought urging action, and action leading to the evolution of still better thought.

But were this freedom to come suddenly, I have no fear of the consequences. Individuals might commit excesses, but there is not only in the sex a reverence for decorums and limits inherited and enhanced from generation to generation, which many years of other life could not efface, but a native love in Woman, as Woman, of proportion, of "the simple art of not too much"—a Greek moderation which would create immediately a restraining party, the natural legislators and instructors of the rest, and would gradually establish such rules as are needed to guard without impeding life.

The Graces would lead the choral dance, and teach the rest to regulate their steps to the measure of beauty.

But if you ask me what offices they may fill, I reply— any. I do not care what case you put; let them be sea-captains, if you will. I do not doubt there are women well fitted for such an office, and if so, I should be as glad to see them in it as to welcome the maid of Saragossa or the maid of Missolonghi or the Suliote heroine or Emily Plater.

I think women need especially at this juncture a much greater range of occupation than they have, to rouse their latent powers. A party of travelers lately visited a lonely hut on a mountain. There they found an old woman, who told them she and her husband had lived there forty years. "Why," they said, "did you choose so barren a spot?" She did not know; *"it was the man's notion."*

And during forty years she had been content to act, without knowing why, upon the "man's notion." I would not have it so.

In families that I know, some little girls like to saw wood, others to use carpenters' tools. Where these tastes are indulged, cheerfulness and good-humor are promoted. Where they are forbidden, because "such things are not proper for girls," they grow sullen and mischievous.

Fourier had observed these wants of women, as no one can fail to do who watches the desires of little girls or knows the ennui that haunts grown women, except where they make to themselves a serene little world by art of some kind. He therefore, in proposing a great variety of employments in manufactures or the care of plants and animals, allows for one third of women as likely to have a taste for masculine pursuits, one third of men for feminine.

Who does not observe the immediate glow and serenity that is diffused over the life of women before restless or fretful by engaging in gardening, building, or the lowest department of art? Here is something that is not routine, something that draws forth life towards the infinite.

I have no doubt, however, that a large proportion of women would give themselves to the same employments as now, because there are circumstances that must lead them. Mothers will delight to make the nest soft and warm. Nature would take care of that; no need to clip the wings of any bird that wants to soar and sing, or finds in itself the strength of pinion for a migratory flight unusual to its kind. The difference would be that *all* need not be constrained to employments for which *some* are unfit.

I have urged upon the sex self-subsistence in its two forms of self-reliance and self-impulse, because I believe them to be the needed means of the present juncture.

I have urged on Woman independence of Man, not that I do not think the sexes mutually needed by one another, but because in Woman this fact has led to an excessive devotion which has cooled love, degraded marriage, and prevented either sex from being what it should be to itself or the other.

I wish Woman to live *first* for God's sake. Then she will not make an imperfect man her god, and thus sink to idolatry. Then she will not take what is not fit for her from a sense of weakness and poverty. Then if she finds what she needs in Man embodied, she will know how to love and be worthy of being loved.

By being more a soul she will not be less Woman, for nature is perfected through spirit.

Now there is no woman, only an overgrown child.

That her hand may be given with dignity, she must be able to stand alone. I wish to see men and women capable of such relations as are depicted by Landor in his *Pericles and Aspasia*, where grace is the natural garb of strength, and the affections are calm, because deep. The softness is that of a firm tissue, as when

> The gods approve
> The depth, but not the tumult of the soul,
> A fervent, not ungovernable love.

A profound thinker has said, "No married woman can represent the female world, for she belongs to her husband. The idea of Woman must be represented by a virgin."

But that is the very fault of marriage and of the present relation between the sexes, that the woman *does* belong to the man instead of forming a whole with him. Were it otherwise, there would be no such limitation to the thought.

Woman, self-centered, would never be absorbed by any relation; it would be only an experience to her as to man. It is a vulgar error that love, *a* love, to Woman is her whole existence; she also is born for Truth and Love in their universal energy. Would she but assume her inheritance, Mary would not be the only virgin mother. Not Manzoni alone would celebrate in his wife the virgin mind with the maternal wisdom and conjugal affections. The soul is ever young, ever virgin.

And will not she soon appear? The woman who shall vindicate their birthright for all women; who shall teach them what to claim, and how to use what they obtain? Shall not her name be for her era Victoria, for her country and life Virginia? Yet predictions are rash; she herself must teach us to give her the fitting name.

An idea not unknown to ancient times has of late been revived, that in the metamorphoses of life the soul assumes the form first of Man, then of Woman, and takes the chances and reaps the benefits of either lot. Why then, say some, lay such emphasis on the rights or needs of Woman? What she wins not as Woman will come to her as Man.

That makes no difference. It is not Woman, but the law of right, the law of growth that speaks in us and demands the perfection of each being in its kind—apple as apple, Woman as Woman. Without adopting your theory, I know that I, a daughter, live through the life of Man; but what concerns me now is that my life be a beautiful, powerful, in a word, a complete life in its kind. Had I but one more moment to live I must wish the same.

Suppose at the end of your cycle, your great world-year, all will be completed whether I exert myself or not (and the supposition is *false*—but suppose it true), am I to be indifferent about it? Not so! I must beat my own pulse true in the heart of the world; for *that* is virtue, excellence, health.

Thou, Lord of Day, didst leave us tonight so calmly glorious, not dismayed that cold winter is coming, not postponing thy beneficence to the fruitful summer! Thou didst smile on thy day's work when it was done, and adorn thy down-going as thy up-rising, for thou art loyal, and it is thy nature to give life, if thou canst, and shine at all events!

I stand in the sunny noon of life. Objects no longer glitter in the dews of morning, neither are yet softened by the shadows of evening. Every spot is seen, every chasm revealed. Climbing the dusty hill, some fair effigies that once stood for symbols of human destiny have been broken; those I still have with me show defects in this broad light. Yet enough is left, even by experience, to point distinctly to the glories of that destiny; faint but not to be mistaken streaks of the future day. I can say with the bard,

Though many have suffered shipwreck, still beat noble hearts.

Always the soul says to us all, cherish your best hopes
as a faith, and abide by them in action. Such shall be
the effectual fervent means to their fulfillment:

> For the Power to whom we bow
> Has given its pledge that, if not now,
> They of pure and steadfast mind,
> By faith exalted, truth refined,
> *Shall* hear all music loud and clear,
> Whose first notes they ventured here.
> Then fear not thou to wind the horn,
> Though elf and gnome thy courage scorn;
> Ask for the castle's King and Queen;
> Though rabble rout may rush between,
> Beat thee senseless to the ground,
> In the dark beset thee round;
> Persist to ask, and it will come;
> Seek not for rest in humbler home;
> So shalt thou see, what few have seen,
> The palace home of King and Queen.

November 15, 1844

2. EMERSON'S ESSAYS

(Text from the New York *Tribune*, December 7,
1844.)

*[Horace Greeley was politically a Whig and considered
himself a conservative, yet his espousal of chimeric causes
resulted in downright consternation among his political
associates. Even more dangerous in their eyes than his
advocacy of Fourierist socialism and vegetarianism was his
preaching of "freedom" for women. In the strength of this
conviction, he hired Margaret Fuller to be the first professional book-reviewer (of either sex) in the country.*

For two years she wrote steadily for the Tribune *despite severe headaches and an intense romantic distraction. Most of the pieces were notices of current books, but she would often meditate on national celebrations or report on her excursions. All other columns in the* Tribune *were, as was then the custom, anonymous; Margaret's was signed with an imperial asterisk. Soon all New York knew the identity of "*". The male journalists derided her unmercifully. (Poe wrote that humanity could be divided into three classes, "men, women, and Margaret Fuller.") Yet a few, including Evert A. Duyckinck, realized the highly professional character of her enterprise. She wrote her pieces in haste and she was habitually verbose, but she turned out sound intelligent essays for the* Tribune *worth ten times her pretentious efforts for the* Dial.

After Greeley had provided for her lodgings in his household on the East River at Turtle Bay, she began work on her first essay for the Tribune, *a critical review of the Second Series of* Essays *by her unconquerable friend in idyllic Concord. She had read them at Fishkill Landing, while writing* Woman *and several of the more irate paragraphs in* Woman *may have been conceived out of revulsion against these* Essays.]*

At the distance of three years this volume follows the first series of essays, which have already made to themselves a circle of readers attentive, thoughtful, more and more intelligent, and this circle is a large one if we consider the circumstances of this country and of England also, at this time.

In England it would seem there are a larger number of persons waiting for an invitation to calm thought and sincere intercourse than among ourselves. Copies of Mr. Emerson's first-published little volume, called *Nature*, have there been sold by thousands in a short time, while one edition has needed seven years to get circulated here. Several of his orations and essays from the *Dial* have also been republished there, and met with a reverent and earnest response.

We suppose that while in England the want of such a voice is as great as here, a larger number are at leisure to recognize that want; a far larger number have set foot in the speculative region and have ears refined to appreciate these melodious accents.

Our people, heated by a partisan spirit, necessarily occupied in these first stages by bringing out the material resources of the land, not generally prepared by early training for the enjoyment of books that require attention and reflection, are still more injured by a large majority of writers and speakers who lend all their efforts to flatter corrupt tastes and mental indolence, instead of feeling it their prerogative and their duty to admonish the community of the danger and arouse it to nobler energy. The aim of the writer or lecturer is not to say the best he knows in as few and well-chosen words as he can, making it his first aim to do justice to the subject. Rather he seeks to beat out a thought as thin as possible, and to consider what the audience will be most willing to receive.

The result of such a course is inevitable. Literature and art must become daily more degraded; philosophy cannot exist. A man who has within his mind some spark of genius or a capacity for the exercises of talent should consider himself as endowed with a sacred commission. He is the natural priest, the shepherd of the people. He must raise his mind as high as he can toward the heaven of truth, and try to draw up with him those less gifted by nature with ethereal lightness. If he does not so, but rather employs his powers to flatter them in their poverty, and to hinder aspiration by useless words and a mere seeming of activity, his sin is great: he is false to God and false to man.

Much of this sin indeed is done ignorantly. The idea that literature calls men to the genuine hierarchy is almost forgotten. One who finds himself able uses his pen as he might a trowel solely to procure himself bread, without having reflected on the position in which he thereby places himself.

Apart from the troop of mercenaries, there is one still larger of those who use their powers merely for local and temporary ends, aiming at no excellence other than may conduce to these. Among these, rank persons of honor and the best intentions, but they neglect the lasting for the transient, as a man neglects to furnish his mind that he may provide the better for the house in which his body is to dwell for a few years.

When these sins and errors are prevalent and threaten to become more so, how can we sufficiently prize and honor a mind which is quite pure from such? When as in the present case we find a man whose only aim is the discernment and interpretation of the spiritual laws by which we live and move and have our being, all whose objects are permanent, and whose every word stands for a fact?

If only as a representative of the claims of individual culture in a nation which tends to lay such stress on artificial organization and external results, Mr. Emerson would be invaluable here. History will inscribe his name as a father of the country, for he is one who pleads her cause against herself.

If New England may be regarded as a chief mental focus of the New World, and many symptoms seem to give her this place, as to other centers the characteristics of heart and lungs to the body politic; if we may believe, as the writer does believe, that what is to be acted out in the country at large is most frequently first indicated there, as all the phenomena of the nervous system in the fantasies of the brain, we may hail as an auspicious omen the influence Mr. Emerson has there obtained, which is deep-rooted, increasing, and over the younger portion of the community far greater than that of any other person.

His books are received there with a more ready intelligence than elsewhere, partly because his range of personal experiences and illustration applies to that region, partly because he has prepared the way for his books to be read by his great powers as a speaker.

The audience that waited for years upon the lectures, a part of which is incorporated into these volumes of essays, was never large, but it was select and it was constant. Among the hearers were some who, attracted by the beauty of character and manner, though they were willing to hear the speaker through, always went away discontented. They were accustomed to an artificial method whose scaffolding could easily be retraced, and desired an obvious sequence of logical inferences. They insisted there was nothing in what they had heard, because they could not give a clear account of its course and purport. They did not see that Pindar's odes might be very well arranged for their own purpose, and yet not bear translating into the methods of Mr. Locke.

Others were content to be benefited by a good influence without a strict analysis of its means. "My wife says it is about the elevation of human nature, and so it seems to me," was a fit reply to some of the critics. Many were satisfied to find themselves excited to congenial thought and nobler life, without an exact catalogue of the thoughts of the speaker.

Those who believed no truth could exist unless encased by the burrs of opinion went away utterly baffled. Sometimes they thought he was on their side, then presently would come something on the other. He really seemed to believe there were two sides to every subject, and even to intimate higher ground from which each might be seen to have an infinite number of sides or bearings, an impertinence not to be endured! The partisan heard but once and returned no more.

But some there were, simple souls, whose life had been perhaps without clear light yet still a search after truth for its own sake, who were able to receive what followed on the suggestion of a subject in a natural manner as a stream of thought. These recognized beneath the veil of words the still small voice of conscience, the vestal fires of lone religious hours, and the mild teachings of the summer woods.

The charm of the elocution too was great. His general manner was that of the reader, occasionally rising into direct address or invocation in passages where tenderness or majesty demanded more energy. At such times both eye and voice called on a remote future to give a worthy reply. A future which shall manifest more largely the universal soul as it was then to this soul. The tone of the voice was a grave body-tone, full and sweet rather than sonorous, yet flexible and haunted by many modulations, as even instruments of wood and brass seem to become after they have been long played on with skill and taste; how much more so the human voice! In the more expressive passages it uttered notes of silvery clearness, winning yet still more commanding. The words uttered in those tones floated awhile above us, then took root in the memory like winged seed.

In the union of an even rustic plainness with lyric inspirations, religious dignity with philosophic calmness, keen sagacity in details with boldness of view, we saw what brought to mind the early poets and legislators of Greece—men who taught their fellows to plow and avoid moral evil, sing hymns to the gods and watch the metamorphoses of nature. Here in civic Boston was such a man —one who could see man in his original grandeur and his original childishness, rooted in simple nature, raising to the heavens the brow and eyes of a poet.

And these lectures seemed not so much lectures as grave didactic poems, theogonies perhaps, adorned by odes when some Power was in question whom the poet had best learned to serve, and with eclogues wisely portraying in familiar tongue the duties of man to man and "harmless animals."

Such was the attitude in which the speaker appeared to

that portion of the audience who have remained permanently attached to him. They value his words as the sig-
nets of reality; receive his influence as a help and incentive
to a nobler discipline than the age in its general aspect
appears to require; and do not fear to anticipate the verdict
of posterity in claiming for him the honors of greatness
and in some respects of a master.

In New England he thus formed for himself a class of
readers who rejoice to study in his books what they already know by heart. For though the thought has become
familiar, its beautiful garb is always fresh and bright in
hue.

A similar circle of like-minded the books must and do
form for themselves, though with a movement less directly powerful, as more distant from its source.

The essays have also been obnoxious to many charges.
To that of obscurity, or want of perfect articulation. Of
"Euphuism," as an excess of fancy in proportion to imagination, and an inclination at times to subtlety at the expense of strength, has been styled. The human heart com-
plains of inadequacy, either in the nature or experience
of the writer, to represent its full vocation and its deeper
needs. Sometimes it speaks of this want as "underdevelop-
ment" or a want of expansion which may yet be remedied;
sometimes doubts whether "in this mansion there be either
hall or portal to receive the loftier of the passions." Sometimes the soul is deified at the expense of nature, then
again nature at that of man, and we are not quite sure
that we can make a true harmony by balance of the statements. This writer has never written one good work, if
such a work be one where the whole commands more attention than the parts, if such an one be produced only
where, after an accumulation of materials, fire enough be
applied to fuse the whole into one new substance. This
second series is superior in this respect to the former, yet
in no one essay is the main stress so obvious as to produce
on the mind the harmonious effect of a noble river or tree

in full leaf. Single passages and sentences engage our attention too much in proportion. These essays, it has been justly said, tire like a string of mosaics or a house built of medals. We miss what we expect in the work of the great poet or the great philosopher, the liberal air of all the zones: the glow, uniform yet various in tint, which is given to a body by free circulation of the heart's blood from the hour of birth. Here is undoubtedly the man of ideas, but we want the ideal man also; want the heart and genius of human life to interpret it, and here our satisfaction is not so perfect. We doubt this friend raised himself too early to the perpendicular and did not lie along the ground long enough to hear the secret whispers of our parent life. We could wish he might be thrown by conflicts on the lap of mother earth, to see if he would not rise again with added powers.

All this we may say, but it cannot excuse us from benefiting by the great gifts that have been given and assigning them their due place.

Some painters paint on a red ground. And this color may be supposed to represent the groundwork most immediately congenial to most men, as it is the color of blood and represents human vitality. The figures traced upon it are instinct with life in its fullness and depths.

But other painters paint on a gold ground. And a very different but no less natural, because also a celestial beauty, is given to their works who choose for their foundation the color of the sunbeam, which nature has preferred for her most precious product, and that which will best bear the test of purification, gold.

If another simile may be allowed, another no less apt is at hand. Wine is the most brilliant and intense expression of the powers of earth—it is her potable fire, her answer to the sun. It exhilarates, it inspires, but then it is liable to fever and intoxicate too the careless partaker.

Mead was the chosen drink of the northern gods. And this essence of the honey of the mountain bee was not thought unworthy to revive the souls of the valiant who had left their bodies on the fields of strife below.

Nectar should combine the virtues of the ruby wine, the golden mead, without their defects or dangers.

Two high claims our writer can vindicate on the attention of his contemporaries. One from his *sincerity*. You have his thought just as it found place in the life of his own soul. Thus, however near or relatively distant its approximation to absolute truth, its action on you cannot fail to be healthful. It is a part of the free air.

He belongs to that band of whom there may be found a few in every age, and who now in known human history may be counted by hundreds, who worship the one God only, the God of Truth. They worship not saints nor creeds nor churches nor relics nor idols in any form. The mind is kept open to truth, and life only valued as a tendency toward it. This must be illustrated by acts and words of love, purity, and intelligence. Such are the salt of the earth; let the minutest crystal of that salt be willingly by us held in solution.

The other is through that part of his life which, if sometimes obstructed or chilled by the critical intellect, is yet the prevalent and the main source of his power. It is that by which he imprisons his hearer only to free him again as a "liberating God" (to use his own words). But indeed let us use them altogether, for none other, ancient or modern, can worthily express how, making present to us the courses and destinies of nature, he invests himself with her serenity and animates us with her joy.

"Poetry was all written before time was, and whenever we are so finely organized that we can penetrate into that region where the air is music, we hear those primal warblings and attempt to write them down, but we lose ever and anon a word or a verse, and substitute something of our own, and thus mistreat the poem. The men of more delicate ear write down these cadences more faithfully, and these transcripts, though imperfect, become the songs of the nations.

"As the eyes of Lyncaeus were said to see through the earth, so the poet turns the world to glass, and shows us all things in their right series and procession. For through that better perception he stands one step nearer to things, and sees the flowing or metamorphosis; perceives that thought is multiform; that within the form of every creature is a force impelling it to ascend into a higher form; and following with his eyes the life, uses the forms which express that life, and so the speech flows with the flowing of nature."

Thus have we in a brief and unworthy manner indicated some views of these books. The only true criticism of these or any good books may be gained by making them the companions of our lives. Does every accession of knowledge or a juster sense of beauty make us prize them more? Then they are good indeed, and more immortal than mortal. Let that test be applied to these; essays which will lead to great and complete poems—somewhere.

3. AMERICANS AND THEIR LOVE OF NATURE

(Text from the New York *Tribune*, January 28, 1845.)

[As a professional, Margaret found herself consigned to giving notice to books that the Dial *would never have so much as recognized. Among the group which supported the* Dial, *read Bryant's poetry, and admired the landscape paintings of the Hudson River School, the comfortable assumption reigned that all Americans truly appreciated "nature." In the conglomeration of New York, Margaret realized—what she had shrewdly suspected—that the popular homage paid to this ritual was mainly lip service.*

Mrs. Lydia Sigourney was the most popular poet of the era, infinitely more so than Longfellow. Although her muse was never hesitant in coming, she varied her output of verse with occasional prose effusions to keep her public responsive. Scenes in My Native Land was one of these, and Margaret now found that she had to make something out of it, if only to fill a space in Greeley's Tribune. Daringly she let her exasperation with regnant hypocrisy find frank expression.]

. . . Only one thing we must speak of,—the apologetic tone for hours passed in the contemplation of natural beauty, and the assumption of calling such a person as the hermit of Niagara "erring brother" because he sequestered some part of his life to this purpose. We have no patience with all this sort of remark, which so strongly marks a gross materialist tendency in our time and place. Mrs. Sigourney does not share it, but is so often conversant with those who do, that she is led to speak of those pure natural enjoyments, meant by Heaven for a great means of education to man for his proper place in the universe, in this dubious or apologetic tone. Let those "erring brethren" apologize who spend their lives in gossip, or money-making; not those who think it worth while to devote some hours to sympathy with the glories that surround them. Is it such a fault, then, to take a little time from the service of Mammon? What do you mean by your "social duties?" What are they good for, except to educate the soul to worship? This mania, as to "social duties," is so fostered among us that for any one to pass a day alone in contemplation of the most sublime work of the Great Spirit is enough to make him pointed or jeered at as "crazy," or (more deadly stigma it would seem,) *"peculiar."* My friends! angels and poets are *peculiar*; and to be gregarious is not the way to be social. Good society can only be composed of intelligent and devout men.

4. TO JAMES NATHAN, March 23, 1845

(Text from *Love-Letters of Margaret Fuller*, New York, 1903, pp. 18–21.)

[Soon after settling in the Greeley household, Margaret Fuller encountered at a literary soiree (she was promptly invited to all such in town) a German-Jewish businessman, aged thirty-four. In February 1845, James Nathan escorted her to an exhibition of a plastic model of the city of Jerusalem. Shortly thereafter she wrote him, "I have long had a presentiment, that I should meet—nearly —one of your race, who would show me how the sun of today shines upon the ancient Temple—but I did not expect so gentle and civilized an apparition and with blue eyes!"

From what we can make out, James Nathan does not emerge from the story with any degree of credit. The Greeleys did not like him. For four intense months Margaret conducted her relations with him through the classic maneuvers of a secret affair—clandestine meetings, exchanges of notes, declarations of passion, and bulletins of recrimination. In June, Nathan sailed for Europe. He had reasons of business for going, but it seems evident—judging from Margaret's letters only—that he was fleeing for his life.

Nathan married while in Europe, returned to America, and resumed his commission business. In 1862 he changed his name to Gotendorf. He then retired to Hamburg, where he died in 1888. He preserved Margaret's letters; a son offered them for sale, and after a complicated history they were published in 1903, as Love-Letters of Margaret Fuller, *with an introduction by Julia Ward Howe.*

Possibly the Greeleys—or at least Mrs. Greeley—guessed the extent of Margaret's involvement with this adventurer.

To the world in general, these letters came as an astounding revelation a half-century after her death.

There is room in this collection for only a sample of the correspondence, enough to show the nature of Margaret's infatuation, the bitterness of her disillusion, and the extra burden that this association added to her effort of commencing a "business" career in the great city.]

. . . The true lovely time is come at last. The leaves and grasses are out, so that the wind can make soft music, as it sweeps along, instead of the rattling and sobbing of winter. A dear little shower is refreshing the trees and they grow greener and fairer every moment in gratitude. (I write so badly, because the wind shakes my paper too as well as the other leaves, but I can't bear to shut the window.)

You must use your moderation about our interviews, and as you know best. I like best to rely entirely upon you, yet keep time as much as possible with the enchanting calls of outward nature. It is nothing to be together in the parlour, or in the street, and we are not enough so among the green things. To-day the lilacs are all in blossom, and the air is full of a perfume which causes ecstasy.

I hear you with awe assert power over me and feel it to be true. It causes awe, but not dread, such as I felt sometimes since at the approach of this mysterious power, for I feel deep confidence in my friend and know that he will lead me on in a spirit of holy love and that all I may learn of nature and the soul will be legitimate. The destiny of each human being is no doubt great and peculiar, however obscure its rudiments to our present sight, but there are also in every age a few in whose lot the meaning of the age is concentrated. I feel I am one of those persons in my age and sex. I feel chosen among women. I have deep mystic feelings in myself and intimations from elsewhere.

I could not, if I would, put into words these spirit facts, indeed they are but swelling germs as yet, and all I do for them is to try to do nothing that might blight them. Yet as you say you need forget your call, so have I need of escaping from this overpowering sense. But when forced back upon myself, as now, though the first turnings of the key were painful, yet the inner door makes rapturous music too upon its golden hinge. What it hides, you perhaps know, as you read me so deeply; indeed, some things you say seem as if you did. Yet do not, unless you must. You look at things so without their veils, yet that seems noble and antique to me. I do it when you hold me by the hand, yet, when I feel how you are thinking, I sometimes only say: Psyche was but a mortal woman, yet as the bride of Love, she became a daughter of the gods too. But had she learned in any other way this secret of herself, all had been lost, the plant and flower and fruit.

But it is impossible to say these things, at least for me. They are myself, but not clearly defined to myself. With you, all seems to assume such palpable reality, though you do not forget its inner sense either. I love to hear you read off the secret, and yet you sometimes make me tremble too. I confide in you, as this bird, now warbling without, confides in me. You will understand my song, but you will not translate it into language too human. I wish, I long to be human, but divinely human. Let the soul invest every act of its abode with somewhat of its own lightness and subtlety. Are you my guardian to domesticate me in the body, and attach it more firmly to earth? Long it seemed, that it was only my destiny, to say a few words to my youth's companions and then depart. I hung lightly as an air-plant. Am I to be rooted on earth, ah! choose for me a good soil and a sunny place, that I may be a green shelter to the weary and bear fruit enough to pay for staying.

Au revoir! Adieu!

5. A TRANSCENDENTAL DEFENSE OF CLASSICAL METRES

(Text from the New York *Tribune*, May 12, 1845.)

*[As the industrial revolution rushed forward in America,
carrying with it a social and intellectual transformation,
the staid eighteenth-century conceptions of education
aroused an increasing amount of public animosity. Charles
Anthon, the scholarly professor of classical literature at
Columbia University, published* A System of Latin Versification *in a gallant effort to stem the rising tide of vulgarity; Timothy Fuller's daughter joined Anthon's barricade, to defend the standards he had strenuously taught
her.]*

. . . A growing prejudice prevails in the more living and
larger portion of our society against the boasted advantages
of a "classical education."—The man brought up in familiarity with outward nature, and to a use of bodily and instinctive powers, feels a contempt for the purblind scholar
who cannot see through his spectacles what is impera-
tively required by a young and growing life like ours. The
man whose mind has been cultivated not classically, nor in
classes, but by earnest seeking and grasping on every side
for what is demanded by the wants of his individual mind,
doubts whether there is time, amid the vast new conquests
of science, the profuse fruits of modern literature and arts,
the needs in a great novel life of original thought and
methods suited to the period, for a careful attention to
the making of verse in the dead languages. He doubts
whether the boy whose eyes have been during his best
years turned too exclusively to the past will ever see as
clear into the present and future as his neighbors, less

schooled in the classics and better in nature and the spirit
of the times.

Yet there is a beautiful propriety in referring back to the
Greeks and Romans, could this but be done with intelligence and in harmony with the other branches of culture.
It is only pedantry and indolence that makes this dangerous. The honey of Hymettus need not spoil the taste of the
American wild bee, but only teach him not to content
himself with the coarsest flowers when he might do better.

Those nations brought some things to a perfection that
the world will probably never see again. We must not
lose the sense of their greatness because our practice is in
a different sphere. For this it is that marks the true eclec-
tic, that he need not cling to the form because he reveres
the spirit that informed it, but treasures the seed of each
plant that bloomed in the garden of Humanity, without
demanding their fruit when the season is past.

"At Christmas he no more desires a rose,
Than asks for ice 'mong June's new-fangled shows."

The metres, the methods of verse that grow up in a
nation are one of the highest expressions of its spirit, one
of the finest organizations of its life. The rules which are
derived from them give the science of life as far as it
can be understood *from without*. Genius needs not to
learn, but will take pleasure in examining them. To make
verse according to rule will enable no man to write one
word of poetry, but it may make him more deeply familiar
with the sense in which poetry has been written, by refining the taste and cultivating the ear. To know these
Greek and Roman writers critically, to imitate by rule
their methods, has the same benefit for the mind, that external association with a graceful person has on the manners. A deeper intimacy may arise; mind may speak to
mind, and grace to love; but, unfortunately, the way in
which acquaintance is begun more frequently hinders than
furthers the higher benefit. The little girl *imitates* the

graceful lady and thus spoils her own manners, instead of,
by intelligent sympathy, awakening within herself that
soul of beauty from which graceful manners flow. The boy
learns how the great poets wrote in measure, and copies
the cadence of their feet, but neither by his tutor is he
taught, nor of his seeking mind does he learn, that metres
are nothing except the harmonious movements of a mind
deeply conscious of the universal harmony, and that only
by adoring and studying that can he really emulate them.
Were this otherwise, were the spirit made known with or
through the letter, classical education, and this branch of
it especially, would be of true and deep value, and demand far less time than it has hitherto, for the mind runs
quick when it apprehends the goal.

6. AMERICAN FACTS

(Text from the New York *Tribune*, May 19, 1845.)

*[The princely American publisher, George Palmer Put-
nam, wrote his* American Facts *after a business trip to
England, where he had become exasperated with British
provinciality. According to Margaret Fuller, he went about
the job in the wrong spirit. (It was to be seen how much
better she would manage.)*

*Putnam, in contrast to the other American publishers,
was a nationalist. His firm, Wiley & Putnam, under the
editorial direction of Evert A. Duyckinck, was the one
house in New York even partially receptive to the cause
of "native" literature—the one house ready to publish,
among others, Margaret Fuller and Herman Melville.*

*Even so, Putnam's solid volume was too drearily factual
for Transcendental Margaret, and in this review she heaps
scorn upon Putnam's statistics; yet her comments suggest
that in New York she was quickly acquiring a more mun-*

dane pride of country than she had learned from Emerson's "The American Scholar." What emerges in this review is not Transcendentalism but the Roman patriotism of the Democrat Timothy Fuller, with the consequent contempt for the vulgarity of work that has failed to measure up to its noblest opportunities.]

Such is the title of a volume just issued from the press; a grand title, which suggests the epic poet or the philosopher. The purpose of the work, however, is modest. It is merely a compilation, from which those who have lived at some distance from the great highway may get answers to their questions, as to events and circumstances which may have escaped them. It is one of those books which will be valued in the backwoods.

It would be a great book indeed, and one that would require the eye and heart of a great man,—great as a judge, great as a seer, and great as a prophet,—that should select for us and present in harmonious outline the true American facts. To choose the right point of view supposes command of the field.

Such a man must be attentive, a quiet observer of the slighter signs of growth. But he must not be one to dwell superstitiously on details, nor one to hasten to conclusions. He must have the eye of the eagle, the courage of the lion, the patience of the worm, and faith such as is the prerogative of man alone, and of man in the highest phase of his culture.

We doubt not the destiny of our country—that she is to accomplish great things for human nature, and be the mother of a nobler race than the world has yet known. But she has been so false to the scheme made out at her nativity, that it is now hard to say which way that destiny points. We can hardly exhibit the true American facts without some idea of the real character of America. Only one thing seems clear—that the energy here at work is very great, though the men employed in carrying out its purposes may have generally no more individual ambition to understand those purposes, or cherish noble ones of their own, than the coral insect through whose restless working new continents are upheaved from ocean's breast.

Such a man, passing in a boat from one extremity of the Mississippi to another, and observing every object on the shore as he passed, would yet learn nothing of universal or general value, because he has no principles, even in hope, by which to classify them. American facts! Why, what has been done that marks individuality? Among men there is Franklin. He is a fact, and an American fact. Niagara is another, in a different style. The way in which newspapers and other periodicals are managed is American; a go-ahead, fearless adroitness is American; so is *not*, exclusively, the want of strict honor. But we look about in vain for traits as characteristic of what may be individually the character of the nation, as we can find at a glance in reference to Spain, England, France, or Turkey. America is as yet but a European babe; some new ways and motions she has, consequent on a new position; but that soul that may shape her mature life scarce begins to know itself yet. One thing is certain; we live in a large place, no less morally than physically: woe to him who lives meanly here, and knows the exhibitions of selfishness and vanity as the only American facts.

7. FOURTH OF JULY, 1845

(Text from the New York *Tribune*, July 4, 1845.)

[This is a still more vigorous assertion of Margaret's increasing comprehension of and sympathy for the cause of American nationalism. Her patriotism now includes both a faith in the multitude and a contempt for the inadequacies of the citizens.]

The bells ring; the cannon rouse the echoes along the river shore; the boys sally forth with shouts and little flags, and crackers enough to frighten all the people they meet from sunrise to sunset. The orator is conning for the last time the speech in which he has vainly attempted to season with some new spice the yearly panegyric upon our country; its happiness and glory; the audience is putting on its best bib and tucker, and its blandest expression to listen.

And yet, no heart, we think, can beat to-day with one pulse of genuine, noble joy. Those who have obtained their selfish objects will not take especial pleasure in thinking of them to-day, while to unbiassed minds must come sad thoughts of national honor soiled in the eyes of other nations, of a great inheritance risked, if not forfeited.

Much has been achieved in this country since the Declaration of Independence. America is rich and strong; she has shown great talent and energy; vast prospects of aggrandizement open before her. But the noble sentiment which she expressed in her early youth is tarnished; she has shown that righteousness is not her chief desire, and her name is no longer a watchword for the highest hopes to the rest of the world. She knows this, but takes it very easily; she feels that she is growing richer and more power-ful, and that seems to suffice her.

These facts are deeply saddening to those who can pro-nounce the words "my country" with pride and peace only so far as steadfast virtues, generous impulses, find their home in that country. They cannot be satisfied with super-ficial benefits, with luxuries and the means of obtaining knowledge which are multiplied for them. They could rejoice in full hands and a busy brain, if the soul were ex-panding and the heart pure; but, the higher conditions being violated, what is done cannot be done for good.

Such thoughts fill patriot minds as the cannon-peal bursts upon the ear. This year, which declares that the people at large consent to cherish and extend slavery as one of our "domestic institutions," takes from the patriot his home. This year, which attests their insatiate love of wealth and power, quenches the flame upon the altar.

Yet there remains that good part which cannot be taken away. If nations go astray, the narrow path may always be found and followed by the individual man. It is hard, hard indeed, when politics and trade are mixed up with evils so mighty that he scarcely dares touch them for fear of being defiled. He finds his activity checked in great nat-ural outlets by the scruples of conscience. He cannot enjoy the free use of his limbs, glowing upon a favorable tide; but struggling, panting, must fix his eyes upon his aim, and fight against the current to reach it. It is not easy, it is very hard just now, to realize the blessings of independ-ence.

For what *is* independence if it do not lead to freedom? —freedom from fraud and meanness, from selfishness, from public opinion so far as it does not agree with the still, small voice of one's better self?

Yet there remains a great and worthy part to play. This country presents great temptations to ill, but also great in-ducements to good. Her health and strength are so remark-able, her youth so full of life, that disease cannot yet have

taken deep hold of her. It has bewildered her brain, made
her steps totter, fevered, but not yet tainted, her blood.
Things are still in that state when ten just men may save
the city. A few men are wanted, able to think and act upon
principles of an eternal value. The safety of the country
must lie in a few such men; men who have achieved the
genuine independence, independence of wrong, of violence, of falsehood.

We want individuals to whom all eyes may turn as
examples of the practicability of virtue. We want shining
examples. We want deeply-rooted characters, who cannot
be moved by flattery, by fear, even by hope, for they work
in faith. The opportunity for such men is great; they will
not be burned at the stake in their prime for bearing
witness to the truth, yet they will be tested most severely
in their adherence to it. There is nothing to hinder them
from learning what is true and best; no physical tortures
will be inflicted on them for expressing it. Let men feel
that in private lives, more than in public measures, must
the salvation of the country lie. If that country has so
widely veered from the course she prescribed to herself,
and that the hope of the world prescribed to her, it must
be because she had not men ripened and confirmed for
better things. They leaned too carelessly on one another;
they had not deepened and purified the private lives from
which the public vitality must spring, as the verdure of
the plain from the fountains of the hills.

What a vast influence is given by sincerity alone. The
bier of General Jackson has lately passed, upbearing a
golden urn. The men who placed it there lament his departure, and esteem the measures which have led this
country to her present position wise and good. The other
side esteem them unwise, unjust, and disastrous in their
consequences. But both respect him thus far, that his conduct was boldly sincere. The sage of Quincy! Men differ
in their estimate of his abilities. None, probably, esteem
his mind as one of the first magnitude. But both sides,

all men, are influenced by the bold integrity of his character. Mr. Calhoun speaks straight out what he thinks. So far as this straightforwardness goes, he confers the benefits of virtue. If a character be uncorrupted, whatever bias it takes, it thus far is good and does good. It may help others to a higher, wiser, larger independence than its own.

We know not where to look for an example of all or many of the virtues we would seek from the man who is to begin the new dynasty that is needed of fathers of the country. The country needs to be born again; she is polluted with the lust of power, the lust of gain. She needs fathers good enough to be godfathers—men who will stand sponsors at the baptism with *all* they possess, with all the goodness they can cherish, and all the wisdom they can win, to lead this child the way she should go, and never one step in another. Are there not in schools and colleges the boys who will become such men? Are there not those on the threshold of manhood who have not yet chosen the broad way into which the multitude rushes, led by the banner on which, strange to say, the royal Eagle is blazoned, together with the word Expediency? Let them decline that road, and take the narrow, thorny path where Integrity leads, though with no prouder emblem than the Dove. They may there find the needed remedy, which, like the white root, detected by the patient and resolved Odysseus, shall have power to restore the herd of men, disguised by the enchantress to whom they had willingly yielded in the forms of brutes, to the stature and beauty of men.

8. POE'S TALES

(Text from the New York *Tribune*, July 11, 1845.)

[Although Poe said many cruel things about Margaret Fuller, she displayed her superiority to insult by treating him—few at the time did—as a serious artist.]

Mr. Poe's tales need no aid of newspaper comment to give them popularity; they have secured it. We are glad to see them given to the public in this neat form, so that thousands more may be entertained by them without injury to their eyesight.

No form of literary activity has so terribly degenerated among us as the tale. Now that everybody who wants a new hat or bonnet takes this way to earn one from the magazines or annuals, we are inundated with the very flimsiest fabrics ever spun by mortal brain. Almost every person of feeling or fancy could supply a few agreeable and natural narratives, but when instead of using their materials spontaneously they set to work with geography in hand to find unexplored nooks of wild scenery in which to locate their Indians or interesting farmers' daughters, or with some abridgment of history to hunt monarchs or heroes yet unused to become the subjects of their crude coloring, the sale-work produced is a sad affair indeed and "gluts the market" to the sorrow both of buyers and lookers-on.

In such a state of things the writings of Mr. Poe are a refreshment, for they are the fruit of genuine observations and experience, combined with an invention which is not "making up," as children call their way of contriving stories, but a penetration into the causes of things which leads to original but credible results. His narrative proceeds with vigor, his colors are applied with discrimination, and where the effects are fantastic they are not unmeaningly so.

The "Murders in the Rue Morgue" especially made a great impression upon those who did not know its author and were not familiar with his mode of treatment. Several of his stories make us wish he would enter the higher walk of the metaphysical novel and, taking a mind of the self-possessed and deeply marked sort that suits him, give us a deeper and longer acquaintance with its life and the springs of its life than is possible in the compass of these tales.

As Mr. Poe is a professed critic and of all the band the most unsparing to others, we are surprised to find some inaccuracies in the use of words, such as these: "he had with him many books, but rarely *employed* them."—"His results have, in truth, the *whole air* of intuition."

The degree of skill shown in the management of revolting or terrible circumstances makes the pieces that have such subjects more interesting than the others. Even the failures are those of an intellect of strong fiber and well-chosen aim.

9. THE PHILOSOPHY OF CRITICISM

(Text from the New York *Tribune*, August 22, 1845.)

[In 1845, a volume entitled Rhymes and Recollections of a Handloom Weaver, *by William Thom, an uneducated factory hand in England, attracted sentimental attention in his own country—where it would be cited both by Tories and Reformers for opposite purposes—but even more praise in America as a vindication of the democratic thesis. Margaret Fuller perceived in Thom's effort a por-*

tent of the nineteenth century. How far she had come since 1840 can be accurately measured by comparing this piece of journalism with her pretentious essay in the Dial *in 1840 (cf. above, pp. 66–74).]*

. . . There are two ways of considering poems, or the products of literature in general. We may tolerate only what is excellent and demand that whatever is consigned to print for the benefit of the human race should exhibit fruits perfect in shape, color, and flavor, enclosing kernels of permanent value.

Those who demand this will be content only with the Iliads and Odysseys of the mind's endeavor.—They can feed no where but at rich men's tables; in the wildest recess of nature, roots and berries will not content them. They say, "If you can thus satiate your appetite it is degrading; we, the highly cultivated in taste and the tissue of the mind, can nowhere be appeased, unless by golden apples, served up on silver dishes."

But on the other hand, literature may be regarded as the great mutual system of interpretation between all kinds and classes of men. It is an epistolary correspondence between brethren of one family, subject to many and wide separations, and anxious to remain in spiritual presence one of another. These letters may be written by the prisoner in soot and water, illustrated by rude sketches in charcoal;—by nature's nobleman, free to use his inheritance, in letters of gold, with the fair margin filled with exquisite miniatures;—to the true man each will have value, *first* in proportion to the degree of its revelation as to the life of the human soul, *second*, in proportion to the perfection of form in which that revelation is expressed.

In like manner are there two modes of criticism. One which tries by the highest standard of literary perfection the critic is capable of conceiving each work which comes in his way; rejecting all that it is possible to reject and reserving for toleration only what is capable of standing the severest test. It crushes to the earth without mercy all the humble buds of Phantasy, all the plants that, though green and fruitful, are also a prey to insects, or have suffered by drouth. It weeds well the garden, and cannot believe that the weed in its native soil may be a pretty graceful plant.

There is another way which enters into the natural history of every thing that breathes and lives, which believes no impulse to be entirely in vain, which scrutinizes circumstances, motive and object before it condemns, and believes there is a beauty in each natural form, if its law and purpose be understood. It does not consider a literature merely as the garden of the nation, but as the growth of the entire region, with all its variety of mountain, forest, pasture, and tillage lands. Those who observe in this spirit will often experience, from some humble offering to the Muses, the delight felt by the naturalist in the grasses and lichens of some otherwise barren spot. These are the earliest and humblest efforts of nature, but to a discerning eye they indicate the entire range of her energies.

These two schools have each their dangers. The first tends to hypercriticism and pedantry, to a cold restriction on the unstudied action of a large and flowing life. In demanding that the stream should always flow transparent over golden sands, it tends to repress its careless majesty, its vigor, and its fertilizing power.

The other shares the usual perils of the genial and affectionate; it tends to indiscriminate indulgence and a leveling of the beautiful with what is merely tolerable. For, indeed the vines need judicious pruning if they are to bring us the ruby wine.

In the golden age to which we are ever looking forward, these two tendencies will be harmonized. The highest

sense of fulfilled excellence will be found to consist with
the largest appreciation of every sign of life. The eye of
man is fitted to range all around no less than to be lifted
on high. Meanwhile the spirit of the time, which is certainly seeking, though by many and strange ways, the
greatest happiness for the greatest number, by discoveries
which facilitate mental no less than bodily communication, till soon it will be almost as easy to get your thought
printed or even engraved on a thousand leaves as to drop
it from the pen on one, and by the simultaneous bubbling
up of rills of thought in a thousand hitherto obscure and
silent places, declares that the genial and generous tendency shall have the lead, at least for the present.

We are not ourselves concerned, lest excellent expression should cease because the power of speech to some
extent becomes more general. The larger the wave and
the more fish it sweeps along the likelier that some ones
should enrich the net. It has always been so. The great
efforts of art belong to artistic regions, where the boys in
the street draw sketches on the wall and torment melodies
on rude flutes; shoals of sonneteers follow in the wake
of the great poet. The electricity which flashes with the
thunderbolts of Jove must first pervade the whole atmosphere.

10. TO JAMES NATHAN, August 31, 1845

(Text from *Love-Letters of Margaret Fuller,* pp. 149–
51.)

*[Nathan, once he had escaped to Europe, proved a poor
hand at writing letters—as we may well understand. After
two months of separation, Margaret began, at immense
emotional cost and while carrying on her duties for the
Tribune, to take his measure.]*

We said farewell the first day of summer and now it
is the last. It is again Sunday, the same hour in the evening. I am by the window in the little study recess with
the tree looking in, and the stars looking through it, "but
where art thou!"

It is gone forever, the beautiful summer, when we might
have been so happy together, and happy in a way, that
neither of us ever will be with any other person. Oh, it
is very sad! My friend, shed some tears with me.

Why, why must you leave me? If you had stayed, I
should have been well and strong by this time, and had
so much natural joy and so many thoughts of childhood!
And you? have you gained much thus far?

I will write no more to-night. I am heart-sick about it
all. I am wishing so much for a letter, yet when it comes,
how little it will be; letters are so little and you do not
love writing; that makes it worse yet. O the summer! "the
green and bowery summer!" gone, irrevocably gone!

Yet, all through it, have I been growing in knowledge of
you. You would be surprised to find how much better I
know you than when we parted. But I should have been
so much more happy in the real than in the ideal intercourse! Why! Why? Yes I must fret, must, must grieve.

11. A FURTHER CAVEAT TO PASTORALISM

(Text from the New York *Tribune*, January 10, 1846.)

[Obliged to review a sentimental and trashy novel,
Ellen: Or, Forgive and Forget, *which offered a particularly
nauseating example of the many degenerate popular imi-
tations of Wordsworth and Emerson, Margaret seized the
chance to put into print the heresy she had written to her
brother in 1841 (cf. above, pp. 75–77). Obviously Marga-*

ret's haunting memories of Groton at the time of her fa-
ther's death come into play here.]

. . . It is a current superstition that country people are
more pure and healthy in mind and body than those who
live in cities. It may be so in countries of old-established
habits, where a genuine peasantry have inherited some of
the practical wisdom and loyalty of the past, with most
of its errors. We have our doubts, though, from the stamp
upon literature, always the nearest evidence of truth we
can get, whether, even there, the difference between town
and country life is as much in favor of the latter as is
generally supposed. But in our land, where the country
is at present filled with a mixed population, who come
seeking to be purified by a better life and culture from
all the ills and diseases of the worst forms of civilization,
things often *look* worse than in the city; perhaps because
men have more time and room to let their faults grow
and offend the light of day.

There are exceptions, and not a few; but, in a very
great proportion of country villages, the habits of the
people, as to food, air, and even exercise, are ignorant
and unhealthy to the last degree. Their want of all pure
faith, and appetite for coarse excitement, is shown by continued intrigues, calumnies, and crimes.

We have lived in a beautiful village, where, more favorably placed than any other person in it, both as to with-
drawal from bad associations and nearness to good, we
heard inevitably, from domestics, work-people, and school-
children, more ill of human nature than we could possibly
sift were we to elect such a task from all the newspapers
of this city in the same space of time.

We believe the amount of ill circulated by means of
anonymous letters, . . . to be as great as can be imported
in all the French novels (and that is a bold word). We
know ourselves of two or three cases of morbid wickedness, displayed by means of anonymous letter, that may

vie with what puzzled the best wits of France in a famous law-suit not long since. It is true, there is, to balance all this, a healthy rebound,—a surprise and a shame; and there are heartily good people, . . . who, having taken a direction upward, keep it, and cannot be bent downward nor aside. But, then, the reverse of the picture is of a blackness that would appall one who came to it with any idyllic ideas of the purity and peaceful loveliness of agricultural life.

But what does this prove? Only the need of a dissemination of all that is best, intellectually and morally, through the whole people. Our groves and fields have no good fairies or genii who teach, by legend or gentle apparition, the truths, the principles, that can alone preserve the village, as the city, from the possession of the fiend. Their place must be taken by the school-master, and he must be one who knows not only "readin', writin', and 'rithmetic," but the service of God and the destiny of man. Our people require a thoroughly-diffused intellectual life, a religious aim, such as no people at large ever possessed before; else they must sink till they become dregs, rather than rise to become the cream of creation, which they are too apt to flatter themselves with the fancy of being already. . . .

12. TYPEE

(Text from the New York *Tribune*, April 4, 1846.)

[The drama behind this brief notice looms larger to our eyes than it would have to those of the participants, including Melville himself, because of the subsequent growth of his literary reputation.

At Evert Duyckinck's suggestion, George Putnam launched an "American Library" at Wiley & Putnam, and

*the firm discarded its business acumen to do so; for the
big money was in pirated English novels and not in the
work of such established American authors as Cooper and
Irving. A program for bringing out minor native writers
was, to say the least, a grave financial risk. Duyckinck
strove manfully, and generally in vain, to win the American public to such authors as Simms, Poe, and Mrs. Kirkland.*

*Among the early gambles in the series was Typee, which
had already been accepted by Murray in London. Putnam
himself grabbed it for the Library, and had it published
in New York on March 17th. It was violently attacked as
no true report but a wanton fabrication, and was further
denounced for its strictures on missionaries. Yet it was one
of the few commercially successful ventures in the Library.*

*As her passion for literary nationalism grew, Margaret
Fuller became friendly with Duyckinck and his "Young
America" band. (Duyckinck reprinted* Summer in New
York, *and held it to be the most "American" book he had
yet published.) In this notice for* Typee, *she did her best
to assist Duyckinck, although she was clearly not convinced
of Melville's veracity, and she did not think highly of the
book as literature. She did take delight in swiping at the
female missionary societies.]*

"Typee" would seem . . . to be the record of imaginary
adventures by some one who had visited those regions.
But it is a very entertaining and pleasing narrative, and
the Happy Valley of the gentle cannibals compares very
well with the best contrivance of the learned Dr. Johnson
to produce similar impressions. Of the power of this writer
to make pretty and spirited pictures as well of his quick
and arch manner generally, a happy specimen may be seen
in the account of the savage climbing the cocoa-tree,
p. 273, vol. 2nd. Many of the observations and narratives
we suppose to be strictly correct. Is the account given of

the result of the missionary enterprises in the Sandwich Islands of this number? We suppose so from what we have heard in other ways. With a view to ascertaining the truth, it would be well if the sewing societies, now engaged in providing funds for such enterprises would read the particulars, they will find in this book beginning p. 249, vol. 2nd., and make inquiries in consequence, before going on with their efforts. Generally, the sewing societies of the country villages will find this the very book they wish to have read while assembled at their work. Othello's hairbreath scapes were nothing to those by this hero in the descent of the cataracts, and many a Desdemona might seriously incline her ear to the description of the lovely Fay-a-way.

13. CHARLES BROCKDEN BROWN

(Text from the New York *Tribune*, July 21, 1846.)

[Brown's melodramatic endeavor in 1798 and 1799 to create an American literature was abortive because he tried to adapt to the native scene the highly artificial conventions of the Gothic romance—already passing out of fashion in England. He was largely forgotten by 1846, and if mentioned at all, only in ridicule. Yet some publisher reissued two of his novels, and Margaret Fuller took the occasion to deliver a lecture on native literary history.]

We rejoice to see these reprints of Brown's novels, as we have long been ashamed that one who ought to be the pride of the country, and who is, in the higher qualities of the mind, so far in advance of our other novelists, should have become almost inaccessible to the public.

It has been the custom to liken Brown to Godwin. But there was no imitation, no second hand in the matter.

They were congenial natures, and whichever had come first might have lent an impulse to the other. Either mind might have been conscious of the possession of that peculiar vein of ore, without thinking of working it for the mint of the world, till the other, led by accident, or overflow of feeling, showed him how easy it was to put the reveries of his solitary hours into words, and upon paper, for the benefit of his fellow-men.

"My mind to me a kingdom is."

Such a man as Brown or Godwin has a right to say that. Their mind is no scanty, turbid rill, rejoicing to be daily fed from a thousand others, or from the clouds. Its plenteous source rushes from a high mountain between bulwarks of stone. Its course, even and full, keeps ever green its banks, and affords the means of life and joy to a million gliding shapes, that fill its deep waters, and twinkle above its golden sands.

Life and Joy! Yes, Joy! These two have been called the dark Masters, because they disclose the twilight recesses of the human heart. Yet the gravest page in the history of such men is joy, compared with the mixed, shallow, uncertain pleasures of vulgar minds. Joy! because they were all alive, and fulfilled the purposes of being. No sham, no imitation, no convention deformed or veiled their native lineaments, or checked the use of their natural force. All alive themselves, they understood that there is no happiness without truth, no perception of it without real life. Unlike most men, existence was to them not a tissue of words and seemings, but a substantial possession.

Born Hegelians, without the pretensions of science, they sought God in their own consciousness, and found him. The heart, because it saw itself so fearfully and wonderfully made, did not disown its Maker. With the highest idea of the dignity, power, and beauty of which human nature is capable, they had courage to see by what an oblique course it proceeds, yet never lose faith that it would reach its destined aim. Thus their darkest disclosures are not hobgoblin shows, but precious revelations.

Brown is great as ever human writer was in showing the self-sustaining force of which a lonely mind is capable. He takes one person, makes him brood like the bee, and extract from the common life before him all its sweetness, its bitterness, and its nourishment.

We say makes *him*, but it increases our own interest in Brown, that, a prophet in this respect of a better era, he has usually placed this thinking, royal mind in the body of a woman. This personage, too, is always feminine, both in her character and circumstances, but a conclusive proof that the term *feminine* is not a synonyme for *weak*. Constantia, Clara Wieland, have loving hearts, graceful and plastic natures, but they have also noble, thinking minds, full of resource, constancy, courage. The Marguerite of Godwin, no less, is all refinement and the purest tenderness; but she is also the soul of honor, capable of deep discernment, and of acting in conformity with the inferences she draws. The Man of Brown and Godwin has not eaten of the fruit of the tree of knowledge, and been driven to sustain himself by the sweat of his brow for nothing, but has learned the structure and laws of things, and become a being, natural, benignant, various, and desirous of supplying the loss of innocence by the attainment of virtue. So his Woman need not be quite so weak as Eve, the slave of feeling or of flattery; she also has learned to guide her helm amid the storm across the troubled waters.

The horrors which mysteriously beset these persons, and against which, so far as outward facts go, they often strive in vain, are but a representation of those powers permitted to work in the same way throughout the affairs of this world. Their demoniacal attributes only represent a morbid state of the intellect, gone to excess from want of balance with the other powers. There is an intellectual as well as a physical drunkenness, and which, no less, impels to crime. Carwin, urged on to use his ventriloquism

till the presence of such a strange agent wakened the
seeds of fanaticism in the breast of Wieland, is in a state
no more foreign to nature than that of the wretch executed
last week, who felt himself drawn as by a spell to murder
his victim, because he had thought of her money and the
pleasures it might bring him, till the feeling possessed his
brain that hurls the gamester to ruin. The victims of such
agency are like the soldier of the Rio Grande, who, both
legs shot off, and his life-blood rushing out with every
pulse, replied serenely to his pitying comrades, that "he
had now that for which the soldier enlisted." The end of
the drama is not in this world, and the fiction which
rounds off the whole to harmony and felicity before the
curtain falls, sins against truth, and deludes the reader.
The Nelsons of the human race are all the more exposed
to the assaults of Fate, that they are decorated with the
badges of well-earned glory. Who but feels as they fall in
death, or rise again to a mutilated existence, that the end
is not yet? Who, that thinks, but must feel that the recompense is, where Brown places it, in the accumulation of
mental treasure, in the severe assay by fire that leaves the
gold pure to be used some time—somewhere?

Brown,—man of the brooding eye, the teeming brain,
the deep and fervent heart,—if thy country prize thee not,
and had almost lost thee out of sight, it is because her
heart is made shallow and cold, her eye dim, by the pomp
of circumstance, the love of gross outward gain. She cannot long continue thus, for it takes a great deal of soul to
keep a huge body from disease and dissolution. As there
is more soul, thou wilt be more sought; and many will yet
sit down with thy Constantia to the meal and water on
which she sustained her full and thoughtful existence, who
could not endure the ennui of aldermanic dinners, or find
any relish in the imitation of French cookery. To-day many
will read the words, and some have a cup large enough to
receive the spirit, before it is lost in the sand on which
their feet are planted.

Brown's high standard of the delights of intellectual communion and of friendship, correspond with the fondest hopes of early days. But in the relations of real life, at present, there is rarely more than one of the parties ready for such intercourse as he describes. On the one side there will be dryness, want of perception, or variety, a stupidity unable to appreciate life's richest boon when offered to its grasp; and the finer nature is doomed to retrace its steps, unhappy as those who, having force to raise a spirit, cannot retain or make it substantial, and stretch out their arms only to bring them back empty to the breast.

We are glad to see these reprints, but sorry to see them so carelessly done. Under the cheap system, the carelessness in printing and translating grows to a greater excess day by day. Please, Public, to remonstrate; else very soon all your books will be offered for two shillings apiece, and none of them in a fit state to be read.

14. AMERICAN LITERATURE. ITS POSITION IN THE PRESENT TIME, AND PROSPECTS FOR THE FUTURE

(Text from *Papers on Literature and Art*, New York, 1846.)

[Marcus Spring was a prosperous New York merchant who combined commercial success with a devotion to Fourierist socialism, in which cause he wrote for Greeley's Tribune. Possibly the explanation is that he was a Quaker. So was his admirable wife, Rebecca (in November 1859, she would be moved to journey to Harpers Ferry and by sheer moral force compel the authorities to grant her an interview with the condemned John Brown). In the early months of 1846, the Springs proposed that Margaret Ful-

*ler come with them, at their expense, to Europe. The
thwarted trip of 1835 could now at last—though possibly
too late!—be realized.*

*Closely associated with Duyckinck in his New York cam-
paign for nativism in literature was a Dickensian figure,
Cornelius Mathews, who served as the butt for innumerable lampoons by the numerous enemies of "Young America." He composed a play about Salem, called* Witchcraft,
*which had been tried out in Philadelphia but was not yet
performed in New York. Margaret again served her
adopted cause by discussing objectively a writer whom
New Yorkers in general considered a clown. (Poe said that
she praised Mathews because he "toadies" to her.)*

*However, quite aside from this bit of logrolling, and
despite the obvious signs (as usual in Margaret's productions) of hasty composition, this essay, in the wide historical perspective, is Margaret Fuller's most important
work. Her two years in New York had carried her fast and
furiously from the Transcendental nationalism of Emerson—which, for all his protestations, remained a species
of New England parochialism—into a truly urban appreciation of the plight of the American artist.*

*In this piece, she renewed the offense she had already
given in the* Tribune *on December 10, 1845, to the hordes
of admirers of Henry Wadsworth Longfellow by her elab-
orately condescending review of his volume of* Poems *for
that year. I feel that here, as a preface to her seminal
essay rather than in the citations, is the place to reproduce
the central passage of that resounding attack:*

> *We must confess a coolness towards Mr. Longfel-
> low, in consequence of the exaggerated praises that
> have been bestowed upon him. When we see a per-
> son of moderate powers receive honors which should
> be reserved for the highest, we feel somewhat like as-
> sailing him and taking from him the crown which
> should be reserved for grander brows. And yet this is,
> perhaps, ungenerous.*

Mr. Longfellow has been accused of plagiarism. We have been surprised that anyone should have been anxious to fasten special charges of this kind upon him, when we had supposed it so obvious that the greater part of his mental stores were derived from the work of others. He has no style of his own, growing out of his own experience and observation of nature. Nature with him, whether human or external, is always seen through the windows of literature.

This want of the free breath of nature, this perpetual borrowing of imagery, this excessive, because superficial, culture which he has derived from an acquaintance with the elegant literature of many nations and men, out of proportion to the experience of life with himself, prevent Mr. Longfellow's verses from ever being a true refreshment to ourselves.

Longfellow being, as Margaret stigmatized him, too much a gentleman to acknowledge a blow, never publicly remonstrated against her censure. But in this essay, as is evident, she paid similar respects to James Russell Lowell; he replied with the savage and ungentlemanly satire upon her as "Miranda" in A Fable for Critics, *1848:*

There is one thing she owns in her own single right,
It is native and germane—namely, her spite.
Though, when acting as censor, she privately blows
A censor of vanity 'neath her own nose.]

Some thinkers may object to this essay, that we are about to write of that which has as yet no existence.

For it does not follow because many books are written by persons born in America that there exists an American literature. Books which imitate or represent the thoughts and life of Europe do not constitute an American literature. Before such can exist, an original idea must animate this nation and fresh currents of life must call into life fresh thoughts along its shores.

We have no sympathy with national vanity. We are not
anxious to prove that there is as yet much American literature. Of those who think and write among us in the methods and of the thoughts of Europe, we are not impatient;
if their minds are still best adapted to such food and such
action. If their books express life of mind and character
in graceful forms, they are good and we like them. We
consider them as colonists and useful schoolmasters to our
people in a transition state; which lasts rather longer than
is occupied in passing bodily the ocean which separates
the New from the Old World.

We have been accused of an undue attachment to foreign continental literature, and it is true that in childhood
we had well nigh "forgotten our English" while constantly
reading in other languages. Still what we loved in the
literature of continental Europe was the range and force
of ideal manifestation in forms of national and individual
greatness. A model was before us in the great Latins of
simple masculine minds seizing upon life with unbroken
power. The stamp both of nationality and individuality
was very strong upon them; their lives and thoughts stood
out in clear and bold relief. The English character has
the iron force of the Latins, but not the frankness and
expansion. Like their fruits, they need a summer sky to
give them more sweetness and a richer flavor. This does
not apply to Shakespeare, who has all the fine side of
English genius, with the rich coloring and more fluent
life of the Catholic countries. Other poets of England also
are expansive more or less, and soar freely to seek the blue
sky, but take it as a whole, there is in English literature,
as in English character, a reminiscence of walls and ceil-
ings, a tendency to the arbitrary and conventional that
repels a mind trained in admiration of the antique spirit.
It is only in later days that we are learning to prize the
peculiar greatness which a thousand times outweighs this
fault, and which has enabled English genius to go forth

from its insular position and conquer such vast dominion in the realms both of matter and of mind.

Yet there is often between child and parent a reaction from excessive influence having been exerted, and such a one we have experienced in behalf of our country against England. We use her language and receive in torrents the influence of her thought, yet it is in many respects uncongenial and injurious to our constitution. What suits Great Britain, with her insular position and consequent need to concentrate and intensify her life, her limited monarchy and spirit of trade, does not suit a mixed race continually enriched with new blood from other stocks the most unlike that of our first descent, with ample field and verge enough to range in and leave every impulse free, and abundant opportunity to develop a genius wide and full as our rivers, flowery, luxuriant, and impassioned as our vast prairies, rooted in strength as the rocks on which the Puritan fathers landed.

That such a genius is to rise and work in this hemisphere we are confident; equally so that scarce the first faint streaks of that day's dawn are yet visible. It is sad for those that foresee, to know they may not live to share its glories, yet it is sweet, too, to know that every act and word uttered in the light of that foresight may tend to hasten or ennoble its fulfillment.

That day will not rise till the fusion of races among us is more complete. It will not rise till this nation shall attain sufficient moral and intellectual dignity to prize moral and intellectual no less highly than political freedom, not till the physical resources of the country being explored, all its regions studded with towns, broken by the plow, netted together by railways and telegraph lines, talent shall be left at leisure to turn its energies upon the higher department of man's existence. Nor then shall it be seen till from the leisurely and yearning soul of that riper time national ideas shall take birth, ideas craving to be clothed in a thousand fresh and original forms.

Without such ideas all attempts to construct a national literature must end in abortions like the monster of Frankenstein, things with forms and the instincts of forms, but soulless and therefore revolting. We cannot have expression till there is something to be expressed.

The symptoms of such a birth may be seen in a longing felt here and there for the sustenance of such ideas. At present it shows itself, where felt, in sympathy with the prevalent tone of society by attempts at external action, such as are classed under the head of social reform. But it needs to go deeper before we can have poets, needs to penetrate beneath the springs of action, to stir and remake the soil as by the action of fire.

Another symptom is the need felt by individuals of being even sternly sincere. This is the one great means by which alone progress can be essentially furthered. Truth is the nursing mother of genius. No man can be absolutely true to himself, eschewing cant, compromise, servile imitation, and complaisance, without becoming original, for there is in every creature a fountain of life which, if not choked back by stones and other dead rubbish, will create a fresh atmosphere and bring to life fresh beauty. And it is the same with the nation as with the individual man.

The best work we do for the future is by such truth. By use of that in whatever way, we harrow the soil and lay it open to the sun and air. The winds from all quarters of the globe bring seed enough, and there is nothing wanting but preparation of the soil and freedom in the atmosphere, for ripening of a new and golden harvest.

We are sad that we cannot be present at the gathering-in of this harvest. And yet we are joyous too, when we think that though our name may not be writ on the pillar of our country's fame, we can really do far more towards rearing it than those who come at a later period and to a seemingly fairer task. *Now*, the humblest effort, made in a noble spirit and with religious hope, cannot fail to be even infinitely useful. Whether we introduce some noble model from another time and clime to encourage aspiration in our own, or cheer into blossom the simplest wood-flower that ever rose from the earth, moved by the genuine impulse to grow, independent of the lures of money or celebrity; whether we speak boldly when fear or doubt keep others silent, or refuse to swell the popular cry upon an unworthy occasion, the spirit of truth, purely worshiped, shall turn our acts and forbearances alike to profit, informing them with oracles which the latest time shall bless.

Under present circumstances the amount of talent and labor given to writing ought to surprise us. Literature is in this dim and struggling state, and its pecuniary results exceedingly pitiful. From many well-known causes it is impossible for ninety-nine out of the hundred who wish to use the pen to ransom by its use the time they need. This state of things will have to be changed in some way. No man of genius writes for money; but it is essential to the free use of his powers that he should be able to disembarrass his life from care and perplexity. This is very difficult here; and the state of things gets worse and worse, as less and less is offered in pecuniary meed for works demanding great devotion of time and labor (to say nothing of the ether engaged) and the publisher, obliged to regard the transaction as a matter of business, demands of the author to give him only what will find an immediate market, for he cannot afford to take anything else. This will not do! When an immortal poet was secure only of a few copyists to circulate his works, there were princes and nobles to patronize literature and the arts. Here is only the public, and the public must learn how to cherish the nobler and rarer plants, and to plant the aloe, able to wait a hundred years for its bloom, or its garden will contain presently nothing but potatoes and potherbs. We shall have in the course of the next two or three years a convention of authors to inquire

into the causes of this state of things and propose measures
for its remedy. Some have already been thought of that
look promising, but we shall not announce them till the
time be ripe; that date is not distant, for the difficulties
increase from day to day in consequence of the system
of cheap publication on a great scale.

The ranks that led the way in the first half century
of this republic were far better situated than we, in this
respect. The country was not so deluged with the dingy
page reprinted from Europe, and patriotic vanity was on
the alert to answer the question, "Who reads an American
book?" And many were the books written as worthy to
be read as any out of the first class in England. They
were, most of them, except in their subject matter, English books.

The list is large, and in making some cursory comments
we do not wish to be understood as designating *all* who
are worthy of notice, but only those who present themselves to our minds with some special claims. In history
there has been nothing done to which the world at large
has not been eager to award the full meed of its deserts.
Mr. Prescott for instance has been greeted with as much
warmth abroad as here. We are not disposed to under-
value his industry and power of clear and elegant arrangement. The richness and freshness of his materials is such
that a sense of enchantment must be felt in their contemplation. We must regret, however, that they should
have been first presented to the public by one who possesses nothing of the higher powers of the historian, great
leading views or discernment as to the motives of action
and the spirit of an era. Considering the splendor of the
materials, the books are wonderfully tame, and everyone
must feel that having once passed through them and got
the sketch in the mind, there is nothing else to which it
will recur. The absence of thought as to that great picture
of Mexican life, with its heroisms, its terrible but deeply

significant superstitions, its admirable civic refinement, seems to be quite unbroken.

Mr. Bancroft is a far more vivid writer; he has great resources and great command of them, and leading thoughts by whose aid he groups his facts. But we cannot speak fully of his historical works, which we have only read and referred to here and there.

In the department of ethics and philosophy we may inscribe two names as likely to live and be blessed and honored in the later time. These are the names of Channing and of Emerson.

Dr. Channing had several leading thoughts which corresponded with the wants of his time, and have made him in it a father of thought. His leading idea of the "dignity of human nature" is one of vast results, and the peculiar form in which he advocated it had a great work to do in this new world. The spiritual beauty of his writings is very great; they are all distinguished for sweetness, elevation, candor, and a severe devotion to truth. On great questions he took middle ground and sought a panoramic view; he wished also to stand high, yet never forgot what was above more than what was around and beneath him. He was not well acquainted with man on the impulsive and passionate side of his nature, so that his view of character was sometimes narrow, but it was always noble. He exercised an expansive and purifying power on the atmosphere, and stands a godfather at the baptism of this country.

The Sage of Concord has a very different mind, in everything except that he has the same disinterestedness and dignity of purpose, the same purity of spirit. He is a profound thinker. He is a man of ideas, and deals with causes rather than effects. His ideas are illustrated from a wide range of literary culture and refined observation, and embodied in a style whose melody and subtle fragrance enchant those who stand stupefied before the thoughts themselves, because their utmost depths do not

enable them to sound his shallows. His influence does
not yet extend over a wide space; he is too far beyond
his place and his time to be felt at once or in full, but it
searches deep, and yearly widens its circles. He is a harbinger of the better day. His beautiful elocution has been
a great aid to him in opening the way for the reception
of his written word.

In that large department of literature which includes
descriptive sketches, whether of character or scenery, we
are already rich. Irving, a genial and fair nature, just what
he ought to be and would have been at any time of the
world, has drawn the scenes amid which his youth was
spent in their primitive lineaments, with all the charms of
his graceful jocund humor. He has his niche and need
never be deposed; it is not one that another could occupy.

The first enthusiasm about Cooper having subsided,
we remember more his faults than his merits. His ready
resentment and way of showing it in cases which it is
the wont of gentlemen to pass by in silence or meet with
a good-humored smile have caused unpleasant associations
with his name, and his fellow-citizens, in danger of being
tormented by suits for libel if they spoke freely of him,
have ceased to speak of him at all. But neither these
causes, nor the baldness of his plots, shallowness of
thought, and poverty in the presentation of character,
should make us forget the grandeur and originality of his
sea-sketches, nor the redemption from oblivion of our
forest-scenery, and the noble romance of the hunter-pio-
neer's life. Already, but for him, this fine page of life's
romance would be almost forgotten. He has done much
to redeem these irrevocable beauties from the corrosive
acid of a semi-civilized invasion.*

* Since writing the above we have read some excellent remarks
by Mr. W. G. Simms on the writings of Cooper. We think the
reasons are given for the powerful interest excited by Hawkeye
and the Pilot, with great discrimination and force.

"They both think and feel, with a highly individual nature,

Miss Sedgwick and others have portrayed with skill and feeling scenes and personages from the revolutionary time. Such have a permanent value in proportion as their subject is fleeting. The same charm attends the spirited delineations of Mrs. Kirkland, and that amusing book, *A New Purchase*. The features of Hoosier, Sucker, and Wolverine life are worth fixing; they are peculiar to the soil and indicate its hidden treasures; they have also that charm which simple life lived for its own sake always has, even in rude and all but brutal forms.

What shall we say of the poets? The list is scanty; amazingly so, for there is nothing in the causes that paralyze other kinds of literature that could affect lyrical and narrative poetry. Men's hearts beat, hope, and suffer always, and they must crave such means to vent them; yet of the myriad leaves garnished with smooth, stereotyped

that has been taught, by constant contemplation, in scenes of solitude. The vast unbroken ranges of forest to its one lonely occupant press upon the mind with the same sort of solemnity which one feels condemned to a life of partial isolation upon the ocean. Both are permitted that degree of commerce with their fellow beings, which suffices to maintain in strength the sweet and sacred sources of their humanity. . . . The very isolation to which, in the most successful of his stories, Mr. Cooper subjects his favorite personages, is, alone, a proof of his strength and genius. While the ordinary writer, the man of mere talent, is compelled to look around him among masses for his material, he contents himself with one man, and flings him upon the wilderness. The picture, then, which follows, must be one of intense individuality. Out of this one man's nature, his moods and fortunes, he spins his story. The agencies and dependencies are few. With self-reliance which is only found in true genius, he goes forward into the wilderness, whether of land or ocean; and the vicissitudes of either region, acting upon the natural resources of one man's mind, furnish the whole material of his work-shop. This mode of performance is highly dramatic, and thus it is that his scout, his trapper, his hunter, his pilot, all live to our eyes and thoughts, the perfect ideals of moral individuality."—*Views and Reviews* by W. G. Simms. [M.F.'s note. Simms' volume was also published by Duyckinck in the America Library.]

rhymes that issue yearly from our press, you will not find, one time in a million, a little piece written from any such impulse or with the least sincerity or sweetness of tone. They are written for the press in the spirit of imitation or vanity, the paltriest offspring of the human brain, for the heart disclaims, as the ear is shut against them. This is the kind of verse which is cherished by the magazines as a correspondent to the tawdry pictures of smiling milliners' dolls in the frontispiece. Like these they are only a fashion, a fashion based on no reality of love or beauty. The inducement to write them consists in a little money, or more frequently the charm of seeing an anonymous name printed at the top in capitals.

We must here in passing advert also to the style of story current in the magazines, flimsy beyond any texture that was ever spun or even dreamed of by the mind of man in any other age and country. They are said to be "written for the seamstresses," but we believe that everyway injured class could relish and digest better fare even at the end of long days of exhausting labor. There are exceptions to this censure; stories by Mrs. Child have been published in the magazines, and now and then good ones by Mrs. Stephens and others; but take them generally, they are calculated to do a positive injury to the public mind, acting as an opiate, and of an adulterated kind too.

But to return to the poets. At their head Mr. Bryant stands alone. His range is not great, nor his genius fertile. But his poetry is purely the language of his inmost nature, and the simple lovely garb in which his thoughts are arranged, a direct gift from the Muse. He has written nothing that is not excellent, and the atmosphere of his verse refreshes and composes the mind, like leaving the highway to enter some green lovely fragrant wood.

Halleck and Willis are poets of society. Though the former has written so little, yet that little is full of fire—elegant, witty, delicate in sentiment. It is an honor to the country that these occasional sparks struck off from the

New York 239

flint of commercial life should have kindled so much flame
as they have. It is always a consolation to see one of them
sparkle amid the rubbish of daily life. One of his poems
has been published within the last year, written in fact
long ago but new to most of us, and it enlivened the
literary thoroughfare as a green wreath might some dusty,
musty hall of legislation.

Willis has not the same terseness or condensed electricity. But he has grace, spirit, at times a winning pensive-
ness, and a lively though almost wholly sensuous delight
in the beautiful.

Dana has written so little that he would hardly be
seen in a more thickly garnished galaxy. But the masculine
strength of feeling, the solemn tenderness and refined
thought displayed in such pieces as the "Dying Raven"
and the "Husband and Wife's Grave" have left a deep
impression on the popular mind.

Longfellow is artificial and imitative. He borrows in-
cessantly, and mixes what he borrows, so that it does not
appear to the best advantage. He is very faulty in using
broken or mixed metaphors. The ethical part of his
writing has a hollow, secondhand sound. He has, however,
elegance, a love of the beautiful, and a fancy for what is
large and manly, if not a full sympathy with it. His verse
breathes at times much sweetness; and if not allowed to
supersede what is better, may promote a taste for good
poetry. Though imitative, he is not mechanical.

We cannot say as much for Lowell, who, we must declare it, though to the grief of some friends and the disgust
of more, is absolutely wanting in the true spirit and tone
of poesy. His interest in the moral questions of the day
has supplied the want of vitality in himself; his great
facility at versification has enabled him to fill the ear
with a copious stream of pleasant sound. But his verse
is stereotyped; his thought sounds no depth; and posterity
will not remember him.

R. W. Emerson, in melody, in subtle beauty of thought
and expression, takes the highest rank upon this list. But

his poems are mostly philosophical, which is not the truest kind of poetry. They want the simple force of nature and passion, and while they charm the ear and interest the mind, fail to wake far-off echoes in the heart. The imagery wears a symbolical air, and serves rather as illustration than to delight us by fresh and glowing forms of life.

We must here mention one whom the country has not yet learned to honor, perhaps never may, for he wants artistic skill to give complete form to his inspiration. This is William Ellery Channing, nephew and namesake of Dr. C., a volume of whose poems, published three or four years ago in Boston, remains unknown except to a few friends, nor if known would they probably excite sympathy, as those which have been published in the periodicals have failed to do so. Yet some of the purest tones of the lyre are his, the finest inspirations as to the feelings and passions of men, deep spiritual insight, and an entire originality in the use of his means. The frequently unfinished and obscure state of his poems, a passion for forcing words out of their usual meaning into one which they may appropriately bear, but which comes upon the reader with an unpleasing and puzzling surprise, may repel at first glance from many of these poems, but do not mar the following sublime description of the beings we want to rule, to redeem, to recreate this nation, and under whose reign alone can there be an American literature, for then only could we have life worth recording. The simple grandeur of this poem as a whole must be felt by everyone, while each line and thought will be found worthy of earnest contemplation and satisfaction after the most earnest life and thought.

> Hearts of Eternity! hearts of the deep!
> Proclaim from land to sea your mighty fate;
> How that for you no living comes too late;
> How ye cannot in Theban labyrinth creep;

How ye great harvests from small surface reap;
Shout, excellent band, in grand primeval strain,
Like midnight winds that foam along the main,
And do all things rather than pause to weep.
A human heart knows naught of littleness,
Suspects no man, compares with no man's ways,
Hath in one hour most glorious length of days,
A recompense, a joy, a loveliness;
Like eaglet keen, shoots into azure far,
And always dwelling nigh is the remotest star.

A series of poems called "Man in the Republic," by Cornelius Mathews, deserves a higher meed of sympathy than it has received. The thoughts and views are strong and noble, the exhibition of them imposing. In plastic power this writer is deficient. His prose works sin in exuberance, and need consolidating and chastening. We find fine things, but not so arranged as to be seen in the right places and by the best light. In his poems Mr. Mathews is unpardonably rough and rugged; the poetic substance finds no musical medium in which to flow. Yet there *is* poetic substance which makes full chords, if not a harmony. He holds a worthy sense of the vocation of the poet, and worthily expresses it thus:

To strike or bear, to conquer or to yield
Teach thou! O topmost crown of duty, teach,
What fancy whispers to the listening ear,
At hours when tongue nor taint of care impeach
The fruitful calm of greatly silent hearts;
When all the stars for happy thought are set,
And, in the secret chambers of the soul,
All blessed powers of joyful truth are met;
Though calm and garlandless thou mayst appear,
The world shall know thee for its crowned seer.

A considerable portion of the hope and energy of this country still turns towards the drama, that greatest achievement when wrought to perfection of human power.

For ourselves, we believe the day of the regular drama to be past; and though we recognize the need of some kind of spectacle and dramatic representation to be absolutely coincident with an animated state of the public mind, we have thought that the opera, ballet, pantomime, and briefer, more elastic forms, like the *vaudeville* of the French theater or the *proverb* of the social party, would take the place of elaborate tragedy and comedy.

But those who find the theaters of this city well filled all the year round by an audience willing to sit out the heroisms of Rolla, and the sentimentalism and stale morality of such a piece as we were doomed to listen to while the Keans were here (*Town and Country* was its name), still think there is room for the regular drama, if genius should engage in its creation. Accordingly there have been in this country, as well as in England, many attempts to produce dramas suitable for action no less than for the closet. The actor Murdoch, about to devote himself with enthusiasm and hope to prop up a falling profession, is to bring out a series of plays written not merely *for* him, but because his devotion is likely to furnish fit occasion for their appearance. The first of these, *Witchcraft, a Tragedy*, brought out successfully upon the boards at Philadelphia, we have read, and it is a work of strong and majestic lineaments; a fine originality is shown in the conception by which the love of a son for a mother is made a sufficient *motiv* (as the Germans call the ruling impulse of a work) in the production of tragic interest; no less original is the attempt, and delightful the success, in making an aged woman a satisfactory heroine to the piece through the greatness of her soul, and the magnetic influence it exerts on all around her, till the ignorant and superstitious fancy that the sky darkens and the winds wait upon her as she walks on the lonely hillside near her hut to commune with the past and seek instruction from Heaven. The working of her character on the other agents of the piece is depicted with force and nobleness. The deep love of her son for her; the little tender, simple ways in which he shows it, having preserved the purity and poetic spirit of childhood by never having been weaned from his first love, a mother's love; the anguish of his soul when he too becomes infected with distrust, and cannot discriminate the natural magnetism of a strong nature from the spells and lures of sorcery; the final triumph of his faith; all offered the highest scope to genius and the power of moral perception in the actor. There are highly poetic intimations of those lowering days with their veiled skies, brassy light, and sadly whispering winds, very common in Massachusetts, so ominous and brooding seen from any point, but from the idea of witchcraft, invested with an awful significance. We do not know, however, that this could bring it beyond what it has appeared to our own sane mind, as if the air was thick with spirits in an equivocal and surely sad condition, whether of purgatory or downfall; and the air was vocal with all manner of dark intimations. We are glad to see this mood of nature so fitly characterized.

The sweetness and naïveté with which the young girl is made to describe the effects of love upon her, as supposing them to proceed from a spell, are also original, and there is no other way in which this revelation could have been induced that would not have injured the beauty of the character and position. Her visionary sense of her lover as an ideal figure is of a high order of poetry, and these facts have very seldom been brought out from the cloisters of the mind into the light of open day.

The play is very deficient as regards rhythm; indeed we might say there is no apparent reason why the lines should begin with capital letters. The minor personages are mere caricatures, very coarsely drawn; all the power is concentrated on the main characters and their emotions. So did not Shakespeare, does not ever the genuine dramatist, whose mind teems with "the fullness of forms." As Raphael in his most crowded groups can put in no

misplaced or imperfect foot or hand, neither neglect to
invest the least important figure of his backgrounds with
every characteristic trait, nor spare the invention of the
most beautiful *coiffure* and accessories for the humblest
handmaid of his Madonnas, so doth the great artist always clothe the whole picture with full and breathing
life, for it appears so before his mental eye. But minds
not perfectly artistic, yet of strong conceptions, subordi-
nate the rest to one or two leading figures, and the imperfectly represented life of the others incloses them as
in a frame.

In originality of conception and resting the main interest upon force of character in a woman, this drama
naturally leads us to revert to a work in the department
of narrative fiction, which on similar grounds comes to
us as a harbinger of the new era. This book is *Margaret,
or the Real and Ideal*, a work which has appeared within
the past year; and, considering its originality and genuine-
ness, has excited admiration and sympathy amazingly soon.
Even some leading reviews of what Byron used to speak
of as the "garrison" class (a class the most opposite
imaginable to that of Garrison abolitionists) have discussed its pretensions and done homage to its merits. It
is a work of great power and richness, a genuine disclosure
of the life of mind and the history of character. Its descriptions of scenery and the common people, in the place
and time it takes up, impart to it the highest value as
a representative of transient existence which had a great
deal of meaning. The beautiful simplicity of action upon
and within the mind of Margaret, Heaven lying so clearly
about her in the infancy of the hut of drunkards, the
woods, the village, and their ignorant, simply human deni-
zens; her unconscious growth to the stature of womanhood, the flow of life impelled by her, the spiritual intimations of her dreams; the prophecies of music in the
character of Chilion; the naïve discussion of the leading
reform movements of the day in their rudimental forms;

the archness, the humor, the profound religious faith, make of this book an aviary from which doves shall go forth to discover and report of all the green spots of promise in the land. Of books like this, as good and still better, our new literature shall be full; and though one swallow does not make a summer, yet we greet in this one "Yankee novel" the sufficient earnest of riches that only need the skill of competent miners to be made current for the benefit of man.

Meanwhile the most important part of our literature, while the work of diffusion is still going on, lies in the journals which monthly, weekly, daily send their messages to every corner of this great land, and form at present the only efficient instrument for the general education of the people.

Among these, the magazines take the lowest rank. Their object is principally to cater for the amusement of vacant hours, and as there is not a great deal of wit and light talent in this country, they do not even this to much advantage. More wit, grace, and elegant trifling embellish the annals of literature in one day of France than in a year of America.

The reviews are more able. If they cannot compare on equal terms with those of France, England, and Germany, where if genius be rare, at least a vast amount of talent and culture is brought to bear upon all the departments of knowledge, they are yet very creditable to a new country where so large a portion of manly ability must be bent on making laws, making speeches, making railroads and canals. They are, however, much injured by a partisan spirit and the fear of censure from their own public. This last is always slow death to a journal; its natural and only safe position is to *lead*; if instead it bows to the will of the multitude, it will find the ostracism of democracy far more dangerous than the worst censure of a tyranny could be. It is not half so dangerous to a man to be immured in a dungeon alone with God and his own clear conscience as to walk the streets fearing the scrutiny of a thousand eyes, ready to veil with anxious care whatever may not suit the many-headed monster in its momentary mood. Gentleness is dignified but caution is debasing; only a noble fearlessness can give wings to the mind, with which to soar beyond the common ken and learn what may be of use to the crowd below. Writers have nothing to do but to love truth fervently, seek justice according to their ability, and then express what is in the mind; they have nothing to do with consequences, God will take care of those. The want of such noble courage, such faith in the power of truth and good desire, paralyzes mind greatly in this country. Publishers are afraid; authors are afraid; and if a worthy resistance is not made by religious souls, there is danger that all the light will soon be put under bushels, lest some wind should waft from it a spark that may kindle dangerous fire.

For want of such faith, and the catholic spirit that flows from it, we have no great leading review. The *North American* was once the best. While under the care of Edward Everett, himself a host in extensive knowledge, grace and adroitness in applying it, and the power of enforcing grave meanings by a light and flexible satire that tickled while it wounded, it boasted more force, more life, a finer scope of power. But now though still exhibiting ability and information upon special points, it is entirely deficient in great leadings and the *vivida vis*, but ambles and jogs at an old gentlemanly pace along a beaten path that leads to no important goal.

Several other journals have more life, energy, and directness than this, but there is none which occupies a truly great and commanding position, a beacon-light to all who sail that way. In order to do this, a journal must know how to cast aside all local and temporary considerations when new convictions command, and allow free range in its columns to all kinds of ability and all ways of viewing subjects. That would give it a life rich, bold, various.

The life of intellect is becoming more and more determined to the weekly and daily papers, whose light leaves fly so rapidly and profusely over the land. Speculations are afloat as to the influence of the electric telegraph upon their destiny, and it seems obvious that it should raise their character by taking from them in some measure the office of gathering and dispersing the news, and requiring of them rather to arrange and interpret it.

This mode of communication is susceptible of great excellence in the way of condensed essay, narrative, criticism, and is the natural receptacle for the lyrics of the day. That so few good ones deck the poet's corner, is because the indifference or unfitness of editors as to choosing and refusing makes this place at present undesirable to the poet. It might be otherwise.

The means which this organ affords of diffusing knowledge and sowing the seeds of thought where they may hardly fail of an infinite harvest, cannot be too highly prized by the discerning and benevolent. Minds of the first class are generally indisposed to this kind of writing; what must be done on the spur of the occasion and cast into the world so incomplete, as the hurried offspring of a day or hour's labor must generally be, cannot satisfy their judgment or do justice to their powers. But he who looks to the benefit of others and sees with what rapidity and ease instruction and thought are assimilated by men, when they come thus as it were on the wings of the wind, may be content, as an unhonored servant to the grand purposes of Destiny, to work in such a way at the Pantheon which the ages shall complete, on which his name may not be inscribed but which will breathe the life of his soul.

The confidence in uprightness of intent and the safety of truth is still more needed here than in the more elaborate kinds of writing, as meanings cannot be fully explained nor expressions revised. Newspaper-writing is next door to conversation, and should be conducted on the

same principles. It has this advantage: we address not
our neighbor, who forces us to remember his limitations
and prejudices, but the ideal presence of human nature
as we feel it ought to be and trust it will be. We address
America rather than Americans.

A worthy account of the vocation and duties of the
journalist is given by Cornelius Mathews. Editors generally could not do better than every New Year's Day to
read and insert the following verses.

As shakes the canvas of a thousand ships,
   Struck by a heavy land-breeze, far at sea,
Ruffle the thousand broad sheets of the land,
   Filled with the people's breath of potency.

A thousand images the hour will take,
   From him who strikes, who rules, who speaks, who sings,
Many within the hour their grave to make,
   Many to live, far in the heart of things.

A dark-dyed spirit he, who coins the time,
   To virtue's wrong, in base disloyal lies,
Who makes the morning's breath, the evening's tide,
   The utterer of his blighting forgeries.

How beautiful who scatters, wide and free,
   The gold-bright seeds of loved and loving truth!
By whose perpetual hand, each day supplied,
   Leaps to new life the empire's heart of youth.

To know the instant and to speak it true,
   Its passing lights of joy, its dark, sad cloud,
To fix upon the unnumbered gazer's view,
   Is to thy ready hand's broad strength allowed.

There is an inwrought life in every hour,
   Fit to be chronicled at large and told.
'Tis thine to pluck to light its secret power,
   And on the air its many-colored heart unfold.

The angel that in sand-dropped minutes lives,
    Demands a message cautious as the ages,
Who stuns, with dusk-red words of hate his ear,
    That mighty power to boundless wrath enrages.

This feeling of the dignity of his office, honor and power in fulfilling it, are not common in the journalist, but where they exist, a mark has been left fully correspondent to the weight of the instrument. The few editors of this country who with mental ability and resource have combined strength of purpose and fairness of conduct, who have never merged the man and the gentleman in the partisan, who have been willing to have all sides fully heard while their convictions were clear on one, who have disdained groundless assaults or angry replies, and have valued what was sincere, characteristic, and free too much to bend to popular errors they felt able to correct, have been so highly prized that it is wonderful that more do not learn the use of this great opportunity. It will be learned yet; the resources of this organ of thought and instruction begin to be understood, and shall yet be brought out and used worthily.

We see we have omitted honored names in this essay. We have not spoken of Brown, as a novelist by far our first in point of genius and instruction as to the soul of things. Yet his works have fallen almost out of print. It is their dark deep gloom that prevents their being popular, for their very beauties are grave and sad. But we see that *Ormond* is being republished at this moment. The picture of Roman character, of the life and resources of a single noble creature, of Constantia alone, should make that book an object of reverence. All these novels should be republished; if not favorites, they should at least not be lost sight of, for there will always be some who find in such powers of mental analysis the only response to their desires.

We have not spoken of Hawthorne, the best writer

of the day, in a similar range with Irving, only touching many more points and discerning far more deeply. But we have omitted many things in this slight sketch, for the subject even in this stage lies as a volume in our mind, and cannot be unrolled in completeness unless time and space were more abundant. Our object was to show that although by a thousand signs the existence is foreshown of those forces which are to animate an American literature, that faith, those hopes are not yet alive which shall usher it into a homogeneous or fully organized state of being. The future is glorious with certainties for those who do their duty in the present, and larklike, seeking the sun, challenge its eagles to an earthward flight, where their nests may be built in our mountains, and their young raise their cry of triumph unchecked by dullness in the echoes.

15. FAREWELL TO NEW YORK

(Text from the New York *Tribune*, August 1, 1846.)

[Horace Greeley agreed to give Margaret Fuller a "leave of absence" from the Tribune *on the condition that she act as a correspondent abroad for his paper. (As a result, Greeley got in the next three years the most superb reports from scenes of action that any American paper could then exhibit.)*

Margaret and the Springs sailed on the steamer Cambria, on August 1, 1846. On that day, by pre-arrangement with Greeley, her farewell to the city appeared in the Tribune. *It tells much, almost all, of what her experiences (including—although, of course, not mentioning directly —James Nathan) in New York had done for her. Duyckinck brought out a collection of her essays, Papers on Literature and Art, in October of 1846.]*

Farewell to New York city, where twenty months have presented me with a richer and more varied exercise for thought and life, than twenty years could in any other part of these United States.

It is the common remark about New York, that it has at least nothing petty or provincial in its methods and habits. The place is large enough: there is room enough, and occupation enough, for men to have no need or excuse for small cavils or scrutinies. A person who is independent, and knows what he wants, may lead his proper life here, unimpeded by others.

Vice and crime, if flagrant and frequent, are less thickly coated by hypocrisy than elsewhere. The air comes sometimes to the most infected subjects.

New York is the focus, the point where American and European interests converge. There is no topic of general interest to men, that will not betimes be brought before the thinker by the quick turning of the wheel.

Too quick that revolution,—some object. Life rushes wide and free, but *too fast.* Yet it is in the power of every one to avert from himself the evil that accompanies the good. He must build for his study, as did the German poet, a house beneath the bridge; and then all that passes above and by him will be heard and seen, but he will not be carried away with it.

Earlier views have been confirmed, and many new ones opened. On two great leadings, the superlative importance of promoting national education by heightening and deepening the cultivation of individual minds, and the part which is assigned to woman in the next stage of human progress in this country, where most important achievements are to be effected, I have received much encouragement, much instruction, and the fairest hopes of more.

On various subjects of minor importance, no less than these, I hope for good results, from observation, with my own eyes, of life in the old world, and to bring home some packages of seed for life in the new.

These words I address to my friends, for I feel that I have some. The degree of sympathetic response to the thoughts and suggestions I have offered, through the columns of the Tribune, has indeed surprised me, conscious as I am of a natural and acquired aloofness from many, if not the most popular tendencies of my time and place. It has greatly encouraged me, for none can sympathize with thoughts like mine, who are permanently insnared in the meshes of sect or party; none who prefer the formation and advancement of mere opinions to the free pursuit of truth. I see, surely, that the topmost bubble or sparkle of the cup is no voucher for the nature of its contents throughout, and shall, in future, feel that in our age, nobler in that respect than most of the preceding ages, each sincere and fervent act or word is secure, not only of a final, but of a speedy response.

I go to behold the wonders of art, and the temples of old religion. But I shall see no forms of beauty and majesty beyond what my country is capable of producing in myriad variety, if she has but the soul to will it; no temple to compare with what she might erect in the ages, if the catchword of the time, a sense of *divine order*, should become no more a mere word of form, but a deeply-rooted and pregnant idea in her life. Beneath the light of a hope that this may be, I say to my friends once more a kind farewell!

CHAPTER V

EUROPE, 1846–1850

1. POVERTY IN ENGLAND

(Text from the New York *Tribune*, letter dated from Paris, November 1846, and reprinted in *At Home and Abroad*, edited by Arthur B. Fuller, Boston, 1860, pp. 159–60, 170–71.)

[Margaret dutifully visited the landmarks of picturesque England, following in the footsteps of Washington Irving, and filled her first letters to the Tribune with conventional sightseeing. She investigated and described —as was expected—rural England; and she, of course, visited Wordsworth at Rydal Mount. But she managed, both in Glasgow and London, to deviate from the prescribed route and catch a glimpse of those areas in which the basic issues of European civilization would shortly be contested.

Margaret was to mail thirty-three dispatches to the Tribune, the last from Rome on July 6, 1849. In the records of American journalism, these communications deserve a greater accolade than historians have given them. They are among the first—and therefore tentative—efforts at reporting. A large amount of the text is thus of interest only historically, but several passages in the narrative still ring true and compel our attention today.]

. . . I understand there is an intellectual society of high merit in Glasgow, but we were there only a few hours,

and did not see any one. Certainly the place, as it may
be judged of merely from the general aspect of the population and such objects as may be seen in the streets, more
resembles an *Inferno* than any other we have yet visited.
The people are more crowded together, and the stamp of
squalid, stolid misery and degradation more obvious and
appalling. The English and Scotch do not take kindly to
poverty, like those of sunnier climes; it makes them fierce
or stupid, and, life presenting no other cheap pleasure,
they take refuge in drinking.

I saw here in Glasgow persons, especially women,
dressed in dirty, wretched tatters, worse than none, and
with an expression of listless, unexpecting woe upon their
faces, far more tragic than the inscription over the gate
of Dante's *Inferno*. To one species of misery suffered here
to the last extent, I shall advert in speaking of London.

But from all these sorrowful tokens I by no means
inferred the falsehood of the information, that here was
to be found a circle rich in intellect and in aspiration.
The manufacturing and commercial towns, burning fo-
cuses of grief and vice, are also the centres of intellectual
life, as in forcing-beds the rarest flowers and fruits are
developed by use of impure and repulsive materials.
Where evil comes to an extreme, Heaven seems busy in
providing means for the remedy. Glaring throughout Scotland and England is the necessity for the devoutest application of intellect and love to the cure of ills that cry
aloud, and, without such application, erelong help *must*
be sought by other means than words. Yet there is every
reason to hope that those who ought to help are seriously,
though slowly, becoming alive to the imperative nature
of this duty; so we must not cease to hope, even in the
streets of Glasgow, and the gin-palaces of Manchester,
and the dreariest recesses of London. . . .

The castle of Stirling is as rich as any place in romantic
associations. We were shown its dungeons and its Court
of Lions, where, says tradition, wild animals, kept in the

grated cells adjacent, were brought out on festival occasions to furnish entertainment for the court. So, while lords and ladies gay danced and sang above, prisoners pined and wild beasts starved below. This, at first blush, looks like a very barbarous state of things, but, on reflection, one does not find that we have outgrown it in our present so-called state of refined civilization, only the present way of expressing the same facts is a little different. Still lords and ladies dance and sing, unknowing or uncaring that the laborers who minister to their luxuries starve or are turned into wild beasts. Man need not boast his condition, methinks, till he can weave his costly tapestry without the side that is kept under looking thus sadly. . . .

To dwell first on London,—London, in itself a world. We arrived at a time which the well-bred Englishman considers as no time at all,—quite out of "the season," when Parliament is in session, and London thronged with the equipages of her aristocracy, her titled wealthy nobles. I was listened to with a smile of contempt when I declared that the stock shows of London would yield me amusement and employment more than sufficient for the time I had to stay. But I found that, with my way of viewing things, it would be to me an inexhaustible studio, and that, if life were only long enough, I would live there for years obscure in some corner, from which I could issue forth day by day to watch unobserved the vast stream of life, or to decipher the hieroglyphics which ages have been inscribing on the walls of this vast palace (I may not call it a temple), which human effort has reared for means, not yet used efficaciously, of human culture.

And though I wish to return to London in "the season," when that city is an adequate representative of the state of things in England, I am glad I did not at first see all that pomp and parade of wealth and luxury in contrast

with the misery, squalid, agonizing, ruffianly, which stares
one in the face in every street of London, and hoots at the
gates of her palaces more ominous a note than ever was
that of owl or raven in the portentous times when empires
and races have crumbled and fallen from inward decay.

It is impossible, however, to take a near view of the
treasures created by English genius, accumulated by English industry, without a prayer, daily more fervent, that
the needful changes in the condition of this people may
be effected by peaceful revolution, which shall destroy
nothing except the shocking inhumanity of exclusiveness,
which now prevents their being used for the benefit of all.
May their present possessors look to it in time! A few
already are earnest in a good spirit. For myself, much as
I pitied the poor, abandoned, hopeless wretches that
swarm in the roads and streets of England, I pity far more
the English noble, with this difficult problem before him,
and such need of a speedy solution. Sad is his life, if a
conscientious man; sadder still, if not. Poverty in England has terrors of which I never dreamed at home. I
felt that it would be terrible to be poor there, but far more
so to be the possessor of that for which so many thousands
are perishing. And the middle class, too, cannot here enjoy
that serenity which the sages have described as naturally
their peculiar blessing. Too close, too dark throng the evils
they cannot obviate, the sorrows they cannot relieve. To
a man of good heart, each day must bring purgatory which
he knows not how to bear, yet to which he fears to become insensible. . . .

2. CARLYLE

(Text from *Letter* VI to the *Tribune*, dated Paris, November 1846. Reprinted in *At Home and Abroad*, pp. 183–85.)

[Emerson had warned Carlyle in advance of Margaret's coming and had written him a description of her. The Carlyles invited Margaret to dinner twice. She gave Emerson a private report of these meetings, but her public account of them is of greater value as an example of Margaret Fuller's journalism.]

I have not yet spoken of one of *our* benefactors, Mr. Carlyle, whom I saw several times. I approached him with more reverence after a little experience of England and Scotland had taught me to appreciate the strength and height of that wall of shams and conventions which he more than any man, or thousand men,—indeed, he almost alone,—has begun to throw down. Wherever there was fresh thought, generous hope, the thought of Carlyle has begun the work. He has torn off the veils from hideous facts; he has burnt away foolish illusions; he has awakened thousands to know what it is to be a man,—that we must live, and not merely pretend to others that we live. He has touched the rocks and they have given forth musical answer; little more was wanting to begin to construct the city.

But that little was wanting, and the work of construction is left to those that come after him: nay, all attempts of the kind he is the readiest to deride, fearing new shams worse than the old, unable to trust the general action of a thought, and finding no heroic man, no natural king, to represent it and challenge his confidence.

Accustomed to the infinite wit and exuberant richness
of his writings, his talk is still an amazement and a splendor scarcely to be faced with steady eyes. He does not
converse,—only harangues. It is the usual misfortune of
such marked men (happily not one invariable or inevitable) that they cannot allow other minds room to breathe
and show themselves in their atmosphere, and thus miss
the refreshment and instruction which the greatest never
cease to need from the experience of the humblest. Carlyle allows no one a chance, but bears down all opposition,
not only by his wit and onset of words, resistless in their
sharpness as so many bayonets, but by actual physical
superiority, raising his voice and rushing on his opponent
with a torrent of sound. This is not the least from unwillingness to allow freedom to others; on the contrary,
no man would more enjoy a manly resistance to his
thought; but it is the impulse of a mind accustomed to
follow out its own impulse as the hawk its prey, and which
knows not how to stop in the chase. Carlyle, indeed, is
arrogant and overbearing, but in his arrogance there is
no littleness or self-love: it is the heroic arrogance of some
old Scandinavian conqueror,—it is his nature and the un-
tamable impulse that has given him power to crush the
dragons. You do not love him, perhaps, nor revere, and
perhaps, also, he would only laugh at you if you did;
but you like him heartily, and like to see him the powerful
smith, the Siegfried, melting all the old iron in his fur-
nace till it glows to a sunset red, and burns you if you
senselessly go too near. He seemed to me quite isolated,
lonely as the desert; yet never was man more fitted to
prize a man, could he find one to match his mood. He
finds such, but only in the past. He sings rather than
talks. He pours upon you a kind of satirical, heroical,
critical poem, with regular cadences, and generally catching up near the beginning some singular epithet, which
serves as a *refrain* when his song is full, or with which
as with a knitting-needle he catches up the stitches if

he has chanced now and then to let fall a row. For the higher kinds of poetry he has no sense, and his talk on that subject is delightfully and gorgeously absurd; he sometimes stops a minute to laugh at it himself, then begins anew with fresh vigor; for all the spirits he is driving before him seem to him as Fata Morganas, ugly masks, in fact, if he can but make them turn about, but he laughs that they seem to others such dainty Ariels. He puts out his chin sometimes till it looks like the beak of a bird, and his eyes flash bright instinctive meanings like Jove's bird; yet he is not calm and grand enough for the eagle: he is more like the falcon, and yet not of gentle blood enough for that either. He is not exactly like anything but himself, and therefore you cannot see him without the most hearty refreshment and good-will, for he is original, rich, and strong enough to afford a thousand faults; one expects some wild land in a rich kingdom. His talk, like his books, is full of pictures, his critical strokes masterly; allow for his point of view, and his survey is admirable. He is a large subject; I cannot speak more or wiselier of him now, nor needs it; his works are true, to blame and praise him, the Siegfried of England, great and powerful, if not quite invulnerable, and of a might rather to destroy evil than legislate for good. At all events, he seems to be what Destiny intended, and represents fully a certain side; so we make no remonstrance as to his being and proceeding for himself, though we sometimes must for us.

3. GEORGE SAND

(Text from a letter to Elizabeth Hoar, Paris, January 18, 1847; Fuller MSS, Harvard College Library. Inaccurately printed in *Memoirs*, II, 193–99.)

[As though it were not enough that Margaret Fuller affronted the prevalent American moral codes by admitting to an admiration for the licentious Madame de Staël, and then added insult to injury by defending Goethe's Elective Affinities, *she invited public censure by becoming almost the sole American advocate for George Sand. The majority of Americans had read nothing of George Sand's—although translations were available—any more than they had read de Staël and Goethe, but they were convinced that she was the worst of a bad lot, and that an American woman who spoke on her behalf must automatically be as depraved as she was.*

In Woman in the Nineteenth Century, *Margaret Fuller deliberately jeopardized her entire plea for female suffrage by citing George Sand's life as the triumphant example of female emancipation (cf. above, p. 160). In the* Tribune *for February 1, 1845, in a courageous essay on French novelists (all of them suspect in America—Balzac, Sue), Miss Fuller calmly mused about George Sand: "It is also known that she had not only broken the marriage-bond, and, since that, formed other connections, independent of the civil and ecclesiastical sanction."*

It must be listed to the credit of Horace Greeley that he let appear in an American newspaper, seeking circulation among American families, this justification of George Sand. As Margaret gently understated the case, "No facts are more adapted to startle every feeling of our com-

munity." Nevertheless, she insisted, some works of George Sand were circulating in America, even though surreptitiously, and so "it would be well they should be read intelligently."

Hence at last came this report to virginal Concord, addressed to Elizabeth Hoar, who had been engaged to marry Emerson's brother and kept her vow until death. Interestingly enough, from Rome on February 8, 1848, where Margaret's education was proceeding apace, she wrote to her brother Richard:

> I liked and loved M. Sand, but should not care particularly to know her more, now I have the true picture of her. She is a woman, who, except by her lovers, may be as known through her books as any other way.]

I went to see her at her house, Place d'Orleans. I found it a handsome modern residence. She had not answered my letter, written about a week before, and I felt a little anxious lest she should not receive me; for she is too much the mark of impertinent curiosity, as well as too busy, to be easily accessible to strangers. I am by no means timid, but I have suffered, for the first time in France, some of the torments of *mauvaise honte*, enough to see what they must be to many.

It is the custom to go and call on those to whom you must bring letters, and push yourself upon their notice; thus you must go quite ignorant whether they are disposed to be cordial. My name is always murdered by the foreign servants who announce me. I speak very bad French; only lately have I sufficient command of it to infuse some of my natural spirit in my discourse. This has been a great trial to me, who am eloquent and free in my own tongue, to be forced to feel my thoughts struggling in vain for utterance.

The servant who admitted me was in the picturesque

costume of a peasant, and, as Madame Sand afterward
told me, her god-daughter, whom she had brought from
her province. She announced me as *"Madame Salere,"*
and returned into the ante-room to tell me, *"Madame
says she does not know you."* I began to think I was
doomed to a rebuff, among the crowd who deserve it.
However, to make assurance sure, I said, "Ask if she has
not received a letter from me." As I spoke Madame S.
opened the door, and stood looking at me an instant.
Our eyes met. I never shall forget her look at that moment.
The doorway made a frame for her figure; she is large,
but well-formed. She was dressed in a robe of dark violet
silk, with a black mantle on her shoulders, her beautiful
hair dressed with the greatest taste, her whole appearance
and attitude, in its simple and lady-like dignity, presenting an almost ludicrous contrast to the vulgar carica-
ture idea of George Sand. Her face is a very little like
the portraits, but much finer; the upper part of the forehead and eyes are beautiful; the lower, strong and masculine, expressive of a hardy temperament and strong passions, but not in the least coarse; the complexion olive,
and the air of the whole head Spanish (as, indeed, she
was born at Madrid, and is only on one side of French
blood). All these details I saw at a glance; but what fixed
my attention was the expression of goodness, nobleness,
and power that pervaded the whole,—the truly human
heart and nature that shone in her eyes. As our eyes met,
she said, *"C'est vous,"* and held out her hand. I took it,
and went into her little study; we sat down a moment,
then I said, *"Il me fait de bien de vous voir,"* and I am
sure I said it with my whole heart, for it made me very
happy to see such a woman, so large and so developed
a character, and everything that *is* good in it so *really*
good. I loved, shall always love her.

She looked away, and said, *"Ah! vous m'avez écrit une
lettre charmante."* This was the preliminary of our talk,

which then went on as if we had always known one another. She told me, before I went away, that she was going that very day to write to me; that when the servant announced me she did not recognize the name, but after a minute it struck her that it might be *La dame Americaine*, as the foreigners very commonly call me, for they find my name hard to remember. She was very much pressed for time, as she was then preparing copy for the printer, and, having just returned, there were many applications to see her, but she wanted me to stay then, saying, "It is better to throw things aside, and seize the present moment." I staid a good part of the day, and was very glad afterwards, for I did not see her again uninterrupted. Another day I was there, and saw her in her circle. Her daughter and another lady were present, and a number of gentlemen. Her position there was of an intellectual woman and good friend,—the same as my own in the circle of my acquaintance as distinguished from my intimates. Her daughter is just about to be married. It is said, there is no congeniality between her and her mother; but for her son she seems to have much love, and he loves and admires her extremely. I understand he has a good and free character, without conspicuous talent.

Her way of talking is just like her writing,—lively, picturesque, with an undertone of deep feeling, and the same skill in striking the nail on the head every now and then with a blow.

We did not talk at all of personal or private matters. I saw, as one sees in her writings, the want of an independent, interior life, but I did not feel it as a fault, there is so much in her of her kind. I heartily enjoyed the sense of so rich, so prolific, so ardent a genius. I liked the woman in her, too, very much; I never liked a woman better.

For the rest I do not care to write about it much, for I cannot, in the room and time I have to spend, express my thoughts as I would; but as near as I can express the sum total, it is this. S——— and others who admire her are anxious to make a fancy picture of her, and represent her as a Helena (in the Seven Chords of the Lyre), all of whose mistakes are the fault of the present state of society. But to me the truth seems to be this. She has that purity in her soul, for she knows well how to love and prize its beauty; but she herself is quite another sort of person. She needs no defence, but only to be understood, for she has bravely acted out her nature, and always with good intentions. She might have loved one man permanently, if she could have found one contemporary with her who could interest and command her throughout her range; but there was hardly a possibility of that, for such a person. Thus she has naturally changed the objects of her affection, and several times. Also, there may have been something of the Bacchante in her life, and of the love of night and storm, and the free raptures amid which roamed on the mountain-tops the followers of Cybele, the great goddess, the great mother. But she was never coarse, never gross, and I am sure her generous heart has not failed to draw some rich drops from every kind of wine-press. When she has done with an intimacy, she likes to break it off suddenly, and this has happened often, both with men and women. Many calumnies upon her are traceable to this cause.

I forgot to mention, that, while talking, she *does* smoke all the time her little cigarette. This is now a common practice among ladies abroad, but I believe it originated with her.

For the rest, she holds her place in the literary and social world of France like a man, and seems full of energy and courage in it. I suppose she has suffered much, but she has also enjoyed and done much, and her expression is one of calmness and happiness. I was sorry to see her *exploitant* her talent so carelessly. She does too much, and this cannot last forever; but "Teverino" and "Mare au Diable," which she has lately published, are as original, as masterly in truth, and as free in invention, as anything she has done.

Afterwards I saw Chopin, not with her, although he lives with her, and has for the last twelve years. I went to see him in his room with one of his friends. He is always ill, and as frail as a snow-drop, but an exquisite genius. He played to me, and I liked his talking scarcely less. Madame S. loved Liszt before him; she has thus been intimate with the two opposite sides of the musical world. Mickiewicz says, "Chopin talks with spirit, and gives us the Ariel view of the universe. Liszt is the eloquent *tribune* to the world of men, a little vulgar and showy certainly, but I like the tribune best." It is said here, that Madame S. has long had only a friendship for Chopin, who, perhaps, on his side prefers to be a lover, and a jealous lover; but she does not leave him, because he needs her care so much, when sick and suffering. About all this, I do not know; you cannot know much about anything in France, except what you see with your two eyes. Lying is ingrained in *"la grande nation,"* as they so plainly show no less in literature than life.

4. NATURE AND ART

(Text from *Letter XI* to the *Tribune*; in *At Home and Abroad*, pp. 198–200, dated February 1847.)

[Just before Margaret and the Springs left Paris on February 25, 1847, Margaret gallantly attempted to summarize the heady effect upon her of the aesthetic debauch of that city. Her appreciation of Turner seems to be independent of Ruskin's, although she must at least

*have heard about Ruskin's thesis, since the first volume
of his* Modern Painters *was published in 1843 and the
second early in 1846.]*

The effort of the French school in Art, as also its main
tendency in literature, seems to be to turn the mind in-
side out, in the coarsest acceptation of such a phrase.
Art can only be truly Art by presenting an adequate outward symbol of some fact in the interior life. But then
it *is* a symbol that Art seeks to present, and not the fact
itself. These French painters seem to have no idea of this;
they have not studied the method of Nature. With the
true artist, as with Nature herself, the more full the representation, the more profound and enchanting is the
sense of mystery. We look and look, as on a flower of
which we cannot scrutinize the secret life, yet by looking
seem constantly drawn nearer to the soul that causes and
governs that life. But in the French pictures suffering is
represented by streams of blood,—wickedness by the most
ghastly contortions.

I saw a movement in the opposite direction in England;
it was in Turner's pictures of the later period. It is well
known that Turner, so long an idol of the English public,
paints now in a manner which has caused the liveliest
dissensions in the world of connoisseurs. There are two
parties, one of which maintains, not only that the pictures
of the late period are not good, but that they are not pictures at all,—that it is impossible to make out the design,
or find what Turner is aiming at by those strange blotches
of color. The other party declare that these pictures are
not only good, but divine,—that whoever looks upon them
in the true manner will not fail to find there somewhat
ineffably and transcendently admirable,—the soul of Art.
Books have been written to defend this side of the question.

I had become much interested about this matter, as
the fervor of feeling on either side seemed to denote that

there was something real and vital going on, and, while time would not permit my visiting other private collections in London and its neighborhood, I insisted on taking it for one of Turner's pictures. It was at the house of one of his devoutest disciples, who has arranged everything in the rooms to harmonize with them. There were a great many of the earlier period; these seemed to me charming, but superficial, views of Nature. They were of a character that he who runs may read,—obvious, simple, graceful. The later pictures were quite a different matter; mysterious-looking things,—hieroglyphics of picture, rather than picture itself. Sometimes you saw a range of red dots, which, after long looking, dawned on you as the roofs of houses,—shining streaks turned out to be most alluring rivulets, if traced with patience and a devout eye. Above all, they charmed the eye and the thought. Still, these pictures, it seems to me, cannot be considered fine works of Art, more than the mystical writing common to a certain class of minds in the United States can be called good writing. A great work of Art demands a great thought, or a thought of beauty adequately expressed. Neither in Art nor literature more than in life can an ordinary thought be made interesting because well dressed. But in a transition state, whether of Art or literature, deeper thoughts are imperfectly expressed, because they cannot yet be held and treated masterly. This seems to be the case with Turner. He has got beyond the English gentleman's conventional view of Nature, which implies a *little* sentiment and a *very* cultivated taste; he has become awake to what is elemental, normal, in Nature,— such, for instance, as one sees in the working of water on the sea-shore. He tries to represent these primitive forms. In the drawings of Piranesi, in the pictures of Rembrandt, one sees this grand language exhibited more truly. It is not picture, but certain primitive and leading effects of light and shadow, or lines and contours, that captivate the attention. I saw a picture of Rembrandt's at the Louvre, whose subject I do not know and have never cared to inquire. I cannot analyze the group, but I understand and feel the thought it embodies. At something similar Turner seems aiming; an aim so opposed to the practical and outward tendency of the English mind, that, as a matter of course, the majority find themselves mystified, and thereby angered, but for the same reason answering to so deep and seldom satisfied a want in the minds of the minority, as to secure the most ardent sympathy where any at all can be elicited.

5. ROUSSEAU

(Text from *Letter XII* to the *Tribune*; in *At Home and Abroad*, p. 207; dated March 1847.)

[From Italy, while greedily gathering a host of new impressions, Margaret did her duty for Horace Greeley by summarizing her last experiences in Paris. Jean Jacques Rousseau was as regularly denounced by righteous Americans as were Goethe, Madame de Staël, and George Sand. Margaret Fuller made her record of dissent from this righteousness complete by publicly saluting him as the begetter of the Romantic spirit.]

To the actually so-called Chamber of Deputies I was indebted for two pleasures. First and greatest, a sight of the manuscripts of Rousseau treasured in their Library. I saw them and touched them,—those manuscripts just as he has celebrated them, written on the fine white paper, tied with ribbon. Yellow and faded age has made them, yet at their touch I seemed to feel the fire of youth, immortally glowing, more and more expansive, with which his soul has pervaded this century. He was the precursor of all we most prize. True, his blood was mixed with madness, and the course of his actual life made some detours through villainous places, but his spirit was intimate with the fundamental truths of human nature, and fraught with prophecy. There is none who has given birth to more life for this age; his gifts are yet untold; they are too present with us; but he who thinks really must often think with Rousseau, and learn of him even more and more: such is the method of genius, to ripen fruit for the crowd of those rays of whose heat they complain.

6. AMERICANS IN EUROPE

(Text from *Letter XVIII* to the *Tribune; in At Home and Abroad,* pp. 250–56, dated November 1847.)

[Margaret and the Springs arrived in Rome in April 1847. Pope Pius IX had promised "reforms," and Margaret felt the people respond with "childlike joy and trust." Then and there, her commitment to the Revolution was made. (It might have been made earlier; she had met Mazzini in London and at once recognized a kindred being.)

In June, she and the Springs went north to Florence and then to Venice, where she fell ill. The Springs had to return to America, but they left her in competent medical hands. She returned to Rome, a dedicated liberal in the grand European tradition, a sworn foe of the Austrian regime in Italy. She believed that any citizen of a democracy, traveling in Europe, must respond to the thrust of revolutionary democracy—a conviction that I should like to believe is shared by all her modern readers.

On October 16th, Margaret wrote her mother that "The Italians sympathize with my character and understand my organization, as no other people ever did; they admire the ready eloquence of my nature, and highly prize my intelligent sympathy (such as they do not often find in foreigners) with their suffering in the past and hopes for the future. . . . My mind made a vast stride in these three months, and my perception of beauty was all the keener for the sickly nervous state I was in."

On October 18th, she sealed her seventeenth Letter to the Tribune, summoning liberal America (which proved completely unresponsive) to some expression, however slight, in support of insurgent Italy. The next month, greatly disillusioned, she made these mordant and astonishingly Jamesian observations on the behavior of Americans in Europe.]

The American in Europe, if a thinking mind, can only become more American. In some respects it is a great pleasure to be here. Although we have an independent political existence, our position toward Europe, as to literature and the arts, is still that of a colony, and one feels the same joy here that is experienced by the colonist in returning to the parent home. What was but picture to us becomes reality; remote allusions and derivations trouble no more: we see the pattern of the stuff, and understand the whole tapestry. There is a gradual clearing up on many points, and many baseless notions and crude fancies are dropped. Even the post-haste passage of the business American through the great cities, escorted by cheating couriers and ignorant *valets de place*, unable to hold intercourse with the natives of the country, and passing all his leisure hours with his countrymen, who know no more than himself, clears his mind of some mistakes,— lifts some mists from his horizon.

There are three species. First, the servile American,— a being utterly shallow, thoughtless, worthless. He comes abroad to spend his money and indulge his tastes. His object in Europe is to have fashionable clothes, good foreign cookery, to know some titled persons, and furnish himself with coffee-house gossip, by retailing which among those less travelled and as uninformed as himself he can win importance at home. I look with unspeakable contempt on this class,—a class which has all the thoughtlessness and partiality of the exclusive classes in Europe, without any of their refinement, or the chivalric feeling which still sparkles among them here and there. However, though these willing serfs in a free age do some little hurt, and cause some annoyance at present, they cannot continue long; our country is fated to a grand, independent existence, and, as its laws develop, these parasites of a bygone period must wither and drop away.

Then there is the conceited American, instinctively bristling and proud of—he knows not what. He does not see, not he, that the history of Humanity for many centuries is likely to have produced results it requires some training, some devotion, to appreciate and profit by. With his great clumsy hands, only fitted to work on a steam-engine, he seizes the old Cremona violin, makes it shriek with anguish in his grasp, and then declares he thought it was all humbug before he came, and now he knows it; that there is not really any music in these old things; that the frogs in one of our swamps make much finer, for they are young and alive. To him the etiquettes of courts and camps, the ritual of the Church, seem simply silly,—and no wonder, profoundly ignorant as he is of their origin and meaning. Just so the legends which are the subjects of pictures, the profound myths which are represented in the antique marbles, amaze and revolt him; as, indeed, such things need to be judged of by another standard than that of the Connecticut Blue-Laws. He criticises severely pictures, feeling quite sure that his natural senses are better means of judgment than the rules of connoisseurs,—not feeling that, to see such objects, mental vision as well as fleshly eyes are needed, and that something is aimed at in Art beyond the imitation of the commonest forms of Nature. This is Jonathan in the sprawling state, the booby truant, not yet aspiring enough to be a good schoolboy. Yet in his folly there is meaning; add thought and culture to his independence, and he will be a man of might: he is not a creature without hope, like the thick-skinned dandy of the class first specified.

The artistes form a class by themselves. Yet among them, though seeking special aims by special means, may also be found the lineaments of these two classes, as well as of the third, of which I am now to speak.

This is that of the thinking American,—a man who, recognizing the immense advantage of being born to a new world and on a virgin soil, yet does not wish one seed from the past to be lost. He is anxious to gather and carry back with him every plant that will bear a new climate and new culture. Some will dwindle; others will attain a bloom and stature unknown before. He wishes to gather them clean, free from noxious insects, and to give them a fair trial in his new world. And that he may know the conditions under which he may best place them in that new world, he does not neglect to study their history in this.

The history of our planet in some moments seems so painfully mean and little,—such terrible bafflings and failures to compensate some brilliant successes,—such a crushing of the mass of men beneath the feet of a few, and these, too, often the least worthy,—such a small drop of honey to each cup of gall, and, in many cases, so mingled that it is never one moment in life purely tasted,—above all, so little achieved for Humanity as a whole, such tides of war and pestilence intervening to blot out the traces of each triumph,—that no wonder if the strongest soul sometimes pauses aghast; no wonder if the many indolently console themselves with gross joys and frivolous prizes. Yes! those men *are* worthy of admiration who can carry this cross faithfully through fifty years; it is a great while for all the agonies that beset a lover of good, a lover of men; it makes a soul worthy of a speedier ascent, a more productive ministry in the next sphere. Blessed are

they who ever keep that portion of pure, generous love
with which they began life! How blessed those who have
deepened the fountains, and have enough to spare for
the thirst of others! Some such there are; and, feeling that,
with all the excuses for failure, still only the sight of
those who triumph gives a meaning to life or makes its
pangs endurable, we must arise and follow.

Eighteen hundred years of this Christian culture in
these European kingdoms, a great theme never lost sight
of, a mighty idea, an adorable history to which the hearts
of men invariably cling, yet are genuine results rare as
grains of gold in the river's sandy bed! Where is the genuine democracy to which the rights of all men are holy?
where the child-like wisdom learning all through life more
and more of the will of God? where the aversion to falsehood, in all its myriad disguises of cant, vanity, covetousness, so clear to be read in all the history of Jesus of
Nazareth? Modern Europe is the sequel to that history,
and see this hollow England, with its monstrous wealth
and cruel poverty, its conventional life, and low, practical
aims! see this poor France, so full of talent, so adroit, yet
so shallow and glossy still, which could not escape from
a false position with all its baptism of blood! see that
lost Poland, and this Italy bound down by treacherous
hands in all the force of genius! see Russia with its brutal
Czar and innumerable slaves! see Austria and its royalty
that represents nothing, and its people, who, as people,
are and have nothing! If we consider the amount of truth
that has really been spoken out in the world, and the
love that has beat in private hearts,—how genius has
decked each spring-time with such splendid flowers, con-
veying each one enough of instruction in its life of harmonious energy, and how continually, unquenchably, the
spark of faith has striven to burst into flame and light
up the universe,—the public failure seems amazing, seems
monstrous.

Still Europe toils and struggles with her idea, and, at

this moment, all things bode and declare a new outbreak of the fire, to destroy old palaces of crime! May it fertilize also many vineyards! Here at this moment a successor of St. Peter, after the lapse of near two thousand years, is called "Utopian" by a part of this Europe, because he strives to get some food to the mouths of the *leaner* of his flock. A wonderful state of things, and which leaves as the best argument against despair, that men do not, *cannot* despair amid such dark experiences. And thou, my Country! wilt thou not be more true? does no greater success await thee? All things have so conspired to teach, to aid! A new world, a new chance, with oceans to wall in the new thought against interference from the old!— treasures of all kinds, gold, silver, corn, marble, to provide for every physical need! A noble, constant, starlike soul, an Italian, led the way to thy shores, and, in the first days, the strong, the pure, those too brave, too sincere, for the life of the Old World, hastened to people them. A generous struggle then shook off what was foreign, and gave the nation a glorious start for a worthy goal. Men rocked the cradle of its hopes, great, firm, disinterested men, who saw, who wrote, as the basis of all that was to be done, a statement of the rights, the *inborn* rights of men, which, if fully interpreted and acted upon, leaves nothing to be desired.

Yet, O Eagle! whose early flight showed this clear sight of the sun, how often dost thou near the ground, how show the vulture in these later days! Thou wert to be the advance-guard of humanity, the herald of all progress; how often hast thou betrayed this high commission! Fain would the tongue in clear, triumphant accents draw example from thy story, to encourage the hearts of those who almost faint and die beneath the old oppressions. But we must stammer and blush when we speak of many things. I take pride here, that I can really say the liberty of the press works well, and that checks and balances are found naturally which suffice to its government. I can say

that the minds of our people are alert, and that talent
has a free chance to rise. This is much. But dare I further
say that political ambition is not as darkly sullied as in
other countries? Dare I say that men of most influence
in political life are those who represent most virtue, or
even intellectual power? Is it easy to find names in that
career of which I can speak with enthusiasm? Must I not
confess to a boundless lust of gain in my country? Must
I not concede the weakest vanity, which bristles and blus-
ters at each foolish taunt of the foreign press, and admit
that the men who make these undignified rejoinders seek
and find popularity so? Can I help admitting that there
is as yet no antidote cordially adopted, which will defend
even that great, rich country against the evils that have
grown out of the commercial system in the Old World?
Can I say our social laws are generally better, or show
a nobler insight into the wants of man and woman? I do,
indeed, say what I believe, that voluntary association for
improvement in these particulars will be the grand means
for my nation to grow, and give a nobler harmony to the
coming age. But it is only of a small minority that I can
say they as yet seriously take to heart these things; that
they earnestly meditate on what is wanted for their country, for mankind,—for our cause is indeed the cause of all
mankind at present. Could we succeed, really succeed,
combine a deep religious love with practical development,
the achievements of genius with the happiness of the multitude, we might believe man had now reached a commanding point in his ascent, and would stumble and faint
no more. Then there is this horrible cancer of slavery, and
the wicked war that has grown out of it. How dare I speak
of these things here? I listen to the same arguments
against the emancipation of Italy, that are used against
the emancipation of our blacks; the same arguments in
favor of the spoliation of Poland, as for the conquest of
Mexico. I find the cause of tyranny and wrong everywhere

the same,—and lo! my country! the darkest offender, because with the least excuse; forsworn to the high calling with which she was called; no champion of the rights of men, but a robber and a jailer; the scourge hid behind her banner; her eyes fixed, not on the stars, but on the possessions of other men.

How it pleases me here to think of the Abolitionists! I could never endure to be with them at home, they were so tedious, often so narrow, always so rabid and exaggerated in their tone. But, after all, they had a high motive, something eternal in their desire and life; and if it was not the only thing worth thinking of, it was really something worth living and dying for, to free a great nation from such a terrible blot, such a threatening plague. God strengthen them, and make them wise to achieve their purpose!

I please myself, too, with remembering some ardent souls among the American youth, who I trust will yet expand, and help to give soul to the huge, over-fed, too hastily grown-up body. May they be constant! "Were man but constant, he were perfect," it has been said; and it is true that he who could be constant to those moments in which he has been truly human, not brutal, not mechanical, is on the sure path to his perfection, and to effectual service of the universe.

It is to the youth that hope addresses itself; to those who yet burn with aspiration, who are not hardened in their sins. But I dare not expect too much of them. I am not very old; yet of those who, in life's morning, I saw touched by the light of a high hope, many have seceded. Some have become voluptuaries; some, mere family men, who think it quite life enough to win bread for half a dozen people, and treat them decently; others are lost through indolence and vacillation. Yet some remain constant;

> "I have witnessed many a shipwreck,
>   Yet still beat noble hearts."

I have found many among the youth of England, of France, of Italy, also, full of high desire; but will they have courage and purity to fight the battle through in the sacred, the immortal band? Of some of them I believe it, and await the proof. If a few succeed amid the trial, we have not lived and loved in vain.

To these, the heart and hope of my country, a happy new year! I do not know what I have written; I have merely yielded to my feelings in thinking of America; but something of true love must be in these lines. Receive them kindly, my friends; it is, of itself, some merit for printed words to be sincere.

7. TO RALPH WALDO EMERSON,
December 20, 1847

(Text from *Memoirs*, II, 224–25; the original seems not to have survived, and one may question whether this is an entirely accurate transcription.)

[By this December, Margaret Fuller, now the impassioned follower of Mazzini and, presumably, the mistress of the Marquis Giovanni Angelo Ossoli, was light-years away from Concord, Massachusetts. Yet she still sought out Emerson to share her pensive movements.]

. . . Nothing less than two or three years, free from care and forced labor, would heal all my hurts, and renew my life-blood at its source. Since Destiny will not grant me that, I hope she will not leave me long in the world, for I am tired of keeping myself up in the water without corks, and without strength to swim. I should like to go to sleep, and be born again into a state where my young life should not be prematurely taxed.

Italy has been glorious to me, and there have been hours in which I received the full benefit of the vision. In Rome, I have known some blessed, quiet days, when I could yield myself to be soothed and instructed by the great thoughts and memories of the place. But those days are swiftly passing. Soon I must begin to exert myself, for there is this incubus of the future, and none to help me, if I am not prudent to face it. So ridiculous, too, this mortal coil, —such small things!

I find how true was the lure that always drew me towards Europe. It was no false instinct that said I might here find an atmosphere to develop me in ways I need. Had I only come ten years earlier! Now my life must be a failure, so much strength has been wasted on abstractions, which only came because I grew not in the right soil. However, it is a less failure than with most others, and not worth thinking twice about. Heaven has room enough, and good chances in store, and I can live a great deal in the years that remain . . .

8. THE REVOLUTION, March and April, 1848

(Text from *Letter XXIII* to the *Tribune*, March 29, 1848; and from *Letter XXIV*, April 19, 1848; in *At Home and Abroad*, pp. 301–27.)

[Through the winter and spring of 1847–48, Margaret Fuller kept the Tribune *informed of the rapid history of the Roman Revolution. Although her accounts are highly emotional, they are extremely vivid reports. (However, because they are so minutely concerned with daily events, they are not very quotable historically.) As news of the French uprising reached her on March 29th, she saw—as few Americans could see—the inner connection of all the*

*revolutionary movements of that tragic year. On April
19th, she realized the depth of her own commitment.]*

. . . The news of the dethronement of Louis Philippe
reached us just after the close of the Carnival. It was just
a year from my leaving Paris. I did not think, as I looked
with such disgust on the empire of sham he had established in France, and saw the soul of the people imprisoned and held fast as in an iron vice, that it would burst
its chains so soon. Whatever be the result, France has
done gloriously; she has declared that she will not be satisfied with pretexts while there are facts in the world,—
that to stop her march is a vain attempt, though the on-
ward path be dangerous and difficult. It is vain to cry,
Peace! peace! when there is no peace. The news from
France, in these days, sounds ominous, though still vague.
It would appear that the political is being merged in the
social struggle: it is well. Whatever blood is to be shed,
whatever altars cast down, those tremendous problems
MUST be solved, whatever be the cost! That cost cannot
fail to break many a bank, many a heart, in Europe, before the good can bud again out of a mighty corruption.
To you, people of America, it may perhaps be given to
look on and learn in time for a preventive wisdom. You
may learn the real meaning of the words FRATERNITY,
EQUALITY: you may, despite the apes of the past who
strive to tutor you, learn the needs of a true democracy.
You may in time learn to reverence, learn to guard, the
true aristocracy of a nation, the only really nobles,—the
LABORING CLASSES. . . .

. . . Hoping this era, I remain at present here. Should
my hopes be dashed to the ground, it will not change my
faith, but the struggle for its manifestation is to me of
vital interest. My friends write to urge my return; they
talk of our country as the land of the future. It is so, but
that spirit which made it all it is of value in my eyes, which

gave all of hope with which I can sympathize for that
future, is more alive here at present than in America. My
country is at present spoiled by prosperity, stupid with
the lust of gain, soiled by crime in its willing perpetuation
of slavery, shamed by an unjust war, noble sentiment much
forgotten even by individuals, the aims of politicians selfish or petty, the literature frivolous and venal. In Europe,
amid the teachings of adversity, a nobler spirit is struggling,—a spirit which cheers and animates mine. I hear
earnest words of pure faith and love. I see deeds of brotherhood. This is what makes *my* America. I do not deeply
distrust my country. She is not dead, but in my time she
sleepeth, and the spirit of our fathers flames no more,
but lies hid beneath the ashes. It will not be so long;
bodies cannot live when the soul gets too overgrown with
gluttony and falsehood. But it is not the making a President out of the Mexican war that would make me wish to
come back. Here things are before my eyes worth recording, and, if I cannot help this work, I would gladly be its
historian. . . .

9. TO RICHARD F. FULLER, February 23, 1849

(Text from the Fuller MSS, Harvard College Library.)

[*In April of 1848, Margaret Fuller became aware that
she had committed herself to more than the Revolution:
she was pregnant.*

*On May 20th she wrote her brother Richard that she
was going into the mountains in order to live cheaply. "I
do not travel this summer, though I have rec'ed several
good invitations, for several reasons, a sufficient one is
the agitated state of Europe." What excuse, if any, she
made to Greeley we do not know. Her next Letter to the
paper was not until December 2nd, and it does not inform*

her public that a son was born to her in Rieti on Septem-
ber 5, 1848.

The twenty-sixth Letter *to the* Tribune, *also dated De-*
cember 2nd, concludes with a Happy New Year's greeting
to America—"may she be worthy of the privileges she pos-
sesses, while others are lavishing their blood to win them."
The next public Letter, *February 20, 1849, barely hints*
at her own activities in the Revolution. All this time she
lived in an agony of apprehension about her child. On
February 23rd she again wrote her brother from Rome,
maintaining at all costs her frantic masquerade.]

. . . The life of the soul is incalculable.

It is something if one can get free foot hold on the
earth, so as not to be jostled out of hearing the music, if
there should be any spirits in the air to make such.

For my part, I have led rather too lonely a life of late.
Before, it seemed as if too many voices of men startled
away inspirations; but having now lived eight months
alone, I doubt that any great good has come of it, and
think to return and herd with others for a little. I have
realized in these last days the thought of Goethe,—"He
who would in loneliness live, ah! he is soon alone. Each
one loves, each one lives, and leaves him to his pain."

I went away and hid, all summer. Not content with
that, I said, on returning to Rome, I must be busy and
receive people [a] little. They have taken me at my word,
and hardly any one comes to see me. Now, if I want some
play and prattle, I shall have to run after them. It is fair
enough that we all, in turn, should be made to feel our
need of one another.

Never was such a winter as this. Ten weeks now of unbroken sunshine and the mildest breezes. Of course, its
price is to be paid. The spring, usually divine here, with
luxuriant foliage and multitudinous roses, will be all
scorched and dusty. There is fear, too, of want of food
for the poor Roman state.

I pass my days in writing, walking, occasional visits to the galleries. I read little, except the newspapers; these take up an hour or two of the day. I am ardently interested in the present struggles of the nations. I have my thoughts fixed daily on the bulletin of men and things. I expect to write the history, but because it is so much in my heart. If you were here, I rather think you would be impassive, like the two most esteemed Americans I see. They do not believe in the sentimental nations. Hungarians, Poles, Italians, are too demonstrative for them, too fiery, too impressible. They like better the loyal, slow-moving Germans; even the Russian with his dog's nose and gentlemanly servility, pleases them better than *my* people. There is an antagonism of race.

10. TO CAROLINE STURGIS TAPPAN,
March 16, 1849

(Text from the Fuller MSS, Harvard College Library.)

[The date on the manuscript of this letter is clearly March 16th. The Memoirs *do not date the letter in which Margaret informed her mother of her "marriage" and the birth of her child (II, 273). The original of that is lost, but it seems Margaret wrote to Caroline about her new son before she told her family. In her Letter XXIX to the* Tribune, *dated March 20, 1849, she conceals her activity in the Revolution and her consuming anxiety about her child behind a solemn critique of American landscape painting!]*

. . . My baby saw mountains when he first looked forward into the world. Rieti, not only an old classic town of Italy, but one founded by what are now called the aborigines, is a hive of very ancient dwellings with soft red brown

roofs, a citadel and several towers. It is in a plain, twelve
miles in diameter one way, not much less the other, entirely encircled with mountains of the noblest form.
Casinos and hermitages gleam here and there on their
lower slopes. The plain is almost the richest in Italy and
full of vineyards. Rieti is near the foot of the hills on one
side, the rapid Velino makes almost the circuit of its walls,
on its way to Terni. I too had my apartment, shut out
from the family on the bank of this river. I too saw the
mountains, as I lay on my restless couch. I had a piazza,
or as they call it here loggia, which hung over the river,
where I walked most of the night, for I was not like you,
I could not sleep at all those months. I do not know how
I lived.

In Rieti, the ancient Umbrians were married thus. In
the presence of friends, the man and maid received together the gifts of fire and water; the bridegroom then
conducted to his house the bride. At the door, he gave
her the keys, and entering threw behind him nuts as a
sign that he renounced all the frivolities of boyhood.

But I intend to write all that relates to the birth of
Angelino in a little book, which I shall, I hope, show you
sometime. I have begun it and then stopped; it seemed
to me he would die. If he lives, I shall finish it, before
the details are at all faded in my mind. Rieti is a place
where I should have liked to have him born, and where I
should like to have him now, but that the people are so
wicked, the most ferocious and mercenary population of
Italy. I did not know this, when I went there, and expected to be solitary and quiet among poor people. But
they looked on *the Marchioness* as an ignorant *Inglese*,
and they fancy all *Inglesi* have wealth untold. Me they
were bent on plundering in every way. They are so still.
They made me suffer terribly in the first days and disturb
me greatly still in visits to my darling. To add to my
trouble, the legion Garibaldi is now stationed there, in
which so many desperadoes are enlisted. The Neapolitan

troops 6 miles off are far worse, and in case of conflict I should fear for the nurse of Angelino, the loveliest young woman there. I cannot take her from her family, I cannot change him to another place without immense difficulty in every way. That I could not nurse him was owing to the wickedness of these people, who threw me into a fever the first days. I shall tell you about it sometime. There is something very singular and fateful in the way all has wrought to give me more and more sorrow and difficulty. Now I live from day to day watching the signs of the times: when I asked you for the money I meant to use it to stay with him in Rieti, but now I do not know whether I can stay there or not. If it proves impossible, I shall at all risks, remove him. I may say every day is to me one of mental doubt and conflict: how it will end, I do not know. I try to hold myself ready every way body and mind for any necessity.

You say no secret can be kept in the civilized world and suppose not long, but it is very important to me to keep this, for the present, if possible, and by and by to have the mode of disclosure at my option. For this I have made the cruellest sacrifices: it will, indeed, be just like the rest, if they are made of none effect.

After I wrote you I went to Rieti. The weather was mild when I set out, but the fatality that has attended me throughout, the night changed to a cold, unknown in Italy and remained so all the time I staid. There was, as is common in Italy, no fire-place except in the kitchen. I suffered much in my room with its brick floor, and windows through which came the cold wind freely. My darling did not suffer, because he was a little swaddled child like this* and robed in wool beside, but I did very much. When I first took him in my arms he made no sound but leaned his head against my bosom, and staid so, he seemed

* Margaret Fuller here pasted on the letter a cheap engraving of the Christ-child heavily swaddled; it is still affixed to the manuscript.

to say how could you abandon me. What I felt you will
know only when you have your own. A little girl who lived
in the house told me all the day of my departure he
would not be comforted, always refusing the breast and
looking at the door; he has been a strangely precocious
infant; I think it was through sympathy with me, and
that in that regard it may be a happiness for him to be
with these more plebeian, instinctive, joyous natures. I saw
he was more serene, that he was not sensitive as when
with me, and slept a great deal more. You speak of my
being happy, all the solid happiness I have known has
been at times when he went to sleep in my arms. You
say when Ellen's beautiful life had been so wasted, it
hardly seemed worth while to begin another. I had all
those feelings too. I do not look forward to his career and
his manly life: it is *now* I want to be with him, before
prescience ends and bafflings begin. If I had a little money
I should go with him into strict retirement for a year or
two and live for him alone. This I cannot do: all life
that has been or could be natural to me is invariably
denied. God knows why, I suppose.

I receive with profound gratitude your thought of taking him, if any thing should happen to us. Should I live,
I don't know whether I should wish him to be an Italian
or American citizen; it depends on the course events take
here politically, but should we die, the person to whom
he would naturally fall is a sister of his father, a person of
great elegance and sweetness but entirely limited in mind.
I should not like that. I shall think about it. Before he
was born I did a great deal, having the idea I might die
and all my spirit remain incarnated in him, but now I
think I shall live and carry him round myself, as I ride
on my ass into Egypt.

You talk about your mangers, Carrie, but that was only
for a little, presently came kings with gold cups and all
sorts of things. Joseph pawned them; with part of the

money he bought this nice donkey for the journey; and
they lived on the rest till Joseph could work at his trade.
We have no donkey and it costs a great deal to travel in
diligences and steamers, and being a nobleman is a poor
trade in a ruined despotism just turning into a Republic.
I often think of Dickens's marchioness playing whist in
the kitchen. So I play whist every where. . . .*

11. THE AGONY OF THE REVOLUTION

(Text from *Letter XXX* to the *Tribune*; in *At Home
and Abroad*, pp. 380–89; dated May 27, 1849.)

*[When she wrote this Letter, Margaret Fuller was serv-
ing as a nurse in the hospital Fate Bene Fratelli. She
beheld, as Whitman was later to do in the hospitals of
Washington, the physical horrors of war.*

*There were to be only three more of these Letters. The
last one, on June 6th, pleaded for America to do something—anything—to help insurgent Hungary and Italy. As
history records, America did nothing.]*

. . . The struggle is now fairly, thoroughly commenced
between the principle of democracy and the old powers,
no longer legitimate. That struggle may last fifty years,
and the earth be watered with the blood and tears of
more than one generation, but the result is sure. All Europe, including Great Britain, where the most bitter re-

* Margaret Fuller refers to a scene in *The Old Curiosity Shop*
in which Charles Dickens (in 1841) has Dick Swiveller promote
the "small servant" into a "Marchioness" (Chapter LVII). Even
in this intimate correspondence, Margaret was yearning for sympathy. The full irony can be appreciated only when we remind
ourselves that in all sincerity she thought she was now legiti-
mately entitled to the distinction.

sistance of all will be made, is to be under republican government in the next century.

"God moves in a mysterious way."

Every struggle made by the old tyrannies, all their Jesuitical deceptions, their rapacity, their imprisonments and executions of the most generous men, only sow more dragon's teeth; the crop shoots up daily more and more plenteous.

When I first arrived in Italy, the vast majority of this people had no wish beyond limited monarchies, constitutional governments. They still respected the famous names of the nobility; they despised the priests, but were still fondly attached to the dogmas and ritual of the Roman Catholic Church. It required King Bomba, the triple treachery of Charles Albert, Pius IX., and the "illustrious Gioberti," the naturally kind-hearted, but, from the necessity of his position, cowardly and false Leopold of Tuscany, the vagabond "serene" meannesses of Parma and Modena, the "fatherly" Radetzsky, and, finally, the imbecile Louis Bonaparte, "would-be Emperor of France," to convince this people that no transition is possible between the old and the new. *The work is done*; the revolution in Italy is now radical, nor can it stop till Italy becomes independent and united as a republic. Protestant she already is, and though the memory of saints and martyrs may continue to be revered, the ideal of woman to be adored under the name of Mary, yet Christ will now begin to be a little thought of; *his* idea has always been kept carefully out of sight under the old *régime*; all the worship being for the Madonna and saints, who were to be well paid for interceding for sinners;—an example which might make men cease to be such, was no way coveted. Now the New Testament has been translated into Italian; copies are already dispersed far and wide; men calling themselves Christians will no longer be left entirely ignorant of the precepts and life of Jesus.

The people of Rome have burnt the Cardinals' carriages. They took the confessionals out of the churches, and made mock confessions in the piazzas, the scope of which was, "I have sinned, father, so and so." "Well, my son, how much will you *pay* to the Church for absolution?" Afterward the people thought of burning the confessionals, or using them for barricades; but at the request of the Triumvirate they desisted, and even put them back into the churches. But it was from no reaction of feeling that they stopped short, only from respect for the government. The "Tartufte" of Molière has been translated into Italian, and was last night performed with great applause at the Valle. Can all this be forgotten? Never! Should guns and bayonets replace the Pope on the throne, he will find its foundations, once deep as modern civilization, now so undermined that it falls with the least awkward movement.

But I cannot believe he will be replaced there. France alone could consummate that crime,—that, for her, most cruel, most infamous treason. The elections in France will decide. In three or four days we shall know whether the French nation at large be guilty or no,—whether it be the will of the nation to aid or strive to ruin a government founded on precisely the same basis as their own.

I do not dare to trust that people. The peasant is yet very ignorant. The suffering workman is frightened as he thinks of the punishments that ensued on the insurrections of May and June. The man of property is full of horror at the brotherly scope of Socialism. The aristocrat dreams of the guillotine always when he hears men speak of the people. The influence of the Jesuits is still immense in France. Both in France and England the grossest falsehoods have been circulated with unwearied diligence about the state of things in Italy. An amusing specimen of what is still done in this line I find just now in a foreign journal, where it says there are red flags on all the houses of Rome; meaning to imply that the Romans are athirst for blood. Now, the fact is, that these flags are put up at the entrance of those streets where there is no barricade, as a signal to coachmen and horsemen that they can pass freely. There is one on the house where I am, in which is no person but myself, who thirst for peace, and the Padrone, who thirsts for money.

Meanwhile the French troops are encamped at a little distance from Rome. Some attempts at fair and equal treaty when their desire to occupy Rome was firmly resisted, Oudinot describes in his despatches as a readiness for *submission*. Having tried in vain to gain this point, he has sent to France for fresh orders. These will be decided by the turn the election takes. Meanwhile the French troops are much exposed to the Roman force where they are. Should the Austrians come up, what will they do? Will they shamelessly fraternize with the French, after pretending and proclaiming that they came here as a check upon their aggressions? Will they oppose them in defence of Rome, with which they are at war?

Ah! the way of falsehood, the way of treachery,—how dark, how full of pitfalls and traps! Heaven defend from it all who are not yet engaged therein!

War near at hand seems to me even more dreadful than I had fancied it. True, it tries men's souls, lays bare selfishness in undeniable deformity. Here it has produced much fruit of noble sentiment, noble act; but still it breeds vice too, drunkenness, mental dissipation, tears asunder the tenderest ties, lavishes the productions of Earth, for which her starving poor stretch out their hands in vain, in the most unprofitable manner. And the ruin that ensues, how terrible! Let those who have ever passed happy days in Rome grieve to hear that the beautiful plantations of Villa Borghese—that chief delight and refreshment of citizens, foreigners, and little children—are laid low, as far as the obelisk. The fountain, singing alone amid the fallen groves, cannot be seen and heard without tears; it seems like some innocent infant calling and crowing amid dead bodies on a field which battle has strewn with the bodies of those who once cherished it. The plantations of Villa Salvage on the Tiber, also, the beautiful trees on the way from St. John Lateran to La Maria Maggiore, the trees of the Forum, are fallen. Rome is shorn of the locks which lent grace to her venerable brow. She looks desolate, profaned. I feel what I never expected to,—as if I might by and by be willing to leave Rome.

Then I have, for the first time, seen what wounded men suffer. The night of the 30th of April I passed in the hospital, and saw the terrible agonies of those dying or who needed amputation, felt their mental pains and longing for the loved ones who were away; for many of these were Lombards, who had come from the field of Novarra to fight with a fairer chance,—many were students of the University, who had enlisted and thrown themselves into the front of the engagement. The impudent falsehoods of the French general's despatches are incredible. The French were never decoyed on in any way. They were received with every possible mark of hostility. They were defeated in open field, the Garibaldi legion rushing out to meet them; and though they suffered much from the walls, they sustained themselves nowhere. They never put up a white flag till they wished to surrender. The vanity that strives to cover over these facts is unworthy of men. The only excuse for the imprudent conduct of the expedition is that they were deceived, not by the Romans here, but by the priests of Gaeta, leading them to expect action in their favor within the walls. These priests themselves were deluded by their hopes and old habits of mind. The troops did not fight well, and General Oudinot abandoned his wounded without proper care. All this says nothing against French valor, proved by ages of glory, beyond the doubt of their worst foes. They were demoralized because they fought in so bad a cause, and there was no sincere ardor or clear hope in any breast.

But to return to the hospitals: these were put in order, and have been kept so, by the Princess Belgioioso. The princess was born of one of the noblest families of the Milanese, a descendant of the great Trivalzio, and inherited a large fortune. Very early she compromised it in liberal movements, and, on their failure, was obliged to fly to Paris, where for a time she maintained herself by writing, and I think by painting also. A princess so placed naturally excited great interest, and she drew around her a little court of celebrated men. After recovering her fortune, she still lived in Paris, distinguished for her talents and munificence, both toward literary men and her exiled countrymen. Later, on her estate, called Locate, between Pavia and Milan, she had made experiments in the Socialist direction with fine judgment and success. Association for education, for labor, for transaction of household affairs, had been carried on for several years; she had spared no devotion of time and money to this object, loved, and was much beloved by, those objects of her care, and said she hoped to die there. All is now despoiled and broken up, though it may be hoped that some seeds of peaceful reform have been sown which will spring to light when least expected. The princess returned to Italy in 1847–8, full of hope in Pius IX. and Charles Albert. She showed her usual energy and truly princely heart, sustaining, at her own expense, a company of soldiers and a journal up to the last sad betrayal of Milan, August 6th. These days undeceived all the people, but few of the noblesse; she was one of the few with mind strong enough to understand the lesson, and is now warmly interested in the republican movement. From Milan she went to France, but, finding it impossible to effect anything serious there in behalf of Italy, returned, and has been in Rome about two months. Since leaving Milan she receives no income, her possessions being in the grasp of Radetzky, and cannot know when, if ever, she will again. But as she worked so largely and well with money, so can she without. She

published an invitation to the Roman women to make
lint and bandages, and offer their services to the wounded;
she put the hospitals in order; in the central one, Trinita
de Pellegrini, once the abode where the pilgrims were received during holy week, and where foreigners were entertained by seeing their feet washed by the noble dames
and dignitaries of Rome, she has remained day and night
since the 30th of April, when the wounded were first
there. Some money she procured at first by going through
Rome, accompanied by two other ladies veiled, to beg it.
Afterward the voluntary contributions were generous;
among the rest, I am proud to say, the Americans in
Rome gave $250, of which a handsome portion came from
Mr. Brown, the Consul.

I value this mark of sympathy more because of the ir-
ritation and surprise occasioned here by the position of
Mr. Cass, the Envoy. It is most unfortunate that we should
have an envoy here for the first time, just to offend and
disappoint the Romans. When all the other ambassadors
are at Gaeta, ours is in Rome, as if by his presence to
discountenance the republican government, which he does
not recognize. Mr. Cass, it seems, is required by his in-
structions not to recognize the government till sure it
can be sustained. Now it seems to me that the only dignified ground for our government, the only legitimate
ground for any republican government, is to recognize for
any nation the government chosen by itself. The suffrage
had been correct here, and the proportion of votes to the
whole population was much larger, it was said by Americans here, than it is in our own country at the time of contested elections. It had elected an Assembly; that Assembly had appointed, to meet the exigencies of this time,
the Triumvirate. If any misrepresentations have induced
America to believe, as France affects to have believed,
that so large a vote could have been obtained by moral
intimidation, the present unanimity of the population in
resisting such immense odds, and the enthusiasm of their

every expression in favor of the present government, puts the matter beyond a doubt. The Roman people claims once more to have a national existence. It declines further serfdom to an ecclesiastical court. It claims liberty of conscience, of action, and of thought. Should it fall from its present position, it will not be from internal dissent, but from foreign oppression.

Since this is the case, surely our country, if no other, is bound to recognize the present government *so long as it can sustain itself*. This position is that to which we have a right: being such, it is no matter how it is viewed by others. But I dare assert it is the only respectable one for our country, in the eyes of the Emperor of Russia himself.

The first, best occasion is past, when Mr. Cass might, had he been empowered to act as Mr. Rush did in France, have morally strengthened the staggering republic, which would have found sympathy where alone it is of permanent value, on the basis of principle. Had it been in vain, what then? America would have acted honorably; as to our being compromised thereby with the Papal government, that fear is idle. Pope and Cardinals have great hopes from America; the giant influence there is kept up with the greatest care; the number of Catholic writers in the United States, too, carefully counted. Had our republican government acknowledged this republican government, the Papal Camarilla would have respected us more, but not loved us less; for have we not the loaves and fishes to give, as well as the precious souls to be saved? Ah! here, indeed, America might go straightforward with all needful impunity. Bishop Hughes himself need not be anxious. That first, best occasion has passed, and the unrecognized, unrecognizing Envoy has given offence, and not comfort, by a presence that seemed constantly to say, I do not think you can sustain yourselves. It has wounded both the heart and the pride of Rome. Some of the lowest people have asked me, "Is it not true that your country had a war to become free?" "Yes." "Then why do they not feel for us?"

Yet even now it is not too late. If America would only hail triumphant, though she could not sustain injured Rome, that would be something. "Can you suppose Rome will triumph," you say, "without money, and against so potent a league of foes?" I am not sure, but I hope, for I believe something in the heart of a people when fairly awakened. I have also a lurking confidence in what our fathers spoke of so constantly, a providential order of things, by which brute force and selfish enterprise are sometimes set at naught by aid which seems to descend from a higher sphere. Even old pagans believed in that, you know; and I was born in America, Christianized by the Puritans,—America, freed by eight years' patient suffering, poverty, and struggle,—America, so cheered in dark days by one spark of sympathy from a foreign shore,— America, first "recognized" by Lafayette. I saw him when traversing our country, then great, rich, and free. Millions of men who owed in part their happiness to what, no doubt, was once sneered at as romantic sympathy, threw garlands in his path. It is natural that I should have some faith.

Send, dear America! to thy ambassadors a talisman precious beyond all that boasted gold of California. Let it loose his tongue to cry, "Long live the Republic, and may God bless the cause of the people, the brotherhood of nations and of men,—the equality of rights for all." *Viva America!*

Hail to my country! May she live a free, a glorious, a loving life, and not perish, like the old dominions, from the leprosy of selfishness. . . .

I have been out on the balcony to look over the city. All sleeps with that peculiar air of serene majesty known to this city only;—this city that has grown, not out of the necessities of commerce nor the luxuries of wealth, but first out of heroism, then out of faith. Swelling domes, roofs softly tinted with yellow moss! what deep meaning, what deep repose, in your faintly seen outline!

The young moon climbs among clouds,—the clouds of a departing thunderstorm. Tender, smiling moon! can it be that thy full orb may look down on a smoking, smouldering Rome, and see her best blood run along the stones, without one nation in the world to defend, one to aid,— scarce one to cry out a tardy "Shame"? We will wait, whisper the nations, and see if they can bear it. Rack them well to see if they are brave. *If they can do without us*, we will help them. Is it thus ye would be served in your turn? Beware!

12. TO RALPH WALDO EMERSON, June 10, 1849

(Text from *At Home and Abroad*, pp. 434–36.)

[This appears to be Margaret Fuller's last attempt to communicate with Emerson. That she should compose it amid a cannonade is perhaps the supreme irony of her highly ironic progression out of New England.]

. . . I received your letter amid the round of cannonade and musketry. It was a terrible battle fought here from the first to the last light of day. I could see all its progress from my balcony. The Italians fought like lions. It is a truly heroic spirit that animates them. They make a stand here for honor and their rights, with little ground for hope that they can resist, now they are betrayed by France.

Since the 30th of April, I go almost daily to the hospitals, and though I have suffered, for I had no idea before how terrible gun-shot wounds and wound-fevers are, yet I have taken pleasure, and great pleasure, in being with the men. There is scarcely one who is not moved by a noble spirit. Many, especially among the Lombards, are the flower of the Italian youth. When they begin to get better, I carry them books and flowers; they read, and we talk.

The palace of the Pope, on the Quirinal, is now used for convalescents. In those beautiful gardens I walk with them, one with his sling, another with his crutch. The gardener plays off all his water-works for the defenders of the country, and gathers flowers for me, their friend.

A day or two since, we sat in the Pope's little pavilion, where he used to give private audience. The sun was going gloriously down over Monte Mario, where gleamed the white tents of the French light-horse among the trees. The cannonade was heard at intervals. Two bright-eyed boys sat at our feet, and gathered up eagerly every word said by the heroes of the day. It was a beautiful hour, stolen from the midst of ruin and sorrow, and tales were told as full of grace and pathos as in the gardens of Boccaccio, only in a very different spirit,—with noble hope for man, and reverence for woman.

The young ladies of the family, very young girls, were filled with enthusiasm for the suffering, wounded patriots, and they wished to go to the hospital, to give their services. Excepting the three superintendents, none but married ladies were permitted to serve there, but their services were accepted. Their governess then wished to go too, and, as she could speak several languages, she was admitted to the rooms of the wounded soldiers, to interpret for them, as the nurses knew nothing but Italian, and many of these poor men were suffering because they could not make their wishes known. Some are French, some Germans, many Poles. Indeed, I am afraid it is too true that there were comparatively few Romans among them. This young lady passed several nights there.

Should I never return, and sometimes I despair of doing so, it seems so far off,—so difficult, I am caught in such a net of ties here,—if ever you know of my life here, I think you will only wonder at the constancy with which I have sustained myself,—the degree of profit to which, amid great difficulties, I have put the time,—at least in the way of observation. Meanwhile, love me all you can. Let me feel that, amid the fearful agitations of the world, there are pure hands, with healthful, even pulse, stretched out toward me, if I claim their grasp.

I feel profoundly for Mazzini. At moments I am tempted to say, "Cursed with every granted prayer,"—so cunning is the demon. Mazzini has become the inspiring soul of his people. He saw Rome, to which all his hopes through life tended, for the first time as a Roman citizen, and to become in a few days its ruler. He has animated, he sustains her to a glorious effort, which, if it fails this time, will not in the age. His country will be free. Yet to me it would be so dreadful to cause all this bloodshed, —to dig the graves of such martyrs!

Then, Rome is being destroyed; her glorious oaks,—her villas, haunts of sacred beauty, that seemed the possession of the world for ever,—the villa of Raphael, the villa of Albani, home of Winckelmann and the best expression of the ideal of modern Rome, and so many other sanctuaries of beauty,—all must perish, lest a foe should level his musket from their shelter. I could not, could not!

I know not, dear friend, whether I shall ever get home across that great ocean, but here in Rome I shall no longer wish to live. O Rome, *my* country! could I imagine that the triumph of what I held dear was to heap such desolation on thy head!

Speaking of the republic, you say, "Do you not wish Italy had a great man?" Mazzini is a great man. In mind, a great, poetic statesman; in heart, a lover; in action, decisive and full of resource as Cæsar. Dearly I love Mazzini. He came in, just as I had finished the first letter to you. His soft, radiant look makes melancholy music in my soul; it consecrates my present life, that, like the Magdalen, I may, at the important hour, shed all the con-

secrated ointment on his head. There is one, Mazzini, who
understands thee well,—who knew thee no less when an
object of popular fear than now of idolatry,—and who, if
the pen be not held too feebly, will help posterity to
know thee too!

13. TO ELLEN CHANNING, June 19, 1849

(Text from *At Home and Abroad*, p. 437.)

*[As Margaret wrote this brief note from Rome, the
French armies were subduing the city and on July 2nd
would take it over, an operation which the liberals of
Europe would regard for the rest of their lives as the
supreme treachery of modern history. Meanwhile, news
of Margaret's romance and of her child was spreading fast
among the literati of America, producing guffaws of Rabe-
laisian laughter along Nassau Street, then the newspaper
row of New York. On this date she contrived to dispatch
a note to her beloved younger sister Ellen, who was as
beautiful as Margaret was plain, and who sacrificed her
sweet nature to the capricious egotism of the younger
Ellery Channing.]*

As was Eve, at first, I suppose every mother is delighted
by the birth of a man-child. There is a hope that he will
conquer more ill, and effect more good, than is expected
from girls. This prejudice in favor of man does not seem
to be destroyed by his shortcomings for ages. Still, each
mother hopes to find in hers an Emanuel. I should like
very much to see your children, but hardly realize I ever
shall. The journey home seems so long, so difficult, so
expensive. I should really like to lie down here, and sleep
my way into another sphere of existence, if I could take

with me one or two that love and need me, and was sure
of a good haven for them on that other side.

The world seems to go so strangely wrong! The bad
side triumphs; the blood and tears of the generous flow
in vain. I assist at many saddest scenes, and suffer for
those whom I knew not before. Those whom I knew
and loved,—who, if they had triumphed, would have
opened for me an easier, broader, higher-mounting road,—
are every day more and more involved in earthly ruin.
Eternity is with us, but there is much darkness and bitterness in this portion of it. A baleful star rose on my birth,
and its hostility, I fear, will never be disarmed while I
walk below.

14. TO WILLIAM HENRY CHANNING,
August 28, 1849

(Text from *Memoirs*, II, 269–70.)

*[In this letter, Margaret Fuller, having fled with Os-
soli from Rome to her baby in the mountains at Rieti,
endeavors to explain the un-Transcendental realities of
European violence to an old friend and fellow-student of
her by then distant Transcendental days.]*

. . . You say, you are glad I have had this great opportunity for carrying out my principles. Would it were
so! I found myself inferior in courage and fortitude to the
occasion. I knew not how to bear the havoc and anguish
incident to the struggle for these principles. I rejoice that
it lay not with me to cut down the trees, to destroy the
Elysian gardens, for the defence of Rome; I do not know
that I could have done it. And the sight of these far nobler
growths, the beautiful young men, mown down in their
stately prime, became too much for me. I forget the great

ideas, to sympathize with the poor mothers, who had nursed their precious forms, only to see them all lopped and gashed. You say, I sustained them; often have they sustained my courage: one, kissing the pieces of bone that were so painfully extracted from his arm, hanging them round his neck to be worn as the true relics of to-day; mementoes that he also had done and borne something for his country and the hopes of humanity. One fair young man, who is made a cripple for life, clasped my hand as he saw me crying over the spasms I could not relieve, and faintly cried, "Viva l'Italia." "Think only, *cara bona donna*," said a poor wounded soldier, "that I can always wear my uniform on *festas*, just as it is now, with the holes where the balls went through, for a memory." "God is good; God knows," they often said to me, when I had not a word to cheer them.

15. TO EMELYN STORY, November 30, 1849

(Text from Fuller MSS, Harvard College Library.)

[William Wetmore Story (1819–95) was the son of the great American jurist Joseph Story. After his father's death he wantonly (in the opinion of his colleagues) threw away a career already well launched in the law and migrated to Rome, in order to study sculpture and write poetry. His wife gallantly approved of this adventure. They were both persons of courage, immense charm and cultivation. Their studio in Rome at once became the center for meetings of American and English intellectuals. They stood solidly with Margaret Fuller.

On the strength of Mrs. Story's assurance that she was shown the marriage certificate of Margaret and Ossoli rests all belief that their child was legitimate. However, it

*may be that Mrs. Story saw only the birth certificate of
the boy. The documents, of course, went down with the*
Elizabeth *on July 19, 1850.]*

. . . Thus far, my friends have received news that
must have been an unpleasant surprise to them, in a way
that, *à moi,* does them great honor. None have shown
littleness or displeasure, at wanting my confidence while
they were giving their own. Many have expressed the
warmest sympathy, and only one has a disposition to trans-
gress the limit I myself had marked and to ask questions.
With her, I think, it was because she was annoyed by
things people said, and wanted to be able to answer them.
I replied to her, that I had communicated already all I
intended, and should not go into details as to the past,—
that when unkind things were said about me, she should
let them pass. Will you, dear Emelyn, do the same? I am
sure your affection for me will prompt you to add, that
you feel confident whatever I have done has been in a
good spirit, and not contrary to *my* ideas of right. For
the rest, you will not admit for me,—as I do not for myself,—the rights of the social inquisition of the United
States to know all the details of my affairs. If my mother
is content, if Ossoli and I are content; if our child, when
grown up, shall be content, that is enough. You and I
know enough of the United States to be sure, that many
persons there will blame whatever is peculiar. The lower
minded persons, everywhere, are sure to think that whatever is mysterious must be bad. But I think there will
remain for me a sufficient number of friends to keep my
heart warm and to help me earn my bread; that is all
that is of any consequence. Ossoli seems to me more lovely
and good every day; our darling child is well now, and
every day more gay and playful. For his sake I shall have
courage; and hope some good angel will show us the way
out of our external difficulties. . . .

16. TO WILLIAM WETMORE STORY,
December 2, 1849

(Text from the Fuller MSS, Harvard College Library; this text is clearly a copy of a lost original; it is not in Margaret Fuller's own hand.)

[Margaret, Ossoli, and the child found lodgings in Florence after their escape from Rome and there Margaret contrived their passage to America. Considering the fidelity the Storys had exhibited in Margaret's cause, we wonder why it took her another week, after telling Mrs. Story, to write to Mr. Story of her marriage. But, as she made clear to even this best of friends, she was resolved to tell only what she wished to tell; with the tale unspoken, she drowned.]

. . . It was like you to receive with such kindness the news of my marriage. A less generous person would have been displeased, that when we had been drawn so together, when we had talked so freely, and you had shown towards me such sweet friendship, I had not told you. Often did I long to do so, but I had, for reasons that seemed important, made a law to myself to keep this secret as rigidly as possible, up to a certain moment. That moment came; its decisions were not such as I had hoped; but it left me at least without that painful burden of secret, which I hope never to bear again. Nature keeps so many secrets, that I had supposed the moral writers exaggerated about the dangers and plagues of keeping them; but they cannot exaggerate. All that can be said about mine is that I at least acted out with to me tragic thoroughness, "The wonder, a woman who keeps a secret." All that can be said of my not telling you is that I was keeping the same information from my family and dearest friends at home, and had you remained near me a very little later, you would have been the first person to whom I should have spoken; and you would have been the first on this side of the water to whom I should have written, had I known where to address you. Yet I hardly hoped for your sympathy, dear William. I am very glad if I have it.

May brotherly love ever be returned unto you in like measure. Ossoli desires his love and respect to be testified to you both. Should he meet you sometime in our land I doubt not the light of your eye will be consoling to him. I feel he will feel very strange and lonely there; indeed I feel much more anxious about his happiness than my own. Still his love for our child is so great and his pleasure in the wood and fields so simple and profound, I hope he will be able to make for himself a life in the unknown country till changes favor return to his own. . . .

17. TO ELLEN CHANNING, December 11, 1849

(Text from the Fuller MSS, Harvard College Library.)

[Margaret and Ossoli were at this time enjoying in Florence what was to be their only respite from anxiety. Probably it was more of a release for him than for her: she not only had to make all the arrangements for their voyage, but to resist the continually darkening cloud of suspicion that surrounded her, of which she evidently kept him in ignorance.

This second letter to her sister reveals the anxious undercurrents of these joyous months in Florence.]

. . . You are anxious, my dear Ellen, to know some details of my past history and I should like to gratify you, but I hardly know how. There are some reasons which I cannot explain further than by the remark that Ossoli is still a member of the Roman Catholic church, why I do not go into all the matter of past history. I cannot, at least at present, tell exactly the facts, so I choose to say nothing. I should be glad if he disengaged himself entirely from the Roman ritual, but I doubt he ever will. His habitual attachment to it is strong, and I do not trouble myself about it as no priest has any influence over his mind.

About him, I do not like to say much, as he is an exceedingly delicate person. He is not precisely reserved, but it is not natural to him to *talk* about the objects of strong affection. I am sure he would not try to describe me to his sister, but would rather she would take her own impression of me; and, as much as possible, I wish to do the same by him. I presume that, to many of my friends, Mr. Emerson for one, he will be nothing, and they will not understand that I should have life in common with him. But I do not think he will care; he has not the slightest tinge of self-love; he has, throughout our intercourse, been used to my having many such ties; he has no wish to be anything to persons with whom he does not feel spontaneously bound, and when I am occupied is happy in himself. But some of my friends and my family, who will see him in the details of practical life, cannot fail to prize the purity and simple strength of his character, and, should he continue to love me as he has done, to consider his companionship will be an inestimable blessing to me. I say *if*, because all human affections are frail, and I have experienced too great revulsions in my own not to know it, yet I feel great confidence in the permanence of his love. It has been unblemished so far, under many trials, especially as I have been more sick, desponding and unreasonable in many ways than I ever was before and more so, I hope, than I ever shall be again. But at all such times, he never had a thought except to sustain and cheer me; he is capable of the sacred

love, the love passing that of women. He showed it to his
father, to Rome, to me. Now he loves his child in the
same way. I think he will be an excellent father, though
he could not speculate about it, or, indeed, about anything.

Our meeting was singular, fateful I may say. Very soon
he offered me his hand through life, but I never dreamed
I should take it. I loved him, and felt very unhappy to
leave, but the connection seemed so every way unfit, I
did not hesitate a moment. He, however, thought I should
return to him, as I did. I acted upon a strong impulse.
I could not analyze at all what passed in my mind. I
neither rejoice nor grieve, for bad or for good, I acted out
my character. Had I never connected myself with any one
my path was clear, now it is all hid, but in that case, my
development must have been partial! As to marriage, I
think the intercourse of heart and mind may be fully
enjoyed without entering into this partnership of daily
life, still I do not find it burdensome. We get along very
well and I find have our better intercourse is much as if
we did not buy unhappiness we have nothing to sell together. The friction that I have seen mar so much the
domestic happiness of others does not occur with us, or at
least, has not. Then there is the pleasure of always being
at hand to help one another.

Still all this I had felt before in some degree. The
great novelty, the immense gain to me is my relation with
my child. I thought the mother's heart lived in me before,
but it did not. I knew nothing about it. Yet before his
birth I dreaded it. I thought I should not survive, but if
I did and my child did, was I not cruel to bring another
into this terrible world[?] I could not at that time get
any other view. When he was born that deep melancholy
changed once into rapture, but did not last long. Then
came the prudential motherhood, then came Mrs. Edg-
worth, Mrs. Smith. I became a coward, a caretaker not
only for the morrow but impiously faithless for twenty

or thirty years ahead. I seemed wicked to have brought the little tender thing into the midst of cares and perplexities we had not feared in the least for ourselves. I imagined everything; he was to be in danger of every enormity the Croats were then committing upon the babies of Lombardy. The house would be burned over his head, but if he escaped, how were we to get money to buy his bibs and primers[?] Then his father was to be killed in the fighting, and I to die of my cough. . . .

During the siege of Rome, I could not see my little boy. What I endured at that time, in various ways not many would survive. In the burning sun, I went every day, to wait, in the crowd, for letters about him. Often they did not come. I saw blood that streamed on the wall where Ossoli was. I have a piece of a bomb that burst close to him. I sought solace in tending the suffering men; but when I beheld the beautiful fair young men bleeding to death, or mutilated for life, I felt the woe of all the mothers who had nursed each to that full flower, to see them thus cut down. I felt the *consolation*, too,—for those youths died worthily. I was a Mater Dolorosa, and I remembered that the midwife who helped Angelino into the world came from the sign of the Mater Dolorosa. I thought, even if he lives, if he comes into the world at this great troubled time, terrible with perplexed duties, it may be to die thus at twenty years, one of a glorious hecatomb, indeed, but still a sacrifice. It seemed then I was willing he should die. But when I really saw him lingering as he did all July and August between life and death, I could not let him go unless I could go with him. . . .

18. TO CAROLINE STURGIS TAPPAN,
December 30, 1849

(Text from the Fuller MSS, Harvard College Library; it is barbarously massacred in *Memoirs*, II, 307–11, 317–18.)

[This letter was written over several troubled and ecstatic days; the last entry is December 30th, but it must have been started a week or more previously. This portion opens with a sudden and unannounced description of the boy, Angelino, now a year and three months old.]

. . . I do not know what to write about him: he changes so much, has so many characters. He is like me in that, his father's character is simple and uniform, though not monotonous, more than are the flowers of spring, flowers of the valley. He is now in the most perfect rosy health, a very gay, impetuous, ardent, but sweet tempered child. He seems to me to have nothing in common with his first baby[hood (?)] with its ecstatic smiles, its exquisite sensitiveness, and a distinction in gesture and attitudes that struck everybody. His temperament seems changed by taking the milk of these robust women. His form is robust. . . .

He is now come to quite a knowing age (fifteen months). In the morning, as soon as dressed, he signs to come into our room; then draws our curtain, kisses me rather violently, pats my face, stretches himself and says *bravo*. Then expects as a reward to be tied in his chair and have his playthings. These engage him busily, but still he calls to us to sing and drum to enliven the scene. Sometimes he calls me to kiss his hand; he laughs very much at this. Enchanting is that baby laugh, all dimples

and glitter, so strangely arch and innocent. Then I wash
and dress him; that is his great time. He makes it [last]
as long as he can, insisting to dress and wash me the
while, kicking, throwing water about, full of all manner
of tricks that I think girls never dream of. Then is his
walk; we have beautiful walks here for him, along the
Arno, by the bridges or the sunny walk at the Cascine,
protected by fine trees, always warm in mid-winter, the
bands playing in the distance and children of all ages
walking and sitting with their nurses. His walk and sleep
give me about three hours in the middle of the day. Then
at eight he goes to bed and we have the [evening]. Otherwise I am always engaged with him. Indeed I often walk
with him, as Italian servants are not to be trusted and I
feel now [the] need of seeing him at each moment.

I feel so refreshed by his young life. Ossoli diffuses such
a power and sweetness over every day that I cannot endure
to think yet of our future. Too much have we suffered
already trying to command it. I do not feel force to make
any effort yet. I suppose that very soon now I must do
something. I hope I shall feel able when the time comes.
I do not yet. My constitution seems making an effort
to rally, by dint of much sleep. I had slept so little
for a year and a half during the last months of pregnancy[,] never an hour in peace after the baby's birth,
such anxiety and anguish, when separated from him, I
was consumed as by nightly fever. I constantly started
up seeming to hear him call me. The last two months
at Rome would have destroyed almost any woman. Then,
when I went to him, he was so ill and I was constantly
up with him at night, carrying him about, feeding him.
At Perugia he began to get better. Then in [September
(manuscript is torn here, but this is the month of their
arrival)] we arrived here. The Police [threatened (?)]
to send us away. It was . . . three weeks before we could
[get] permission to stay. Now for two months we have
been tranquil; we have resolved to repose and enjoy being

together as much as we can, in this brief interval, perhaps all we shall ever know of peace. It is very sad we have no money, we could be so quietly happy a while. I rejoice in all Ossoli did but the results, in this our earthly state are disastrous, especially as my strength is now so much impaired. This much I do hope, in life or death, to be no more separated from Angelino.

Last winter I made the most vehement efforts at least to redeem the time, hoping thus good for the future. But, of at least two volumes written at that time, no line seems of any worth. I had suffered much constraint, much that was uncongenial, harassing, even agonizing, but this kind of pain found me unprepared. The position of a mother separated from her only child is too frightfully un-natural. . . .

What you say of the meddling curiosity of people re-pels me. It is so different here. When I made my appear-ance with a husband and a child of a year old nobody did the least act to annoy me. All were most cordial, none asked or implied questions. Yet there were not a few who might justly have complained that when they were con-fiding to me all their affairs and doing much to serve me, I had observed absolute silence to them. Others might for more than one reason be displeased at the choice I made. All have acted in the kindliest and most refined manner. An Italian lady with whom I was intimate[,] who might be qualified in the court journal as one of the highest rank sustained by the most scrupulous decorum,* when I wrote, "Dear Friend, I am married. I have a child. There are particulars, as to my reasons for keeping this secret I do not wish to tell. This is rather an odd affair, will it make any difference in our relations?" She answered, "What difference can it make, except that I shall love you more, now that we can sympathize as mothers?" Her first

* Margaret Fuller undoubtedly means Madame Arconati (cf. *Memoirs*, II, 233, 240-41, 242-43, 257-59).

visit here was to me; she adopted at once Ossoli and the child to her love.

Emelyn Story wrote me that William was a little hurt at first that I did not tell him even in the trying days of Rome, but left him to hear it, as he unluckily did, at the *table d'hôte* in Venice. But his second and prevailing thought was regret that he had not known it so as to soothe and aid me, to visit Ossoli at his post, to go to the child in the country. Wholly in that spirit was the fine letter he wrote me, one of my treasures. His character has come out beautifully at times in Europe. He has had his ordeals. The little American society have been most cordial and attentive; one lady who has been most intimate with me dripped a tear over the difficulties before me but she said, "Since you have seen fit to take the step, all your friends have to do, now, is to make it as easy for you as they can." . . .

19. TO RICHARD F. FULLER, January 8, 1850

(Text from the Fuller MSS, Harvard College Library.)

[What could by now have been the destiny in America of these three vagrants?]

. . . The way you speak now of my marriage is such as I expected from you. Now that we have once exchanged some words on these important changes in our lives, it matters little to write letters, too much has happened, and the changes have been too great to be made clear in writing. I doubt not when we have met face to face, we shall be friends the same as ever, or better than before.

It would not be worthwhile to keep the family thinking of me. I cannot fix precisely the period of my return, though at present it seems to me probable we may make the voyage in May or June. At first we should wish to go and make a little visit to Mother. I should take counsel with various friends before fixing myself in any place, see what openings there are for me, &c. I cannot judge at all before I am personally in the United States, and wish to engage myself noway. Should I finally decide on the neighborhood of New York I should see you all often. I wish, however, to live with Mother, if possible. We will discuss it on all sides when I come. Climate is one thing I must think of. The change from the Roman winter to that of New England might be very trying for Ossoli. In New York he would see Italians, often hear his native tongue and feel less exiled. If we had our affairs in New York and live in the country, we could find places as quiet as Canton, more beautiful, and from which access to a city would be as easy by means of steam. On the other hand my family and most cherished friends are in New England. I shall weigh all advantages at the time, and choose as may then seem best.

I feel also the great responsibility about a child, and the mixture of solemn feeling with the joy its sweet ways and caresses give. Yet this is only different in degree, not in kind, from what we should feel in other relations. The destiny of all we come in contact with we may more or less impede or brighten. Much as the child lies in our power, still God and Nature are there, furnishing a thousand masters to correct our erroneous, fill up our imperfect, teachings. I feel impelled to try for good, for the sake of my child, most powerfully, but if I fail, I trust help will be tendered to him from some other quarter. I do not wish to trouble myself more than is inevitable or lose the simple, innocent pleasure of watching his growth from day to day by thinking of his future. At present my care of him is to keep him clean body and mind, to give for body and mind simple nutriment when he demands it, and to play with him. Now he learns [by] playing as we all shall when we enter a higher state. With him my intercourse thus far has been satisfactory and if I do not well for *him* he at least has taught *me* a great deal. . . .

Ossoli sends his love to you. I may say of him, as you say of your wife, it would be difficult to [do] other than like him, so sweet is his disposition, so without an effort disinterested, so simply wise his daily conduct, so harmonious his whole nature. Add he is a perfectly unconscious character, and never dreams that he does well. He is studying English but makes little progress. For a good while you may not be able to talk with him, but you will like showing him some of your favorite haunts: he is so happy in nature, in sweet tranquil places. . . .

20. TO MARCUS AND REBECCA SPRING,
February 5, 1850

(Text from the Fuller MSS, Harvard College Library. The manuscript is copied; it is not in Margaret Fuller's original hand.)

[Here Margaret confronted the prospect of her future in America—not knowing that it would remain forever unrealized. For those who had been her benefactors and were to remain her champions, this letter becomes by virtue of the accident an epitaph.]

. . . You have no doubt ere this received a letter written I think in December, but I must suddenly write again to thank you for the New Years letter. It was a sweet impulse that led you all to write together, and had its full reward in the pleasure you gave. I am glad it entered into the heart of Emelyn Story to write that letter: it was in the spirit of that tender and generous friendship that both she and her husband always showed me. I trust that the [bond(?)] formed between us will last as long

as our lives. It is also pleasant that it should be the Lowells
that took pains to show the letter. As to its subject matter
I have written as little as possible about Ossoli and our
relation, wishing my old friends to form their own impressions naturally when they see us together. I have faith
that all who ever really knew me would feel that I have
become somewhat milder, kinder, and more worthy to
serve all who need for my new relations. I have expected
that those who have cared for me chiefly for my activity
of intellect would not care for him, but that those in
whom the moral nature predominates would gradually
learn to love and admire him, and see what a treasure
his affection must be to me. But that would be only gradually, for it is by acts, not by words, that one so simple,
true, delicate and retiring can be known. For me while
some of my friends have thought me exacting, I may say
Ossoli has always outgone my expectations in the disinterestedness, the uncompromising bounty of his every
act. He was the same to his father as to me. His affections are few, but profound, and thoroughly acted out.
His permanent affections are few, but his heart is always open to the humble, suffering, heavy-laden. His
mind has little habitual action, except in a simple natural
poetry that one not very intimate with him would never
know anything about. But one opened to a great impulse
as it was to the hope of freeing his country it rose to
the height of the occasion and staid there. His enthusiasm
was quiet, but unsleeping. He is very unlike most Italians,
but very unlike most Americans, too. I do not expect all
who cared for me to care for him, nor is it of importance
to him; he is wholly without vanity. He is too truly the
gentleman not to be respected by all persons of refinement: For the rest if my life is free and not too much
troubled, if he can enjoy his domestic affections, and fulfill his duties in his own way, he will be content. Can
we find this much for ourselves in bustling America for
the next three or four years? I know not but think we

shall come and try. I wish much to see you all, and exchange the kiss of peace. There will, I trust, be peace within if not without. I thank you warmly for your gift; be assured it will turn to great profit. I have learned to be a great adept in economy by looking at my little boy. I cannot bear to spend a cent for fear he may come to want it. I understand how the family men get so mean. I shall have to begin soon to pray against that danger. . . .

My little Nino as we call him for house and pet name is now in perfect health. I wash and dress and sew for him and think I see a great deal more of his little cunning ways and shall know him better for doing all for him, though 'tis inconvenient and fatiguing at times. His head is singularly formed. I fear the faculties are not in very good balance. He is very gay and laughing, sometimes violent, for he has come to the age when he wants everything in his own hand, but on the whole sweet as yet and very fond of me. He often calls me to kiss him. He says *kiss* in preference to the Italian word bacio. I do not cherish sanguine visions about him. I shall try to do my best by him and enjoy the present moment. . . .

21. TO EMELYN STORY, April 11, 1850

(Text from the Fuller MSS, Harvard College Library.)

[The surviving text is a copy; the date may be earlier. There was no reason to suppose that the trip to America itself would be more hazardous than any other—although Atlantic crossings were then always dangerous. But Margaret reveals here that she was intensely aware that this trip would require of her the ultimate courage.]

. . . I go home prepared to expect everything that is painful and difficult. . . . I am glad to have people favorably impressed, because I feel lazy and weak, unlike the trouble of friction or the pain of conquest. Still I feel a good deal of contempt for those so easily disconcerted or reassured. I was not a child; I had lived in the midst of that New England society in a way that entitled me to esteem and a favorable interpretation where there was doubt about my motives or actions. I pity those who are inclined to think ill, when they might as well have inclined the other way. However, let them go: there are many in the world who stand the test, enough to keep us from shivering to death. I am on the whole fortunate in friends that I can truly esteem where I know the kernel and substance of their being too well to be misled by seemings.

22. PROPHECY

(Text from *Memoirs*, II, 377, presumably just before the *Elizabeth* sailed from Leghorn on May 17, 1850.)

[The Memoirs, *as usually, but here most exasperatingly, do not indicate the source of the quotation or to whom it was addressed; nor do they offer us a guarantee of the textual accuracy. The shipwreck and the extinction of the three pilgrims came off the shore of Fire Island near New York City, on July 19, 1850.]*

I am absurdly fearful, and various omens have combined to give me a dark feeling. I am become indeed a miserable coward, for the sake of Angelino. I fear heat and cold, fear the voyage, fear biting poverty. I hope I shall not be forced to be brave for him, as I have been for myself, and that, if I succeed to rear him, he will be neither a weak nor a bad man. But I love him too much! In case of mishap, however, I shall perish with my husband and my child, and we may be transferred to some happier state. . . . I feel perfectly willing to stay my threescore years and ten, if it be thought I need so much tuition on this planet; but it seems to me that my future upon earth will soon close. It may be terribly trying, but it will not be so very long now. God will transplant the root, if he will to rear it into fruit-bearing. . . . I have a vague expectation of some crisis,—I know not what. But it has long seemed that, in the year 1850, I should stand on a plateau in the ascent of life, where I should be allowed to pause for a while, and take more clear and commanding view than ever before. My life proceeds as regularly as the fates of a Greek tragedy, and I can but accept the pages as they turn. . . .

BIBLIOGRAPHICAL SOURCES
AND ACKNOWLEDGMENTS

The indispensable source book for the study of the life and mind of Margaret Fuller is the two-volume *Memoirs of Margaret Fuller Ossoli*, compiled in 1852 by Ralph Waldo Emerson, William Henry Channing, and James Freeman Clarke. These three had not only deep affection for her but also manly respect for her intellect and courage. They made a gallant effort to treat her as a Romantic heroine, to tell all the truth and to show in their tone that they were men of the world.

Unfortunately their standards of scholarship were those of their age, of a culture in which there had not yet emerged professional canons. It is not so much that they suppressed unpleasant passages, and it must be said on their behalf that they were not, where they might have been, censorious. But they eviscerated her journals, rewrote her letters, and sent to the printer her actual papers cluttered with their editorial notes. As a result of their appalling handling, most originals have disappeared and many fragments that happen to remain are in a shocking physical condition.

Other letters used by her brother in his editions of the works have also disappeared, but to judge from manuscripts that have not been destroyed, he was somewhat more accurate.

Wherever I could find a holograph, I have taken it

for my text, with a minimum of editing. I have silently put in the obvious punctuation marks where she in her haste—she was always in haste when she got a pen in her hand—forgot them. Otherwise I have made a literal transcription even when, as often, Margaret's sentences will hardly parse by the ordinary rules of grammar.

I am grateful to the Harvard College Library and to the Boston Public Library for permission to study and use the Fuller manuscripts in their possession.

Most of Margaret Fuller's letters to Emerson are given in faithful transcripts by Ralph L. Rusk, *The Letters of Ralph Waldo Emerson,* 6 Vols., 1939.

The works of Margaret Fuller, in chronological sequence, are:

Eckermann's Conversations with Goethe, Boston, 1839.
Correspondence of Fräulein Günderode and Bettina von Arnim, Boston, 1842.
Summer on the Lakes, Boston, 1844.
Woman in the Nineteenth Century, New York, 1845.
Papers on Literature and Art, New York, 1856.
At Home and Abroad, edited by A. B. Fuller, Boston, 1856.
Life Without and Life Within, edited by A. B. Fuller, Boston, 1859.
Love-Letters of Margaret Fuller, 1845–1846, Introduction by Julia Ward Howe, New York, 1903.

The principal biographies, in addition to the *Memoirs,* are:

Julia Ward Howe, *Margaret Fuller (Marchesa Ossoli),* Boston, 1883.
Thomas Wentworth Higginson, *Margaret Fuller Ossoli,* Boston, 1884.
Caroline W. Healey, *Margaret and Her Friends,* Boston, 1895.
Andrew MacPhail, *Essays on Puritanism,* Boston, 1905.

Katharine Anthony, *Margaret Fuller, a Psychological Biography*, New York, 1920.

Margaret Bell, *Margaret Fuller*, New York, 1930.

Mason Wade, *Margaret Fuller: Whetstone of Genius*, New York, 1940.

Madeleine B. Stern, *The Life of Margaret Fuller*, New York, 1942.

My own foreword to this collection is a reworking of an essay I wrote about her in *American Heritage*, VIII (February 1957), 22–25, 96–99.

The literature by and about the New England Transcendentalists is, of course, vast; I suggest that a guide through it may be found in my *The Transcendentalists: An Anthology*, Cambridge, Massachusetts, 1950; or, in a shortened form, in *The American Transcendentalists: Their Prose and Poetry*, Anchor Books A119, New York, 1957.

ANCHOR BOOKS

ADAMS, HENRY   Democracy *and* Esther A243
———————   A Henry Adams Reader A177
———————   Mont-Saint-Michel and Chartres A166
ALAIN-FOURNIER, HENRI   The Wanderer A14
ALBRIGHT, W. F.   From the Stone Age to Christianity A100
ALEXANDER, ROBERT J.   Today's Latin America A327
ALLPORT, GORDON W.   The Nature of Prejudice A149
ANDRADE, E. N. DA C.   An Approach to Modern Physics A111
———————   Sir Isaac Newton A151
ARENDT, HANNAH   The Human Condition A182
ARISTOPHANES   Five Comedies A57
ARON, RAYMOND   On War A171
AUDEN, W. H.; GREENBERG, NOAH; KALLMAN, CHESTER   An Eliza-
    bethan Song Book A56
AUERBACH, ERICH   Mimesis A107
BARK, WILLIAM CARROLL   Origins of the Medieval World A190
BARKER, ALAN   The Civil War in America A274
BARRETT, WILLIAM   Irrational Man A321
BARTH, KARL   Community, State and Church A221
BARZUN, JACQUES   Classic, Romantic and Modern A255
———————   Darwin, Marx, Wagner A127
———————   Teacher in America A25
BATE, WALTER JACKSON   Prefaces to Criticism A165
BAUDELAIRE, CHARLES   The Mirror of Art A84
BEDIER, JOSEPH   The Romance of Tristan and Iseult A2
BEERBOHM, MAX   A Selection from "Around Theatres" A226
BEETHOVEN   Letters, Journals and Conversations A206
BENDIX, REINHARD   Max Weber: An Intellectual Portrait A281
BENTLEY, ERIC (Ed.)   The Classic Theatre I: Six Italian Plays A155a
———————   The Classic Theatre II: Five German Plays A155b
———————   The Classic Theatre III: Six Spanish Plays A155c
———————   The Classic Theatre IV: Six French Plays A155d
BENTLEY, ERIC (Ed.)   The Modern Theatre I, II, III, IV, V, VI A48a,
    A48b, A48c, A48d, A48e, A48f
———————   From the American Drama (The Modern Theatre IV) A48d
BERENSON, BERNARD   Aesthetics and History A36
BERGIN, THOMAS GODDARD and MAX HAROLD FISCH   The New
    Science of Giambattista Vico A254
BERGSON, HENRI   "Laughter" in Comedy A87
———————   Matter and Memory A172
———————   The Two Sources of Morality and Religion A28
BETTELHEIM, BRUNO   Paul and Mary: Two Case Histories from
    Truants from Life A237
BISHOP, AMASA   Project Sherwood, A202
BLACKMUR, R. P.   Form and Value in Modern Poetry A96
BRANDEIS, IRMA   The Ladder of Vision A320
BRENNER, CHARLES   An Elementary Textbook of Psychoanalysis A102
BROGAN, D. W.   Politics in America, A198
BROOKS, VAN WYCK   America's Coming of Age A129
BROWN, ROBERT McAFEE and GUSTAVE WEIGEL, S.J.
    An American Dialogue A257
BULLITT, STIMSON   To Be A Politician A264
BURCKHARDT, JACOB   The Age of Constantine the Great A65
BURTT, EDWIN ARTHUR   The Metaphysical Foundations of Modern
    Science A41
BUTTERFIELD, HERBERT and OTHERS   A Short History of Science
    A180
CABLE, GEORGE W.   Creoles and Cajuns A179
———————   The Negro Question A144

CARY, JOYCE Art and Reality A260
———————— A Fearful Joy A242
———————— A House of Children A315
———————— The Moonlight A292
CASSON, LIONEL (Trans.) Selected Satires of Lucian A295
CASTIGLIONE, BALDESAR The Book of the Courtier A186
CHASE, RICHARD The American Novel and Its Tradition A116
CHAUCER, GEOFFREY The Canterbury Tales of Geoffrey Chaucer
    (Daniel Cook, Ed.) A265
CHEKHOV, ANTON Early Stories A261
———————— Peasants and Other Stories A66
CHEVALIER, MICHAEL Society, Manners and Politics in the United
    States (John William Ward, Ed.) A259
CLARK, KENNETH The Nude A168
COLETTE My Mother's House and The Vagabond A62
CONANT, JAMES B. Modern Science and Modern Man A10
CONNOLLY, CYRIL Enemies of Promise and Other Essays, A194
CONRAD, JOSEPH Chance A113
———————— A Mirror of the Sea and A Personal Record A207
———————— The Rescue, A199
———————— The Rover A240
———————— The Secret Agent A8
———————— The Shadow-Line and Two Other Tales A178
———————— Tales of Heroes and History A228
———————— Tales of the East A256
———————— Victory A106
———————— Youth: A Narrative and Two Other Stories A173
CORNFORD, FRANCIS M. The Origin of Attic Comedy (Ed. by Theodor
    H. Gaster) A263
COULANGES, FUSTEL DE The Ancient City A76
CRANE, HART The Complete Poems of Hart Crane A128
CROMBIE, A. C. Medieval and Early Modern Science: I, II A167a, A167b
CROSS, FRANK MOORE JR. The Ancient Library of Qumran A272
DANTZIG, TOBIAS Number, the Language of Science A67
DICKINSON, EMILY Selected Poems and Letters A192
DOLLARD, JOHN Caste and Class in a Southern Town A95
DOSTOEVSKY, FYODOR Three Short Novels A193
DOUGHTY, C. M. Travels in Arabia Deserta A50
DUBOS, RENE Mirage of Health A258
DUMAS, ALEXANDRE Adventures in Spain A211
DUPEE, F. W. Henry James A68
EDEL, LEON Literary Biography A188
EISELEY, LOREN Darwin's Century A244
ESSLIN, MARTIN Brecht: The Man and His Work A245
———————— The Theatre of the Absurd A279
FERGUSSON, FRANCIS The Human Image in Dramatic Literature A124
———————— The Idea of a Theatre A4
FINCH, JAMES K. The Story of Engineering A214
FLORES, ANGEL (Ed.) An Anthology of French Poetry A134
———————— An Anthology of German Poetry A197
———————— An Anthology of Spanish Poetry A268
———————— Nineteenth Century French Tales A217
———————— Nineteenth Century German Tales A184
FLORNOY, BERTRAND The World of the Inca A137
FORSTER, E. M. Alexandria: A History and a Guide A231
FORTUNE, EDITORS OF The Exploding Metropolis A146
FRANKFORT, HENRI The Birth of Civilization in the Near East A89
FRAZER, J. G. The New Golden Bough (Theodor H. Gaster, Ed.) A270
FREUD, SIGMUND The Future of an Illusion A99
———————— A General Selection from the Works of A115
FROMM, ERICH May Man Prevail? A275
FRY, ROGER Transformations A77

GALILEO Discoveries and Opinions A94
GARNETT, DAVID Pocahontas A157
GASTER, T. H. The Dead Sea Scriptures in English Translation A92
———————— Thespis A230
GEIRINGER, KARL Brahms A248
GOFFMAN, ERVING Asylums: Essays on the Social Situation of Patients and Other Inmates A277
———————— The Presentation of Self in Everyday Life A174
GOGOL, NICOLAI Tales of Good and Evil A120
GONCOURT, EDMOND and JULES DE The Goncourt Journals A158
GOYA, FRANCISCO DE The Disasters of War AA1
GRANICK, DAVID The Red Executive A246
GRANVILLE-BARKER, H. and HARRISON, G. B. A Companion to Shakespeare Studies, A191
GRAVES, ROBERT Good-Bye to All That A123
———————— The Poems of Robert Graves—Chosen by Himself A139
GRAVES, ROBERT (Ed.) The Comedies of Terence A305
GREEN, HENRY Loving A18
HADAS, MOSES (Ed.) A History of Rome A78
————————(Ed) The Stoic Philosophy of Seneca A148
HAGGIN, B. H. The Listener's Musical Companion A183
HAHN, WALTER F. and NEFF, JOHN C. American Strategy for the Nuclear Age A224
HALL, ROBERT A. JR. Linguistics and Your Language A201
HAMILTON, ALEXANDER, MADISON, JAMES, and JAY, JOHN The Federalist Papers (Edited by Roy P. Fairfield) A239
HANDLIN, OSCAR The Newcomers A283
———————— Race and Nationality in American Life A110
HARRIS, MARK Bang the Drum Slowly A324
HEARD, ALEXANDER The Costs of Democracy A288
HEIDEGGER, MARTIN Introduction to Metaphysics A251
HENDERSON, HAROLD An Introduction to Haiku A150
HERBERG, WILL Four Existentialist Theologians A141
———————— Protestant, Catholic, Jew A195
HIMMELFARB, GERTRUDE Darwin and the Darwinian Revolution A325
HINDEMITH, PAUL A Composer's World A235
HOFFMAN, DANIEL (Ed.) American Poetry and Poetics A304
HOLT, ELIZABETH GILMORE A Documentary History of Art: I, II A114a, A114b
HOOVER, CALVIN B. The Economy, Liberty and the State A241
HOOVER, EDGAR M. and VERNON, RAYMOND Anatomy of a Metropolis A298
HUIZINGA, J. The Waning of the Middle Ages A42
HYTIER, JEAN Andre Gide (Trans. by Richard Howard) A307
IBSEN, HENRIK Brand A215
———————— Hedda Gabler and Three Other Plays A215c
———————— When We Dead Awaken and Three Other Plays A215b
JAMES, HENRY The Art of Travel (Ed. by Morton Dauwen Zabel) A306
———————— The Awkward Age A138
———————— In the Cage and Other Tales A131
———————— Selected Letters, A204
———————— What Maisie Knew A43
JARRELL, RANDALL (Ed.) The Anchor Book of Stories A145
JASPERS, KARL Man in the Modern Age A101
JESPERSEN, OTTO Growth and Structure of the English Language A46
JEWETT, SARAH ORNE The Country of the Pointed Firs A26
JONES, ERNEST Hamlet and Oedipus A31
JUNG, C. G. Psyche and Symbol A136
KAUFMANN, WALTER Critique of Religion and Philosophy A252
———————— From Shakespeare to Existentialism A213
KAZIN, ALFRED On Native Grounds A69

KEATS, JOHN   Selected Letters A70
KIERKEGAARD, SOREN   Either/Or, I, II A181a, A181b
————————   Fear and Trembling and The Sickness Unto Death A30
————————   Selections from the Writings of Kierkegaard A210
KIMBLE, GEORGE H. T.   Tropical Africa (2 volumes) A303a, A303b
KIPLING, RUDYARD   A Choice of Kipling's Verse (Ed. by T. S. Eliot) A301
KISSINGER, HENRY A.   The Necessity for Choice A282
————————   Nuclear Weapons and Foreign Policy A152
KITTO, H. D. F.   Greek Tragedy A38
KOUWENHOVEN, JOHN   Made in America A300
KRAMER, SAMUEL NOAH   History Begins at Sumer A175
————————   (Ed.)   Mythologies of the Ancient World A229
KRONENBERGER, LOUIS (Ed.)   Novelists on Novelists A293
KROPOTKIN, PETER   Memoirs of a Revolutionist (Ed. by James Allen Rogers) A287
LAWFORD, GIOVANNA   The Human Frame A234
LAWRENCE, D. H.   Selected Letters of D. H. Lawrence (Edited by Diana Trilling) A236
————————   Studies in Classic American Literature A5
LERMONTOV, MIHAIL   A Hero of Our Time A133
LETWIN, WILLIAM (Ed.)   A Documentary History of American Economic Policy since 1789 A280
LEWIS, D. B. WYNDHAM   François Villon A147
LEWIS, W. H.   The Splendid Century A122
LIPSET, S. M., TROW, M. A. and COLEMAN, J. S.   Union Democracy A296
LITTELL, FRANKLIN H.   From State Church to Pluralism A294
LOWRIE, WALTER   A Short Life of Kierkegaard A273
LUBELL, SAMUEL   The Future of American Politics A71
LUKACS, JOHN   A History of the Cold War A322
LUTHER, MARTIN   Martin Luther: Selections from His Writings (John Dillenberger, Ed.) A271
LYNN, KENNETH S.   The Comic Tradition in America A187
MALINOWSKI, BRONISLAW   Magic, Science and Religion A23
MARTINEAU, HARRIET   Society in America (Ed. by S. M. Lipset) A302
MARX, KARL and ENGELS, FRIEDRICH   Basic Writings on Politics and Philosophy A185
MATTINGLY, HAROLD   Roman Imperial Civilisation A160
MAURIAC, FRANCOIS   Thérèse A79
McCORMICK, JOHN and MacINNES, MAIRI (Eds.)   Versions of Censorship A297
MELVILLE, HERMAN   Redburn: His First Voyage A118
MEREDITH, GEORGE   "An Essay on Comedy" in Comedy A87
MERWIN, W. S. (Trans.)   The Life of Lazarillo de Tormes A316
————————   Spanish Ballads A253
MEYERHOFF, HANS (Ed.)   The Philosophy of History in Our Time A164
MILLER, PERRY (Ed.)   The American Puritans: Their Prose and Poetry A80
————————(Ed.)   The American Transcendentalists: Their Prose and Poetry A119
————————   (Ed.)   The Legal Mind in America — From Independence to the Civil War A313
MONTAIGNE, MICHEL DE   The Complete Essays, Vols. I, II, III A227a, A227b, A227c
MOORE, W. G.   Moliere: A New Criticism A291
MORRIS, WRIGHT (Ed.)   A Mississippi River Reader A299
MOSCATI, SABATINO   The Face of the Ancient Orient A289
MURASAKI, LADY   The Tale of Genji A55
————————   The Tale of Genji, Part II A176
MURRAY, GILBERT   Five Stages of Greek Religion A51
MURRAY, MARGARET   The God of the Witches A212

NEALE, J. E. Queen Elizabeth I A105
NEGLEY, GLENN and PATRICK, J. MAX (Eds.) The Quest for Utopia A326
NEHRU, JAWAHARLAL Discovery of India, A200
NEVINS, ALLAN The Gateway to History A314
NICOLSON, HAROLD Tennyson A284
NIETZSCHE, FRIEDRICH The Birth of Tragedy and The Genealogy of Morals A81
OBLER, PAUL C. and ESTRIN, HERMAN A. (Eds.) The New Scientist A319
ORTEGA Y GASSET, JOSE The Dehumanization of Art A72
ORWELL, GEORGE A Collection of Essays A29
PANOFSKY, ERWIN Meaning in the Visual Arts A59
PAOLUCCI, HENRY and ANNE (Eds.) Hegel on Tragedy A276
PEIRCE, CHARLES S. Values in a Universe of Chance A126
PETERSEN, WILLIAM (Ed.) American Social Patterns A86
PETERSON, SPIRO (Ed.) The Counterfeit Lady Unveiled and Other Criminal Fiction of Seventeenth-Century England A232
PHILLIPS, DR. HARLAN B. (Ed.) Felix Frankfurter Reminisces A310
PIERSON, GEORGE W. and LUNT, DUDLEY C. Tocqueville in America A189
PIRENNE, HENRI A History of Europe: I, II A156a, A156b
—————— Medieval Cities A82
POLYA, G. How to Solve It A93
POWER, EILEEN Medieval People A32
PROUST, MARCEL Pleasures and Days and Other Writings A97
RAAB, EARL (Ed.) American Race Relations Today A318
RAHV, PHILIP Discovery of Europe A208
REPS, PAUL (Ed.) Zen Flesh, Zen Bones A233
RIEFF, PHILIP Freud: The Mind of the Moralist A278
RIESMAN, DAVID Constraint and Variety in American Education A135
—————— Selected Essays from Individualism Reconsidered A58
RILKE, RAINER MARIA Selected Letters A223
ROBINSON, MARSHAL A., MORTON, HERBERT C. and CALDERWOOD, JAMES D. An Introduction to Economic Reasoning A338
ROOSEVELT, JAMES (Ed.) The Liberal Papers A290
ROURKE, CONSTANCE American Humor A12
RUSSELL, BERTRAND Mysticism and Logic A104
SANTAYANA, GEORGE Character and Opinion in the United States A73
—————— Three Philosophical Poets A17
SCHOPENHAUER, ARTHUR The Will to Live: Selected Writings of Arthur Schopenhauer (Ed. by Richard Taylor) A266
SCHRODINGER, ERWIN What Is Life? A88
SCIAMA, D. W. The Unity of the Universe A247
SCOTT, GEOFFREY The Architecture of Humanism A33
SHATTUCK, ROGER The Banquet Years A238
SHAW, BERNARD Shaw on Music A53
SIGAL, CLANCY Weekend in Dinlock A269
SIGERIST, HENRY E. The Great Doctors A140
SNOW, C. P. The Masters: A Novel A162
SOMERS, HERMAN MILES and ANNE RAMSAY Doctors, Patients and Health Insurance A309
STEEGMULLER, FRANCIS The Grand Mademoiselle A205
STENDHAL The Charterhouse of Parma A1
—————— Five Short Novels of Stendhal A153
—————— On Love A103
STRINDBERG, AUGUST Six Plays A54
—————— Five Plays A219
SUZUKI, D. T. Zen Buddhism A90
SYPHER, WYLIE (Ed.) Comedy A87
—————— Four Stages of Renaissance Style A45
TAYLOR, A. E. Socrates A9
TITCHMARSH, E. C. Mathematics for the General Reader A169

TOCQUEVILLE, ALEXIS DE The European Revolution and the Corre-
————— spondence with Gobineau A163
————— The Old Regime and the French Revolution A60
TOKLAS, ALICE B. The Alice B. Toklas Cook Book A196
TRAVERSI, D. A. An Approach to Shakespeare A74
TRELAWNEY, E. J. The Last Days of Shelley and Byron A225
TREVELYAN, G. M. History of England I, II, III A22a, A22b, A22c
TRILLING, LIONEL The Liberal Imagination A13
————— The Middle of the Journey A98
TROTSKY, LEON The Russian Revolution A170
TSAO HSUEH-CHIN Dream of the Red Chamber A159
TURGENEV, IVAN Selected Tales A203
VAN DOREN, MARK Shakespeare A11
VIDICH, ARTHUR J. and BENSMAN, JOSEPH Small Town in Mass
————— Society A216
VIRGIL The Aeneid A20
WADDELL, HELEN The Wandering Scholars A63
WALEY, ARTHUR Three Ways of Thought in Ancient China A75
WAYNE, PHILIP (Trans.) A Hundred Fables from La Fontaine A267
WELSFORD, ENID The Fool A262
WESTON, JESSIE From Ritual to Romance A125
WHYTE, LANCELOT LAW The Unconscious Before Freud A266
WHYTE, WILLIAM H., JR. The Organization Man A117
WIENER, NORBERT The Human Use of Human Beings A34
WILDER, THORNTON Heaven's My Destination A209
WILLEY, BASIL The Seventeenth Century Background A19
WILLIAMS, RAYMOND Culture and Society 1780–1950 A220
WILSON, EDMUND A Literary Chronicle: 1920–1950 A85
————— A Piece of My Mind A143
————— To the Finland Station A6
WOODWARD C. VANN Reunion and Reaction A83
WRIGHT, G. ERNEST and DAVID NOEL FREEDMAN (Eds.)
————— The Biblical Archaeologist Reader A250
WRIGHT, G. ERNEST and FULLER, REGINALD H. The Book of the
————— Acts of God A222
YEATS, WILLIAM BUTLER The Autobiography of William Butler Yeats
————— A142
YARMOLINSKY, AVRAHM (Ed.) An Anthology of Russian Verse,
————— 1812–1960 A285
————— (Ed.) Soviet Short Stories A218